Fraud Examination
Casebook with Documents

Founded in 1807, John Wiley & Sons is the oldest independent publishing company in the United States. With offices in North America, Europe, Asia, and Australia, Wiley is globally committed to developing and marketing print and electronic products and services for our customers' professional and personal knowledge and understanding.

The Wiley Corporate F&A series provides information, tools, and insights to corporate professionals responsible for issues affecting the profitability of their company, from accounting and finance to internal controls and performance management.

Fraud Examination Casebook with Documents

A Hands-on Approach

WILLIAM H. BEECKEN, CFE, CPA
CLARK A. BEECKEN, CFE

WILEY

For general information on our other products and services or for technical support, please contact our Customer Care Department within the United States at (800) 762-2974, outside the United States at (317) 572-3993 or fax (317) 572-4002.

Wiley publishes in a variety of print and electronic formats and by print-on-demand. Some material included with standard print versions of this book may not be included in e-books or in print-on-demand. If this book refers to media such as a CD or DVD that is not included in the version you purchased, you may download this material at http://booksupport.wiley.com. For more information about Wiley products, visit www.wiley.com.

Library of Congress Cataloging-in-Publication Data is available:

ISBN 9781119349990 (Hardcover)
ISBN 9781119349952 (epdf)
ISBN 9781119349877 (epub)

Cover Design: Wiley
Cover Image: © Nomad_Soul/Shutterstock

10 9 8 7 6 5 4 3 2 1

Contents

Foreword

I am pleased to write this foreword to the *Fraud Examination Casebook with Documents: A Hands-on Approach* by William H. Beecken and Clark A. Beecken, a redoubtable father-son team of forensic accountants. Bill has been a seasoned forensic professional employed many years with the Federal Deposit Insurance Corporation (FDIC) Office of Inspector General, as well as the Bureau of Alcohol, Tobacco, Firearms and Explosives (ATF). Clark is currently working as a forensic auditor for the federal government.

Several years ago, as a faculty member in the School of Accountancy at Kennesaw State University (KSU), I came to know Bill as a popular faculty member at Southern Polytechnic State University—now the KSU Marietta campus—who taught forensic accounting in an innovative way. At the end of his course, it was part of the students' end-of-term assignment to go through the real-world experience of being deposed as an "expert witness" by the local district attorney and overseen by a judge in the actual environs of the Marietta, Georgia, courthouse. A couple of times, I was a member of the audience in the courthouse, rather envious of Bill's students who were being exposed to a mock-trial scenario. Hence, I enthusiastically commend and recommend Bill's idiosyncratic interpretation of a hands-on approach!

From my very first meeting, Clark appeared to be a chip off the old block, cut of the same cloth, the apple that doesn't fall far from the tree, etc.—sharp, incisive, and blessed with the technological adeptness and adroitness that comes with having grown up digital. So, I am not surprised that he has left his indelible mark on the book by focusing on Microsoft Excel, the industry standard for spreadsheets, featuring calculation, graphing tools, pivot tables, and such.

Among other things, this practical fraud casebook does a wonderful job of showing how Excel PivotTables may be profitably deployed—not only to summarize a huge amount of data but also to help trace Excel Pivot red flags back to source documents to understand the flow of money. After all, much of forensic accounting can be usefully described as the work of understanding and investigating people, money, and associated patterns of behavior with great tenacity—colloquially described as the "follow the money" approach. Such work cannot be carried out without sophisticated data analysis in today's data rich, information poor (DRIP) world.

It is one thing to appreciate the scope and reach of forensic accounting at a conceptual level; quite another to get your hands dirty with data, and recognize the power of data-driven insights and solutions. This book admirably makes that bridge from theory to practice happen. Rather than "hand waving," you become hands-on—you don't just talk, for talk is cheap, but you actually perform analyses and learn to manipulate data statistically to yield relevant and meaningful information. This information helps you gather evidence and arrive at inferences that support or challenge your hypotheses—a most exciting endeavor. After all, it is such information that can greatly help buttress one's arguments, defend one's position, persuade others in courtroom contexts, and thus, help win cases.

Dr. Sridhar Ramamoorti, ACA, CPA/CITP/CFF/CGMA, CIA, CFSA, CGAP, CRMA, CFE, CGFM, CRP, MAFF

Associate Professor of Accounting, School of Business Administration, University of Dayton, Ohio

Managing Principal, The Behavioral Forensics Group, LLC (www.bringingfreudtofraud.com)

MEMBERSHIPS

Standing Advisory Group, Public Company Accounting Oversight Board, 2014–2016
Forensic Accounting Advisory Board, Georgia Southern University, 2015–
Board of Trustees, Financial Executives Research Foundation, 2016–
Litigation Forensics Board, National Association of Certified Valuators & Analysts, 2016–
Lead author, *A.B.C.'s of Behavioral Forensics* (Hoboken, NJ: John Wiley & Sons, 2013)

Preface

Professors of graduate and undergraduate Fraud Examination courses often instruct students from a survey-level textbook and, if available, supplement their course with guest lecturers who work in the field. Those new to Fraud Examination often simply read a Fraud Examination textbook, specialized book dealing with some aspect of fraud, or study for the CFE Exam. Students usually complete a typical Fraud Examination course with general knowledge of complex human behaviors like greed and deception, a broad understanding of what fraud is and how fraud is committed, prevented, and resolved. However, they gain little or no hands-on experience using life-like accounting documents, databases, or witness interviews. They also do not learn how to apply Fraud Examination techniques like horizontal, vertical, and ratio analysis. Learning Fraud Examination theory is not enough to do the job effectively; "knowing" is different from "applying."

This casebook was developed with a hands-on concept similar to that used to train federal special agents. It provides students and those new to Fraud Examination with cases based on real Fraud Examinations. The exercises take them from predication (e.g., receipt of allegations given in a case scenario) through producing a written report, schedules, and court-room ready audio-visuals, which are ready for examination and cross-examination by attorneys in depositions, hearings, or trials. It gives the students and those new to Fraud Examination cradle-to-grave experience, painstakingly spreading and analyzing accounting documentation and related data, preparing audio-visuals to simplify the complex, and preparing a report that adequately discusses the Fraud Examination, schedules, and audio-visuals to an uninformed reader (e.g., an attorney). Students and those new to Fraud Examination learn such Fraud Examination techniques as horizontal and vertical analysis, examining the front and back of canceled checks, decoding debit card transactions, vouching to supporting documents, examining edits to digital information, using simple data analytics, and preparation of audio-visuals to simplify the complex. As with real Fraud Examinations, the students and those new to Fraud Examination must think outside of the box and connect the dots, often reading and rereading the scenario and examining and reexamining the accounting documents and witness interviews. Like in real life, they do not receive all of the information they would like to have.

The information they need is present in the case, but they have to dig deeply to find it all. In those courses where the professor uses a mock fraud trial as an additional teaching tool, a prosecutor and defense attorney can use the finished product to painfully examine and cross-examine students on the results of their completion of these exercises (Fraud Examination reports, schedules, and audiovisuals).

This work is the outgrowth of three earlier versions of the first two fraud cases, which were used to augment Fraud Examination courses at a state university (on-the-ground) and private university (online). Starting with the first Fraud Examination course students in the on-the-ground course were required to prepare reports, schedules, and audiovisuals and then meet in groups to prepare for the final examination: a mock fraud trial before a real judge, prosecutor, and defense attorney. During the pre-trial period, teams were selected for the defense and prosecution attorneys, and team reports, schedules, and audiovisuals were exchanged under discovery. Attorneys taught a session in how to testify as an expert witness and films were shown on the tips, tricks, and traps of testifying. During cross-examination, students quickly found out how inadequate work, misspoken words, and/or fear of the unknown impacted the effectiveness of their testimony on the results of their Fraud Examinations. Those teams that prepared most often did the best.

Based on prior experience, the first two cases are the most that should be used to supplement an undergraduate Fraud Examination course. It takes four to eight hours for each assignment to individually complete with worksheets and another eight to ten hours for teams to prepare reports, schedules, and audiovisuals. Considering the more intense writing requirements for graduate programs, graduate Fraud Examination students can and should work all five cases. Those new to Fraud Examination may take more or less hours depending on their experience level. Expect the first set of reports, schedules, and audiovisuals (fraud case 1) to be substandard. However, those that follow review comments often provide much improved products with the second set of reports, schedules, and audiovisuals (fraud case 2). The forensic data analytics case (case 4) is provided so business schools can introduce students to forensic data analytics. The "how-to" session provides an overview of Excel

Pivot. Finally, the conspiracy/loan fraud case was added to bring the serial cases full circle and emphasize that frauds may not be committed alone.

Writing this book came out of a need to provide students with a working knowledge of simple fraud cases and an avenue to quickly become Fraud Examiners. From past experience, graduates must first work as auditors, claims adjusters, forensic accountants, investigators, and so forth before getting an opportunity to enter the field. To get them entry-level positions right out of college required a large number of volunteers: guest lecturers, employers with Fraud Examination internships, and attorneys and CFEs willing to spend hours holding a mock fraud trial where students would testify as expert witnesses.

The following spoke about their real-world experience: Lew Brendle, J.D., Laurie Dyke, CFE CPA, Karen Fortune, CFE CPA, James F. Hart, CPA/ABV, CFE, Scott Hilsen, J.D, CFE, Tim Huhn, CFE, Phil Hurd, CISSP CIA, Deputy Chief Assistant District Attorney (White Collar Crime) John Melvin, J.D., David Sawyer, CFE, CPA, Special Agent Gary Sherrill, CFE, and Thomas Taylor, CFE. The Cobb County District Attorney's Office, Georgia Institute of Technology, and IAG Forensics & Valuation provided Fraud Examination internships. The following CFEs devoted days getting students prepared to testify as expert witnesses: Laurie Dyke, CFE CPA, Karen Fortune, CFE CPA, Luke Thomas, CFE CPA, and many of their junior associates with IAG Forensics & Valuation. The following attorneys and magistrates participated as judges and attorneys at the annual mock fraud trials: John Capo, J.D., Scott Poole, J.D., and Chief Judge Allen Wigington (Pickens County), Victor Hartman, J.D., CFE, CPA (former FBI District Counsel), and District Attorney Victor Reynolds, J.D., Deputy Chief Assistant District Attorney (White Collar Crime) John Melvin, J.D., Deputy Chief Assistant District Attorney (Major Litigation) Michael Carlson, J.D., and Assistant District Attorney Jason Marbutt, J.D. (Cobb County). In addition, thanks to the academic assistance provided by Donald Ariail, Ph.D., CFE, CPA and Sridhar Ramamoorti, Ph.D., CFE, CPA, CIA.

Finally, Clark and I want to thank Jeanne, our mother and wife, respectively. She has had to persevere through countless hours of solitary living while we wrote this casebook. Without her love and understanding, this casebook would not have been written.

Fraud Examination
Casebook with Documents

Overview of the Serial Fraud Cases
(A Family of Fraudsters)

WHEN YOU EXAMINE AN ALLEGED FRAUD, many of the facts are not readily apparent. Fraud examiners must dig up the hidden facts. In this casebook, you will learn a few fraud examiner tools and how to prepare a fraud examination report, associated schedules, and trial-ready audiovisuals.

Fraud examiners work in public and private entities: law enforcement agencies, insurance companies, Certified Public Accounting (CPA) firms, Certified Fraud Examination (CFE) firms, consulting firms, and corporate and university internal audit departments, to name a few. In these cases, you are working for an independent forensic accounting firm that specializes in forensic accounting and fraud examination. You work for an attorney under attorney-client privilege (i.e., your report is not readily available to other parties).

Fraudsters have hidden personal and/or financial problems that function as the pressure (motive) for committing the fraud. In these cases, you must discover their hidden problems by response to the requirements of the insurance contract, subpoena, and after serving a properly signed authorization to release financial records to the correct source and requesting the correct information. If you want to learn more about hidden personal and/or financial problems, review the doctoral research of Donald R. Cressey.

All five cases in this book are connected via marriage. Greg and Tonya Larsen are husband and wife and their finances are intertwined. Greg's finances impacts Tonya's finances, and vice versa. Greg owns and operates Larsen Convenience Store, Canton, Georgia, as a sole proprietorship. Tonya is the office manager for Anderson Internal Medicine in Lawrenceville, Georgia. As a sole proprietor, Greg must file an Internal Revenue Service (IRS) Schedule C (Profit or Loss from Business—Sole Proprietorship) with his personal federal income taxes.

1

FRAUDULENT FINANCIAL STATEMENTS

Around midnight on December 31, 2015, a fire breaks out at Larsen Convenience Store.

Under his business insurance policy, Greg must submit a proof of loss and financial documents to his insurance company and submit to an examination under oath (EUO). Insurance companies often hire independent forensic accounting firms to perform a business interruption (BI) calculation that covers the loss of income as a result of the disaster. The BI calculation, which is also used as a fraud examination tool, includes net profits that would have been earned, fixed costs that continue to be incurred during the business interruption, and reimbursement of reasonable extra expenses. The calculation starts with a horizontal and vertical analysis of several months, quarters, or years of financial statements (whatever is available). This analysis often detects anomalies for closer examination and is used to calculate an estimate of the actual loss. It also detects trends (e.g., seasonality, increases/decreases in revenue and expenses) and can be compared to benchmarks (comparisons with similar-sized companies in the same industry), budgets, and required reports to franchisers and industry suppliers.

In large or suspicious disasters, insurance companies also hire attorneys to conduct the EUO. Crucial to developing EUO questions is the BI and/or fraud examination report.

The BI calculation often takes four to eight months because of delays in receiving needed financial information. During this period, the insured often receives no income from the business.

CHECK FRAUD, DEBIT CARD FRAUD, CASH LARCENY

Just after Greg submits the proof of loss and requested financial documents (last three IRS individual tax returns [including Schedules C] and last three SBA personal financial statements) to the insurance company in late March, Anderson Internal Medicine receives a call from its banker. The business checking account is overdrawn by thousands of dollars. Working late into the night, Tonya changes IDs and passwords, shreds patient billing files, and quits.

FRAUDULENT EDITS/ADJUSTING JOURNAL ENTRIES TO CASH RECEIPTS

After Tonya quits, Jennifer Anderson discovers adjustments to cash receipts.

You previously noted from your bank reconciliation that there is a significant amount of missing cash. You follow up on Dr. Anderson's discovery and perform additional work to identify the reason for the difference, the method of concealing the difference, and quantity of the money stolen.

EXCEL PIVOT ANALYZES AND SUMMARIZES A HUGE AMOUNT OF DATA

You have spread six months of transactions (October through February) from the Anderson Internal Medicine bank statement. What does it mean? What other trends or interesting facts do you find? You will learn and use Excel Pivot, an easy to use data analytics function inside of Excel. It is easy to use and quickly analyzes, summarizes, and presents your data in a simplified format.

Dig deep! Not all company names listed on the bank statements are what they seem. For example, a $3,000 debit payment to MG Sports Grill is actually $3,000 paid to Marti Gras Atlanta (a strip club). You might find purchases for expensive entertainment, food and drinks, or travel. Are they applicable to Anderson Internal Medicine?

TRACING EXCEL PIVOT RED FLAGS BACK TO SOURCE DOCUMENTS AND DOCUMENTING THE FLOW OF MONEY

In analyzing six months of transactions from the Anderson Internal Medicine bank statement, you detect a $36,000.00 deposit from Greg Larsen and a number of disbursements that appear to benefit Greg Larsen, including one to a casino. What do these red flags mean? Why are these transactions funneled through Anderson Internal Medicine instead of Larsen Convenience Store? Is there a conspiracy, money laundering, or some other activity involved?

Although you thought you had completed Larsen Convenience long ago, these provide new leads that must be followed. Learn how to prepare the wording for subpoenas so you can trace forwards and backwards to the originating transaction. Learn how to document the flow of money from several bank accounts on schedules and simplify the movement via audiovisuals. Do you need an addendum to your report?

CHAPTER ONE

Case 1: Fraudulent Financial Statements

1-1 LARSEN CONVENIENCE STORE: USING ANALYTICAL PROCEDURES IN DETECTING FINANCIAL STATEMENT FRAUD

Learning Objective

After completing and discussing this case, you should be able to:

1. Review and analyze financial statement information relating to a company's balance sheet and income statement accounts using horizontal and vertical analysis method.
2. Identify potential fraudulent financial accounts for closer scrutiny.
3. Understand one method used to estimate the loss from the destruction of the out-of-sight (destroyed) inventory (cost of goods sold as a percent of gross receipts).
4. Be able to use one ratio (days sales of inventory) to detect potentially misstated inventory balances.

HISTORY BEHIND THE FRAUD CASE:

In one of the author's fraud cases, an incendiary device destroyed a franchised grocery store at 3:00 a.m. on December 31. The Special Agent in Charge (SAC) of the investigation wanted the case agent to close the case because the store experienced its best year ever. Why would the owner destroy a profitable business? At the time the request was made, two cause-and-origin teams concluded that the torches poured over 30 gallons of gasoline that caused a massive explosion, which blew the front windows several hundred feet into the parking lot, warped huge girders, and propelled a concrete wall into the street almost killing a motorist. The case agent pleaded with the author to give the financial information a second look to avoid closing the criminal investigation.

A quick horizontal and vertical analysis of gross receipts, beginning and ending inventory, cost of goods sold, and gross receipts highlighted a potential material misstatement with the ending inventory. Ending inventory was over $300,000 higher and gross and net profits were substantially higher than in the prior three years. Telephone calls to the primary vendors revealed that the owner was delinquent and they had forced him to sign promissory notes and pay for all future shipments cash-on-delivery (COD). Agent interviews documented that the shelves were almost bare at the time of the fire.

A physical inventory taken at night 90 days before the fire was unusual. Instead of being taken during the day by professional inventory takers, it was allegedly taken by the owner and his tax accountant (a felon) late at night on a weekend. A handwriting analysis of the physical inventory tapes indicated that the tapes were not made by the owner or tax accountant. Thinking that the handwriting was that of the head teller, the case agent and author interviewed her. When confronted, she cried and then admitted to making up the ending inventory after the fire (and not 90 days before the fire) in the tax accountant's office a week after the fire. The fraud examination of the bank checking account and loan records revealed over 600 insufficient funds charges involving the owner and tax accountant and a bank loan made before the fire to help stop a constant overdraft of the owner's checking account. It also detected check kiting between the owner and tax accountant. A painstaking roll-forward of the inventory from the prior accounting period and benchmarks confirmed the material overstatement. The author testified as an expert witness for four days.

The jury convicted both the owner and tax accountant. The judge sentenced both to ten years; however, both were paroled after three years. Because the owner did not pay the $1 million in restitution that started on the day he was released, a probation revocation hearing was held. During his incarceration, the owner's wife and daughter liquidated and spent his assets. The judge sent the owner back to prison for the remainder of his sentence.

Introduction

Analytical procedures are powerful forensic accounting tools in conducting a fraud examination. When financial statements (balance sheet, income statement, and statement of changes) are available in whole or in part, analytical procedures can be useful as a starting point in a Fraud Examination. In an ideal world, the fraud examiner has a full set of financial statements (audited statements, reviewed statements, or compiled statements that are neither audited nor reviewed). In some cases, the fraud examiner has to work with only partial financial statements, for example, income statements (e.g., IRS Schedules C, proprietorship income tax returns) or balance sheets (e.g., personal financial statements given to a financial institution).

Analysis of these documents can provide leads and/or corroborative evidence that support other types of evidence (e.g., interviews and supporting financial documentation).

This case teaches the use of horizontal and vertical analysis of an income statement and personal financial statement. It also teaches the calculation of selected financial ratios to augment the horizontal and vertical analysis. In addition, it teaches one method for estimating out-of-sight inventories (e.g., inventories destroyed by fire, flood, or other catastrophe) using the cost of goods sold to gross revenues method. For extra credit (25 points), you may research and roll-forward the October 31, 2016, physical inventory to the date of destruction; adding purchases (which are at cost) and subtracting sales (which must be reduced from retail price at cost).

Normally, income statements prepared for tax purposes and personal financial statements are prepared separately and at different times of year and cannot be used together. In some cases, you can use both. Therefore, when conducting a fraud examination, you need to step back and determine what financial documents can be connected.

From experience with arson-for-profit cases, many proprietorship arsons take place at or near the end of the year. According to IRS regulations, ending inventory should be at or near yearend. Financial institutions often require its commercial loan customers to provide them with Small Business Administration (SBA) (or similar) personal financial statements at the beginning of the year. Since both documents are prepared around the same time, you may be able to use one (IRS Schedule C) as an income statement and the other personal financial statement) as the related balance sheet for ratio purposes. Note: Bank personal financial statements may not be a true balance sheet—the personal financial statement when a proprietorship is involved often includes both personal and business assets and liabilities as well as personal sources of income (e.g., a spouse's salary). Accordingly, you may have to separate the personal and business assets and liabilities, as you will do in this case.

Net profit and loss and assets and liabilities may not be accurate. Through the following analyses, you will detect material abnormal balances from the facts of the case as well as by vouching[1] the totals listed on the statements back to original accounting documents (e.g., vendor bills, invoices, and summary statements, bank/mortgage loan statements, etc.) and determine what additional fraud examination steps, if any, should be taken.

Background

Three months before Tonya Larsen walked out of Anderson Internal Medicine, a suspicious incendiary fire took place at her husband's convenience store in Canton, Georgia. As with most casualty claims, the examination of the claim takes months to complete as the company files a proof of loss and provides requested documentation, fraud examiners prepare business interruption calculations, and the attorney prepares for and then takes the insured's examination under oath (EUO). Under the standard insurance contract, the insured (Greg Larsen) must (1) provide requested financial documents and (2) submit to a EUO by an attorney hired by the insurance company. If the insured does not, he/she will not be paid for their loss.

The fire started at Larsen Convenience Store in Canton, Georgia, around midnight on December 31, 2015, and completely burned all of the structure and contents to the ground. Agents from the State Fire Marshal's office and independent cause and origin experts hired by the insurance company conducted a cause and origin investigation of the fire scene and determined that the fire was incendiary (i.e., intentionally set as opposed to being caused by natural, mechanical, or electrical causes). The deputy fire marshals and experts found four sources of ignition. Georgia Bureau of Investigation chemists analyzed carpet and wood samples identified by arson dogs at the fire scene and found the samples to contain hydrocarbons in the same category as gasoline. Insurance company special agents also asked Greg Larsen the following questions:

1. Who discovered the fire?
2. How was he notified of the fire?

---

[1] Vouching is an auditing term indicating the examination of a number of a financial statement (total number or individual transaction) back to documentary evidence or supporting documentation.

3. Who was the last person in the building?
4. Who has keys to the building?
5. Did he notice any unusual activity before the fire?
6. Is he the owner or the tenant?
7. What is the location of flammables, utilities, etc.?
8. Did he know of any fire hazards and flammable liquid storage?
9. How were the business and his personal finances at the time of the fire?

Among his answers, Greg Larsen said that he (his business) had just completed its best year ever, sales and net profits were significantly higher than prior years. Larsen also stated that he rented the building from J. L. Jensen LLC for $1,000 a month and had 24 months left on his lease. Larsen told the agents that surely a pyromaniac or someone with a grudge lit the fire.

Because the cause was an incendiary fire, Southern Appalachian Insurance assigned the follow-up civil investigation to its Special Investigative Unit (SIU) and expanded the services of Alexander Z. Boone to include the casualty loss claim. On March 18, 2016, Greg Larsen filed the proof of loss with Southern Appalachian Insurance for the loss of his inventory, shelving, and leasehold improvements and business interruption (lost net profits and continuing expenses). As requested by the attorney, Greg Larsen also provided financial records, including the 2013, 2014, and 2015 federal income tax returns and January 7, 2014, 2015, and 2016 SBA personal financial statements filed with Sharptop Bank, and a physical inventory he took on October 31, 2015. The 2015 federal income tax return shows that Greg Larsen had his best year ever, having net income totaling $130,458. With such a great net income, Attorney Boone thought that Greg Larsen had no financial motive to burn his store.

Thus far, the SIU special agents found:

1. Greg Larsen primary suppliers, Georgia-Tennessee Fuel Partners, Shamrock Groceries, Discount Tobacco Supply, Marietta Beverage Company, and Jenkins Media Services had required Greg Larsen in early November 2015 to sign promissory notes for their respective unpaid balances. Instead of cutting him off, each made future deliveries subject to cash on delivery. The special agents had Greg Larsen sign an Authorization to Release Financial Records and obtained records from the vendors and Georgia Department of Revenue.
2. Regular customers of Larsen Convenience stated that in the days leading up to the fire, Larsen did not carry their brand of beer, snacks, and tobacco.

In fact, the beer and tobacco inventory looked low (i.e., half the tobacco bins behind the counter were empty).

3. Larsen had a sale on paper towels, which sat on a pallet in the center of the store.
4. Several years ago, Greg Larsen had a heated argument with his nephew, an employee of the store, in the parking lot. Greg Larsen jumped into his truck, backed it up in anger, and accidently ran over and killed his nephew. His sister and brother-in-law sued him in state court for wrongful death and won a $500,000 judgment. The state court judge handed down his decision in mid-October 2013. The appellate court affirmed the lower court decision in September 2014, and the Georgia Supreme Court denied certiorari in May 2015. The denial of certiorari had the direct effect of upholding the appellate court's decision and making the $500,000 judgment a collectible debt. In July 2015, Southern Appalachian Insurance paid his sister and brother-in-law $75,000, the limit of the business liability insurance policy. In September 2015, his sister and brother-in-law obtained a court order and subsequently seized the funds in his business bank account and put a lien on his business assets.
5. Greg and Tonya Larsen were in arrears on their mortgage at the end of December and potentially facing foreclosure unless they came up with several thousand dollars.

Summary Requirements

Your role in the examination of the Greg Larsen has been expanded by Alexander Z. Boone to perform the following under attorney-client privilege:

- ▨ A financial condition (solvency) analysis of Greg Larsen's business (Larsen Convenience Store) at the time of the fire
- ▨ Review the claimed casualty loss and determine the estimated inventory loss on the fire date

Before proceeding, read the documents in Chapter 7, section 7-1, "Larsen Convenience Store." As you work the case, you will have to read and reread the documents to fully understand the evidence.

Study section 1-2 on *How to Perform a Vertical and Horizontal Analysis* that follows this case before conducting the specific requirements relating to this analysis.

The results of your assignment will be used by the attorney during the EUO. Your assignment (in general) is, as follows:

1. Perform a financial condition analysis of Larsen Convenience as of the fire date, using the tax returns, SBA personal financial statements, October 31, 2015, physical inventory, and all information at your disposal. Among other procedures,
   a. Perform two separate vertical and horizontal analyses of the 2013–2015 Schedules C and January 7, 2014, 2015, and 2016 SBA personal financial statements. Highlight material differences.
   b. Calculate the 2015 estimated ending inventory using the cost of goods sold/gross revenues method using the tax returns:
      i. Calculate the average cost of each product line (e.g., beverages, groceries, tobacco) and associated average gross revenue (e.g., revenue groceries/food) for 2013 and 2014 by adding the totals for both years and dividing result by 2.
      ii. Divide the average cost of each product line by the average gross revenue.
      iii. Multiply the result by the associated 2015 gross revenue to derive the estimated 2015 cost of product line (e.g., cost of beverages, groceries, and tobacco).
      iv. Back into the estimated 2015 ending inventory by adding beginning inventory and purchases and then subtracting the estimated 2015 cost of product.
      v. Recalculate the gross profit and net profit.
      vi. Repeat for each of the ending inventories that appear to be overstated.
2. Calculate the Days Sales of Inventory ratio for December 31, 2013, 2014, and 2015 for total, groceries, beverages, and tobacco sales.
3. Determine the types of alleged frauds perpetrated by Greg Larsen related to reporting the financial data for Larsen Convenience. ***DO NOT allege arson!***
4. Prepare a report and associated schedules using the sample report and schedules.
5. Prepare audiovisuals (e.g., charts, summary schedules, and/or graphs of your choice) to simplify these complex accounting issues. Hint: Comparison of balance sheet and income statement assertions (e.g., inventory at the end of the years 2013, 2014, and 2015) make easy to understand audiovisuals.

The initial steps (see exercises) are to be completed individually. You may confer online on strategy, but do your own work. In particular, each student is to schedule and analyze the tax returns and SBA personal financial statements using Excel, calculate the days sales of inventory ratio, and submit their Excel working papers for grades. These steps will be performed as a series of graded exercises designed to walk you through the process.

The final exercise is a team project. Each team will submit a final examination report addressed to the attorney for Southern Appalachian Insurance, accompanying set of schedules, and audiovisuals for a grade. Each team is to select a team leader, who assigns various tasks to each member of the team, emails a list of each student's assignment, and emails the final deliverables. The team leader is responsible for quality control and should not take on any additional tasks.

Accuracy Certifications and Potential False Statements

When examining financial statements, be aware that most common financial documents have certifications as to the accuracy of the submitted information above or below the signature line. Whoever knowingly prepares and/or submits MATERIALLY untrue, inaccurate, incomplete, or misleading information can be prosecuted for making MATERIAL misstatements.

In this case, you will examine IRS Forms 1040, SBA Personal Financial Statements, and a Sworn Statement in Proof of Loss. All three have accuracy certifications.

IRS Form 1040

> Under penalties of perjury, I declare that I have examined this return and accompanying schedules and statements, and to the best of my knowledge and belief, they are true, correct, and complete. Declaration of preparer (other than taxpayers) is based on all information of which preparer has any knowledge.

Small Business Administration (SBA) Personal Financial Statement

CERTIFICATION: (to be completed by each person submitting the information requested on this form)

> By signing this form, I certify under penalty of criminal prosecution that all information on this form and any additional supporting information submitted with this form is true and complete to the best of my knowledge. I understand that SBA or its participating Lenders or

Certified Development Companies or Surety Companies will rely on this information when making decisions regarding an application for a loan or a surety bond. I further certify that I have read the attached statements required by law and executive order.

Sworn Statement in Proof of Loss

Any person who knowingly and with intent to injure, defraud or deceive any insurance company files a statement of claim containing any false, incomplete or misleading information is guilty of a felony of the third degree.

When Contacting Law Enforcement, Do Not Forget the IRS Criminal Investigation Division (CID)

When you have completed your fraud examination, your client, employer, or insurance may want to refer your findings to local law enforcement. Often, alleged fraud cases prosecuted at the local level result in probation and no prison due to overcrowding. Fraudsters are not violent criminals. IRS regulations require that ill-gotten gains be reported on the fraudster's income tax return. However, when fraudsters steal money, they often do not report it on their income tax returns. If IRS CID takes the tax evasion case and it goes to trial, fraudsters often receive sentences of 44 to 48 months incarceration. In one fraud examination, the fraudster stole an average of $12,000 a month for three years. The local detective said he had never seen more than probation given. IRS CID took the case, and two years later the fraudster was convicted and sent to jail for 44 months.

1-2 HOW TO PERFORM A HORIZONTAL, VERTICAL, AND RATIO ANALYSIS

Learning Objective

After reading this synopsis, you should be able to:

1. Horizontally spread fraudulent data (e.g., from balance sheets, income statements, monthly inventory summaries).
2. Where applicable, add common-sized ratios.
3. Identify horizontal and vertical anomalies (e.g., an account where the balance materially increased or decreased in comparison with prior periods) and/or trends (e.g., seasonality in the revenue account).
4. Estimate the actual amount of a material anomaly (e.g., ending inventory).

Introduction

Horizontal and vertical analysis is a tool to compare common financial information that is recorded monthly, quarterly, and/or annually. The more data points available (36 monthly versus three annual financial statements) the better the analysis of trends (e.g., seasonality, steadily increasing or decreasing revenues, steadily increasing or decreasing expenses) and abrupt changes (e.g., huge quarterly decreases in certain expenses like salaries and wages). By itself, or combined with ratio analysis between financial statements (e.g., days sales in inventory and days sales in receivables), the fraud examiner can use this tool to pinpoint accounts that require further examination (e.g., obtaining and examining documents and/or conducting interviews).

Below is a discussion of horizontal, vertical, and ratio analysis using only three annual income statements (IRS Schedules C, Profit or Loss for a Proprietorship). Similar analysis can be performed for 12 quarterly or 36 monthly unaudited financial statements (balance sheet, income statement, and statement of cash flow) as well as other financial information like comparative physical inventories.

Steps in Performing a Horizontal and Vertical Analysis

Performing a horizontal and vertical analysis on a spreadsheet is a multistep process.

STEP 1: Schedule the Data

Schedule the financial information. Below is an IRS Schedule C (Proprietorship Profit & Loss Statement) from an individual's tax return. You can schedule other sets of financial information like balance sheets, specific account totals by month, quarter, or year (e.g., customer accounts receivable totals, accounts payable totals, inventory totals, monthly purchases by type).

	From Schedules C		
	2013	**2014**	**2015**
Gross receipts	$320,000	$350,000	$300,000
Beginning inventory	90,000	95,000	99,000
Purchases	250,000	275,000	235,000
Ending inventory	95,000	99,000	145,000
Cost of goods sold	**$245,000**	**$271,000**	**$189,000**
Gross profit	**$75,000**	**$79,000**	**$111,000**

	From Schedules C		
	2013	**2014**	**2015**
Advertising	700	900	1,000
Car & truck expenses	6,000	6,000	6,000
Insurance	3,000	3,000	4,000
Interest—other	100	1,600	1,800
Legal & professional	750	750	15,000
Office	395	950	550
Rent	10,800	10,800	10,975
Repairs	900	1,200	1,655
Supplies	1,500	1,668	3,000
Taxes & licenses	1,800	1,200	1,500
Utilities	4,000	4,000	5,900
Wages	4,000	4,000	1,666
Total expenses	**$33,945**	**$36,068**	**$53,046**
Net profit/loss	**$41,055**	**$42,932**	**$57,954**

STEP 2: Add Common-sized Ratios

Add common-sized percentages (e.g., use *gross receipts* as the base for income statements, *total assets* as the base for balance sheets, *total inventory* for inventory summaries). Do not clutter the percent column with unneeded decimals (like 28.1% or 28.15%). Round up unless specificity is needed.

	From Schedules C					
	2013	**%**	**2014**	**%**	**2015**	**%**
Gross receipts	$320,000	100%	$350,000	100%	$300,000	100%
Beginning inventory	90,000	28%	95,000	27%	99,000	33%
Purchases	250,000	78%	275,000	79%	235,000	78%
Ending inventory	95,000	30%	99,000	28%	145,000	48%
Cost of goods sold	**$245,000**	**77%**	**$271,000**	**77%**	**$189,000**	**63%**
Gross profit	**$75,000**	**23%**	**$79,000**	**23%**	**$111,000**	**37%**

(*continued*)

	From Schedules C					
	2013	**%**	**2014**	**%**	**2015**	**%**
Advertising	700	0%	900	0%	1,000	0%
Car & truck expenses	6,000	2%	6,000	2%	6,000	2%
Insurance	3,000	1%	3,000	1%	4,000	1%
Interest—other	100	0%	1,600	0%	1,800	1%
Legal & professional	750	0%	750	0%	15,000	5%
Office	395	0%	950	0%	550	0%
Rent	10,800	3%	10,800	3%	10,975	4%
Repairs	900	0%	1,200	0%	1,655	1%
Supplies	1,500	0%	1,668	0%	3,000	1%
Taxes & licenses	1,800	1%	1,200	0%	1,500	1%
Utilities	4,000	1%	4,000	1%	5,900	2%
Wages	4,000	1%	4,000	1%	1,666	1%
Total expenses	**$33,945**	11%	**$36,068**	10%	**$53,046**	18%
Net profit/loss	**$41,055**	13%	**$42,932**	12%	**$57,954**	19%

STEP 3: Analyze Dollars and Percentages Horizontally and Vertically

Analyze vertically and horizontally for anomalies in dollars and by percentages (e.g., trends up or down, abnormal common-sized ratios, abrupt changes in account totals). In the following example, the 2015 ending inventory is significantly higher than the prior two years in both dollars and as a percent of gross receipts. Similarly, interest is up slightly, but legal and professional expenses increased significantly, while wages are materially lower.

	From Schedules C					
	2013	**%**	**2014**	**%**	**2015**	**%**
Gross receipts	$320,000	100%	$350,000	100%	**$300,000**	100%
Beginning inventory	90,000	28%	95,000	27%	99,000	**33%**
Purchases	250,000	78%	275,000	79%	235,000	78%

	2013	%	2014	%	2015	%
			From Schedules C			
Ending inventory	95,000	30%	99,000	28%	**145,000**	**48%**
Cost of goods sold	$245,000	77%	$271,000	77%	**$189,000**	**63%**
Gross profit	$75,000	23%	$79,000	23%	**$111,000**	**37%**
Advertising	700	0%	900	0%	1,000	0%
Car & truck expenses	6,000	2%	6,000	2%	6,000	2%
Insurance	3,000	1%	3,000	1%	4,000	1%
Interest—other	100	0%	1,600	0%	1,800	1%
Legal & professional	750	0%	750	0%	**15,000**	**5%**
Office	395	0%	950	0%	550	0%
Rent	10,800	3%	10,800	3%	10,975	4%
Repairs	900	0%	1,200	0%	1,655	1%
Supplies	1,500	0%	1,668	0%	3,000	1%
Taxes & licenses	1,800	1%	1,200	0%	1,500	1%
Utilities	4,000	1%	4,000	1%	5,900	2%
Wages	4,000	1%	4,000	1%	**1,666**	1%
Total expenses	$33,945	11%	$36,068	10%	**$53,046**	**18%**
Net profit/loss	$41,055	13%	$42,932	12%	**$57,954**	**19%**

STEP 4: (Optional) Estimate the Impact of the Anomaly

The previous analysis detects some material differences. In the example above, ending inventory is a material anomaly (45% of gross receipts versus 28–30% of gross receipts in prior years). This anomaly *overstates* assets on the balance sheet (ending inventory) and *understates* gross and net profit on the income statement. In such circumstances you may want to *estimate the impact* of the anomalies. One method for estimating the ending inventory is the cost of goods sold/gross receipts method, which is demonstrated as follows.

Using the Periodic Inventory Formula

NOTE: Below is an example of the periodic inventory method where the company takes a physical inventory. The physical inventory is subtracted from the goods available for sale.

Take a Physical Inventory	Example
Beginning inventory	$100,000
Plus: Purchases	300,000
Equals: Goods available for sale	400,000
Minus: Ending inventory (B/S)	(75,000)
Equals: Cost of goods sold (I/S)	$325,000

NOTE: The periodic inventory method is *reversed* when the company cannot take an ending inventory (e.g., inventory is destroyed). The example takes numbers for the comparative schedules above.

First, *estimate* the cost of goods sold by dividing the average cost of goods sold by the average gross receipts from prior periods (using the previous example).

	2013	2014	Average
Cost of goods sold	$245,000	$271,000	$258,000
Gross receipts	$320,000	$350,000	$335,000
Percentage (CGS/Gross receipts)			77%
2015 Gross receipts		×	$300,000
2015 Estimated cost of goods sold			$231,000

Second, plug the estimated cost of goods sold into the formula to get the estimated ending inventory.

Inventory Destroyed	Example	
Beginning inventory	$99,000	
Plus: Purchases	235,000	
Minus: Est. Cost of goods sold	(231,000)	**Estimate using prior COGS/Gross Revenue** ⇐
Equals: Est. Ending inventory	$103,000	

1-3 EXERCISES—FRAUDULENT FINANCIAL STATEMENTS (LARSEN CONVENIENCE STORE)

Exercise 1: Individual Assignment

1. Input the IRS Schedules C from the 2013–2015 income tax returns into a spreadsheet.
   a. Add percent columns to the right of dollar column for each year.
   b. Calculate common-sized percentages in the percent columns [divide each number for that year (e.g., 2013) by gross receipts for that year (e.g., 2013)].
   c. Review the dollars horizontally across the three years and vertically down each year and identify any material irregularities.
   d. Review the percentages horizontally across the three years and vertically down each year and identify any material irregularities.
   e. Are there any material trends or material single-year changes (e.g., material increases or decreases)?
2. Input the other metrics from the individual tax returns (e.g., income from wages and salaries, interest earned, and estimated tax payments).
   a. Review the dollars horizontally across the three years and vertically down each year and identify any material irregularities.
   b. Compare estimated tax payments with total taxes for the year (vertically during the same year).
   c. Are there any material trends or material single-year changes (e.g., material increases or decreases)?
3. Because you did not observe the inventory, which was destroyed in the fire, estimate ending inventory using the 2013 and 2014 dollars and percentages (**Method #1: Cost of goods sold to gross receipts ratio**).

a. Because you did not observe the inventory, estimate the ending inventory for 2015 by:
   i. Averaging the 2013 and 2014 cost of goods sold and 2013 and 2014 gross receipts, and then dividing the average cost of goods sold by the average gross receipts. You cannot use an average of an average (e.g., Cost of goods sold/Gross receipts ratios for 2013 and 2014), which can distort the average. You must calculate the average for each and then the Cost of goods sold/Gross receipts ratio.
   ii. Multiply the resultant percentage from 3.a.i. by the 2015 gross receipts to get an estimated 2015 cost of goods sold total in dollars.

4. How does the estimated ending inventory impact the individual income tax return ending inventory, cost of goods sold, net profit, and net income? Find out by adding an additional column for 2015 and recalculate cost of goods sold using the estimates calculated above. Every number in that column is identical to the recorded 2015 column except estimated inventory, cost of goods sold, gross profit, and net profit.

5. Compare your recalculated ending inventory to that given to Sharptop Bank and to Southern Appalachian Insurance. Is either estimated ending inventory materially different from that reported on the 2015 IRS Schedule C?

6. OPTIONAL *(extra credit points determined by professor)* Because you did not observe the inventory, which was destroyed in the fire, estimate ending inventory by rolling the October 31, 2015, physical inventory totals forward (**method #2**).
   a. Starting with the October 31, 2015, physical inventory, roll the inventory forward at cost by adding the purchases from November 1, 2015, through December 31, 2015 (according to the various wholesaler purchase records), to the December 31, 2015, physical inventory totals. This results in the inventory available for sale during 2015.
   b. Then, reduce the inventory available for sale by the sales from November and December 2015 Georgia Sales and Use Tax Returns. Note: These sales are at retail price and must be reduced to wholesale cost. Use the Cost of goods sold/Gross receipts ratio determined in 3.a.i.

7. OPTIONAL *(extra credit points determined by professor)* Go to a business library or university librarian and locate RMA Annual Financial Statement Studies or a similar publication and locate convenience stores and comparable ratios (e.g., cost of goods sold to total revenues). How does the cost of goods sold to total receipts ratio in that publication compare to the ratios on the 2015 IRS Schedule C?

Exercise 2: Individual Assignment

1. Input information from the SBA Personal Financial Statements given to Sharptop Bank into a spreadsheet.
   a. Separate personal items (e.g., residence) from business items (e.g., inventory).
   b. Calculate common-sized percentages (divide each number by gross receipts for income statement items and total assets for balance sheet items for that particular year).
   c. Review the dollars horizontally across the three years and vertically down each year and identify any material irregularities.
   d. Review the percentages horizontally across the three years and vertically down each year and identify any material irregularities.
   e. Trace business items (e.g., accounts payable) to information provided by suppliers (e.g., fuel, groceries, beverage, tobacco, and print media sales summaries). Calculate any differences.
   f. Compare the reported inventory to the income tax returns and proof of loss (e.g., ending inventory). Calculate any differences.
2. If the tax return or insurance claim is misstated, did Greg Larsen commit some form of financial statement fraud?
3. What accuracy certifications on the tax return and bank financial statement address providing materially inaccurate information?
4. Was Larsen Convenience solvent on January 7, 2016? Solvency is defined three ways: (a) having more assets (particularly current assets) than liabilities (particularly current liabilities), or (b) Larsen Convenience cannot pay its debts when the dates come due, or (c) both (a) and (b).
5. How does Greg Larsen's business solvency impact his wife Tonya Larsen?

Exercise 3: Group Assignment—Writing Report and Associated Schedules

1. Prepare a final examination report to the attorney for Southern Appalachian Insurance and an accompanying set of schedules.
2. Prepare court-ready audiovisuals (e.g., one-page chart of talking points, summary schedule of the categories of the alleged material misstatements or omissions, comparative bar chart of a single item like ending inventory or net profit). Reference the schedules and audiovisuals in the report.

1-4 EXERCISE TEMPLATES

Larsen Convenience Store—Exercise #1

Financial Statement Fraud, Exercise #1 — Template

	From Schedules C (AS REPORTED)						REVISED based on Estimated Ending Inventory	
	2013	%	2014	%	2015	%	2015	%
Revenue								
Fuel revenue								
Beginning inventory								
+ Purchases								
= Ending inventory								
Cost of fuel								
Gross profit								
Groceries/food revenue								
Beginning inventory								
+ Purchases								
= Ending inventory								
Cost of groceries								
Gross profit								
Beverages revenue								
Beginning inventory								
+ Purchases								
= Ending inventory								
Cost of beverages								
Gross profit								
Tobacco revenue								
Beginning inventory								
+ Purchases								
= Ending inventory								
Cost of tobacco								
Gross profit								
Print media revenue								
Beginning inventory								
+ Purchases								
= Ending inventory								
Cost of print media								
Gross profit								
Bank ATM rents								
Beginning inventory								
+ Purchases								
= Ending inventory								
Cost of bank ATM rents								
Gross profit								
Total revenue								
Beginning inventory								
+ Purchases								
= Ending inventory								
Total cost of goods sold								
Total gross profit								
Expenses								
Administration fee								
Advertisement								
Cash over/short								
Credit card fees								
Rent expense								
Equipment station repair								
Expense items								
Insurance								
NSF checks expense								

Payroll tax expense					
Permits/legal					
Salaries					
Taxes					
Utilities					
Total All Expenses					
Net Profit (REPORTED)					
Net Profit (REVISED)					—
Difference (Reported, Less/ Estimated)					

(a) Ending Inventory Is Estimated using Cost of Goods Sold/Gross Receipts Method				% PROOF
	2013	**2014**	**2013–2014 Avg.**	**2015 (Estimated)**
Cost of groceries				
Gross Revenue - Groceries/Food				
2013–2014 Percent COGS/Gross receipts				
Cost of beverages				
Gross Revenue - Beverages				
2013–2014 Percent COGS/Gross receipts				
Cost of tobacco				
Gross Revenue - Tobacco				
2013–2014 Percent COGS/Gross receipts				

DAYS SALES OF INVENTORY CALCULATION				% PROOF
	2013	**2014**	**2015 (Reported)**	**2015 (Estimated)**
TOTAL INVENTORY				
Inventory	$ –	$ –	$ –	$ –
/ Cost of Sales	–	–	–	–
X 365 Days Sales of Inventory				
GROCERIES INVENTORY				
Inventory				
/ Cost of Sales				
X 365 Days Sales of Inventory				
BEVERAGES INVENTORY				
Inventory				
/ Cost of Sales				
X 365 Days Sales of Inventory				
TOBACCO INVENTORY				
Inventory				
/ Cost of Sales				
X 365 Days Sales of Inventory				

OTHER INCOME TAX RETURN INFORMATION - NOT IN SCHEDULES C			
	2013	**2014**	**2015 (Reported)**
Wages, salaries			
Interest			
Estimated Tax Payments			

Larsen Convenience Store—Exercise #2

Financial Statement Fraud, Exercise #2 — Template

January 2014, 2015, 2016 Financial Statements
Larsen Convenience
Source: Sharptop Bank

1.a. - 1.b.	As Given (Reported) to Sharptop Bank		
	1/7/2014	1/7/2015	1/7/2016
Residence - 213 Underwood Street, Canton, Georgia			
Cash - Savings			
Cash - Sharptop Bank (Larsen Convenience)			
2011 Jeep Grand Cherokee			
2014 Ford F-150			
Household goods			
Leasehold improvements			
Inventory (Larsen Convenience)			
Total assets	$ –	$ –	$ –
Credit card - Sharptop Bank			
Automobile loan - Sharptop Bank			
Truck loan - Sharptop Bank			
Accounts payable - Shamrock Groceries			
Accounts payable - Discount Tobacco Supply			
Accounts payable - Marietta Beverage Co.			
Accounts payable - Georgia-Tennese Fuel			
Accounts payable - Jenkins Media Services			
State sales and use taxes payable			
SBA note payable			
Mortgage - Integrity Mortgage			
Total liabilities	$ –	$ –	$ –
Total equity	$ –	$ –	$ –
Total liabilities and equity (equals total assets)	$ –	$ –	$ –

	Business Assets & Liabilities Only			REVISED (Per Source Docs.)
	1/7/2014	1/7/2015	1/7/2016	1/7/2016
Cash - Sharptop Bank (Larsen Convenience)				
Leasehold improvements				
Inventory (Larsen Convenience)				
Total assets	$ –	$ –	$ –	$ –
Accounts payable - Shamrock Groceries				
Accounts payable - Discount Tobacco Supply				
Accounts payable - Marietta Beverage Co.				
Accounts payable - Georgia-Tennese Fuel				
Accounts payable - Jenkins Media Services				
State sales and use taxes payable				
Note payable				
Wrongful death liability				
Total liabilities	$ –	$ –	$ –	
Total equity	$ –	$ –	$ –	
Total liabilities and equity (equals total assets)	$ –	$ –	$ –	

| | Personal Assets & Liabilities Only | | |
	1/7/2014	1/7/2015	1/7/2016
Residence - 213 Underwood Street, Canton, Georgia			
Cash - Sharptop Bank (Tonya)			
2011 Jeep Grand Cherokee			
2014 Ford F-150			
Household goods			
Total assets	$ –	$ –	$ –
Credit card - Sharptop Bank			
Automobile loan - Sharptop Bank			
Truck loan - Sharptop Bank			
Mortgage - Integrity Mortgage			
Total liabilities	$ –	$ –	$ –
Total equity	$ –	$ –	$ –
Total liabilities and equity (equals total assets)	$ –	$ –	$ –

1.c. - 1.d.

Horizontal and vertical analysis:
Business (1/7/16 v. prior years):

Personal:

1.e. - Accounts Payable Under-Statement	**Date**	**Amount**	**Difference**	
Shamrock Groceries per Financial Statement			//////	
Shamrock Groceries per Sales Summary				
Discount Tobacco per Financial Statement			//////	
Discount Tobacco per Sales Summary				
Marietta Beverage per Financial Statement			//////	**Total**
Marietta Beverage per Sales Summary				**Accounts**
Georgia-Tennessee per Financial Statement			//////	**Payable**
Georgia-Tennessee per Sales Summary				**Under-Statement**
Jenkins Media Sales per Financial Statement			//////	$ –
Jenkins Media Sales per Sales Summary				

1.f. - Ending Inventory Over-Statement	**Date**	**Amount**	**Difference**	
Ending Inv. - Estimated			//////	
Ending Inv. - Schedule C				**Ending Inventory**
Ending Inv. - Sharptop Bank				**Over-Statement**
Ending Inv. - Proof of Loss				$ –

2

If the tax return or insurance claim is misstated, did Greg Larsen commit some form of financial statement fraud? If so, what kind of fraud? Explain.

3

What accurary certifications (e.g., penalties of perjury, false statements) on tax return and bank financial statement address materially inaccurate information?

4

Was Larsen Convenience solvent on January 7, 2016? Explain.

5

How does Greg Larsen's solvency impact Tonya Larsen?

1-5   REVIEW QUESTIONS—FRAUDULENT FINANCIAL STATEMENTS (LARSEN CONVENIENCE STORE)

1. In the case scenario, Greg Larsen lost a wrongful death lawsuit for killing his nephew and is required to pay $500,000. The Georgia Supreme Court denied certiorari in May 2015 to hear an appeal to overturn the appellate court's affirmation of the lower court decision. When should the $500,000 judgment be shown on Larsen's personal financial statements?
   A. Subsequent to September 2013, when the state court judge handed down his decision.
   B. After October 2014, when the appellate court affirmed the lower court.
   C. Subsequent to May 2015, when the Georgia Supreme Court denied certiorari.
   D. He should have listed the $500,000 as a debt on all personal financial statements filed after September 2013.
2. Which types of financial statements do not have certifications about the accuracy of information listed on or submitted with the financial statements?
   A. Income tax forms (e.g., IRS Forms 1040, 1065, and 1120)
   B. Unaudited financial statements
   C. Credit applications or financial statements given to financial institutions
   D. Sworn statements in proof of loss submitted to insurance companies
3. In calculating common-sized ratios in a vertical and horizontal analysis, what is the base for calculating common-sized ratios for the balance sheet?
   A. Total assets
   B. Gross receipts
   C. Total liabilities
   D. Retained earnings
4. When compared to prior years' income statements (IRS Schedules C), the IRS Schedule C for the year ending 2015 shows net profit (and associated income taxes on the net profit) that far exceed prior years. In short, Greg Larsen had his best year yet. Based on that net profit and associated income taxes, you:
   A. Do not have to further investigate his finances because only a fool would overstate his/her net income and pay more income taxes than required.
   B. Should investigate Greg Larsen's finances further because his net income may be overstated (net income is easily overstated in a number

of ways including overstating ending inventory, which understates cost of goods sold and overstates gross income and net income).

C. Need to investigate further because Greg Larsen's primary suppliers made him sign promissory notes for unpaid balances.

D. Both B and C.

5. In calculating common-sized ratios in a vertical and horizontal analysis, what is the base for calculating common-sized ratios for the income statement?

A. Gross receipts

B. Total assets

C. Total liabilities

D. Retained earnings

6. When analyzing financial statements (e.g., unaudited financial statements and income tax returns), which of the following is correct?

A. Vertically analyze only the dollars.

B. Vertically and horizontally examine just the common-sized percentages looking for irregularities.

C. Vertically and horizontally analyze for anomalies in dollars and by percentages.

D. Scan for irregularities of all kinds.

7. In conducting a vertical and horizontal analysis, you can estimate the impact of irregularities (e.g., material differences in inventory balances) by:

A. Materially changing a suspected anomaly like ending inventory on a financial statement (e.g., the Balance Sheet) and determining its impact on related financial statements (e.g., the Income Statement and Statement of Retained Earnings).

B. Estimating the impact of the suspected irregularity by calculating what the anomaly would have been using prior-period information, ratios, and benchmarks.

C. Calculating the impact of the suspicious abnormal number by rolling forward the number from prior accounting periods using verifiable information like sales reported to taxing authorities and purchases from vendors.

D. All of the above.

CHAPTER TWO

Case 2: Check Fraud, Debit Card Fraud, Cash Larceny

2-1 ANDERSON INTERNAL MEDICINE: PREPARING A BANK RECONCILIATION AND SPREADING/ ANALYZING TRANSACTIONS ON MONTHLY STATEMENTS FROM FINANCIAL INSTITUTIONS

Learning Objective

After completing and discussing this case, you should be able to:

1. Prepare a bank reconciliation between the bank records and company's accounting records to determine the existence of unaccounted transactions that have not been recorded in the:
   - Bank statements (but have been recorded in the company's point-of-sale [POS] computer program), deposits in transit (i.e., deposits recorded on the company's books but not presented to the bank), and outstanding checks (i.e., checks recorded on the company's books but not presented to the bank); and/or,
   - Company's accounting records (but may have been recorded in the bank statements), including unrecorded fees (e.g., insufficient funds charges, monthly account fees, and other debit memorandums)

and unrecorded income (e.g., interest earned and other credit memorandums).

2. Enter into a spreadsheet debits and credits from financial institution monthly statements, identify the payee, maker, and endorsee on checks, read the transaction information on the back of checks, read the coding associated with debit (or ATM) card charges listed on the statements, read deposit slips, and then analyze the information.

3. Vouch transactions on the monthly statements to accounting records (e.g., cash receipts and cash disbursement journals).

4. Identify irregularities in payee, maker, and endorsee on checks, coding associated with debit (or ATM) card charges (e.g., when and where charged, timing) and the amount and type of deposits.

HISTORY BEHIND THE FRAUD CASE:

This is a combination of two fraud cases involving dental / medical practitioners. In one case, an oral surgeon arrived at his office on Monday morning and found that (1) his patient records had been shredded and (2) the passwords to access his computer dental accounting program and payroll accounting program had been changed. He called a forensic computer expert, who unlocked the computer only to find that the data had been wiped clean. A subsequent criminal background check found that the office manager had been convicted twice of fraud for thefts as a bookkeeper for two other businesses. In each case, the courts sentenced her to probation and restitution. It took one year to physically reconstruct the records and document substantial larceny and skimming. Local law enforcement eventually located her in another state and arranged to have her extradited to stand trial.

In the other fraud case, drug diversion agents arrested the office manager for attempting to use drug prescription pads taken from one of her doctors to obtain controlled painkillers. The agents conducted a physical inventory of the controlled substance locker at the doctors' office and found material shortages of painkillers. A week later, checks started bouncing. The new office manager spent months documenting the extent of the frauds—additional payroll checks made payable to the former office manager, checks made to payable to various companies on behalf of the former office manager, obtaining and using an unauthorized ATM / Debit Card to obtain cash, groceries, and other goods at locations over 30 miles from the doctors' office, and shorting cash from daily deposits. She pleaded guilty to the drug diversion charges.

As is common with small businesses, internal controls, particularly segregation of duties, were weak at both offices. Both former office managers had full custody of all assets, controlled all of the accounting duties, and authorized almost all receipts and disbursements, except for signing checks. They regularly fanned out checks during busy periods to get the doctors' signatures. Both doctors seldom asked for or reviewed any documentation. In addition, the edit function of the accounting programs allowed the office managers to print checks made payable to whomever they wanted and then in the edit run to change the payee name and accounting classification. As a result, the payee names on the canceled checks and in the cash disbursement journals were different.

Introduction

This case teaches you to prepare: (1) a bank reconciliation and (2) a spreadsheet with transactions listed on monthly statements. You will also examine the front and back of checks, the coding associated with debit card transactions, deposit tickets, as well as vouch the checks and debit card transactions to the cash disbursements journal and the deposits to the cash receipts journal.

Bank reconciliations account for the differences between the month-end balance shown on the financial institution statement and the corresponding total shown in the company's books of record (i.e., cash and related accounts). Completion of the bank reconciliation requires a number of adjustments for timing differences and items found on the statement or books of record (e.g., checks or deposits listed on the books but yet to be received by the bank, and interest earned at the financial institution that has yet to be recorded on the books). When all adjustments have been made, there might still be a yet-to-be-explained difference. When two or more bank reconciliations (e.g., prior and current reconciliation) result in large unaccounted-for differences, the differences might be larceny, lapping, another type of cash fraud, or material accounting error. Such large unaccounted-for differences require additional fraud examination work (e.g., interviewing those who handle cash, examination of individual receivable accounts, reviewing adjusting journal entries and account edits).

Monthly statements from financial institutions (e.g., bank, credit unions, savings and loan associations, and stock brokerage firms) offer a great deal of information, some of which reflects how the alleged fraudster or company spent its money (e.g., personal as opposed to business expenses). It can also detect such illegal activities as unauthorized use of debit (or ATM) cards, check kiting, money laundering, and so on.

Balances in the general ledger and trial balance accounts are not always what they seem. Through the following analyses, you will detect receipts and disbursements that do not agree with the cash receipts and disbursement journal descriptions, unauthorized use of debit cards, and the possibility of larceny.

Background

Greg and Tonya Larsen are being investigated by law enforcement and Southern Appalachian Insurance Company, the company that insured Anderson Internal Medicine (AIM).

Early on Friday, April 1, 2016, the branch manager of the Bank of Lawrenceville called Jennifer Anderson, MD, the CEO of Anderson Internal Medicine, to inform her that the medical practice's checking account was overdrawn by $5,945.43. Late last night, the bank paid as a courtesy four charges that overdrew the account ($2,339.50, $2,501.66, $2,497.89, and $280.00). In addition, it returned four checks totaling $6,159.75 ($1,534.73, $1,783.83, $1,341.19, and $1,500.00). Dr. Anderson spoke with Tonya Larsen when she arrived. Tonya quickly performed a bank reconciliation and announced that the shortage was the result of several missing deposits because she had not deposited some receipts, which were in her credenza. Tonya promised to track down and deposit the missing deposits and personally cover the insufficient funds (NSF) charges. The two agreed to go over the books early on Monday morning. Tonya Larsen spent the remainder of the day in her office with her door closed and stayed behind after the last patient and all employees left for the day.

Dr. Anderson arrived early on Monday and went straight to Ms. Larsen's desk. She found a wastebasket overflowing with shredded paper. She immediately went to the file room, where she found a giant trash bag also overflowing with shredded paper and empty patient file folders tossed haphazardly all around the file room. Dr. Anderson attempted to access the point-of-sale, accounting, and payroll systems, but could not get into either computer system—none of the passwords worked. She called in a forensic computer examiner, who successfully unlocked the computer, but found that much of the data on the hard drive had been erased. Over several days, he was able to un-erase some of the data.

Late on Monday, a lawyer emailed Dr. Anderson and left a voice message on her personal cell phone that he represented Greg and Tonya Larsen and left instructions that no one was allowed to talk with either of them. Any inquiries that she or anyone else had MUST go through him.

AIM's new office manager spent two weeks attempting to make sense out of the mess and file an employee dishonesty claim with Southern Appalachian Insurance Company. She found $260.00 in cash, $2,210.00 in patient and insurance company checks, and two business debit cards in Tonya Larsen's file cabinet. She also confirmed that the ending balance in the cash account for the point-of-sale system was $901.47 in the general ledger. After getting a copy of an order form from the Bank of Lawrenceville, the new office manager discovered that Tonya Larsen obtained the two debit cards without the authorization of Dr. Anderson. She also obtained facsimiles of canceled and dishonored checks and deposit tickets for March 2016.

The special agents with the insurance company's Special Investigative Unit (SIU) found that:

Tonya previously worked for Absolute Orthopedics, Marietta, Georgia, as the office manager. She resigned at the end of March 2015 after the practice started bouncing checks. Absolute Orthopedics' CPA determined that over $30,000.00 was missing. The practice filed an employee dishonesty claim with its insurance company (not Southern Appalachian Insurance Company), but could not definitively determine who caused the loss. The case was referred to the Cobb County Sheriff's Office. Their investigation is still open.

Notes

1. AIM uses a point-of-sale (POS) computer program to record the cash receipts, debit card, credit card (e.g., AMEX, Discover, MasterCard, VISA), and insurance charges (e.g., Blue Cross Blue Shield, Medicare, Medicaid, Tricare) for patient services. *Only the daily cash receipts are deposited to the checking account at Sharptop Bank.* The deposits of subsequent settlement payments for credit card charges and insurance charges are deposited in a separate bank lock box that monitors charge transactions.
2. Dr. Anderson owns a Lexus RX 350, which she finances with Sharptop Bank.

Summary Requirements

You have been retained by Alexander Z. Boone, Esq., the independent attorney hired by Southern Appalachian Insurance Company, to examine an employee dishonesty claim filed by Anderson Internal Medicine. You work under attorney-client privilege (i.e., your work is not made available to opposing counsel until authorized by Alexander Boone).

Before proceeding, read the documents in Chapter 7, section 7-2, "Anderson Internal Medicine." As with the prior case, you will have to read and reread the documents to fully understand the evidence.

On your own, research how to prepare a bank reconciliation. It can easily be found online. Study sections 2-3 and 2-4, *How to Read Checks and Decode Debit Card Transactions* and *How to Spread and Analyze Check and Debit Card Transactions* before conducting the specific requirements of this case.

The results of your assignment will be used by the attorney. Your assignment (in general) is, as follows:

1. Determine the types of employee dishonestly frauds allegedly perpetrated by Tonya Larsen on Anderson Internal Medicine. Determine how the alleged fraud could have occurred at the medical practice (e.g., weak internal controls) and what Anderson Internal Medicine needs to do to deter future frauds.
2. Determine the amount of verifiable loss from alleged employee dishonesty at Anderson Internal Medicine.
3. Determine what additional steps need to be taken to examine the yet-to-be-determined difference detected by the bank reconciliation.
4. Prepare a report and associated schedules using the sample report and schedules.
5. Prepare audiovisuals (e.g., charts, summary schedules, and/or graphs of your choice) to simplify these complex accounting issues.

The initial steps (see exercises) are to be completed individually. You may confer online about examination strategy, but must do your own work. In particular, each student is to perform the various fraud examination steps and submit their Excel working papers (e.g., schedules) for grades. These steps will be performed as a series of graded exercises designed to walk you through the process.

The final exercise is a team project. Each team will submit a final examination report addressed to the attorney for Southern Appalachian Insurance Company, accompanying set of schedules, and audiovisuals for a grade. Each team is to select a team leader, assign various tasks to each member of the team, and email a list of each student's assignment. Pick your team leader wisely, as he/she is responsible for quality control and should not take on any additional tasks. The team leader makes sure that deliverables are received in a timely manner (i.e., schedules, audiovisuals, and report in that order) and proofreads the report before submission.

Look Closer at Repeating Debit Card Transactions at Big Box Stores and Chain Grocery Stores

If you examine checking accounts of persons suspected of money laundering and find small, repeating debit card transactions (say $25 to $75) at big-box stores or chain grocery stores, you might be witnessing the 5 percent fee charged by customer service for loading prepaid cards valued from $500 to $1,500. Similarly, large dollar transactions at grocery stores (say $1,575 or $2,337) may not be for groceries. Yes, persons might spend $400 or more for the monthly groceries, but not $2,337. Something else is transpiring. You might be witnessing the conversion of cash to stored value cards for shipment outside the United States. What is a 5 percent fee to a fraudster if they can convert it to an easily transportable medium that does not come under the U.S. Treasury Cash Transaction Regulations (CTR). Explore those transactions further. Call or visit the big-box store or chain grocery store and get their policies concerning converting cash to stored value cards. Also, inquire about the store's retention of electronic records of these transactions, which can be obtained by subpoena. Some stores also have video cameras that surveil customer service.

2-2 HOW TO PERFORM A BANK RECONCILIATION

Learning Objective

After reading this synopsis, you should be able to:

1. Better understand the purpose of a bank reconciliation.
2. Be able to complete a bank reconciliation.

Introduction

Bank reconciliations are an accounting tool used to schedule differences between the company's books and records and the bank's books and records on a specific day (e.g., last day of the month) for an individual account held by a financial institution. Where the company owns more than one account at a financial institution, bank reconciliations must be performed for each account. To a large degree, the differences between the two sets of records involve timing (e.g., items in transit between the company and financial institution) and unrecorded transactions (e.g., interest earned in a bank account that has yet to be recorded on the company's books and records).

When a bank reconciliation detects an unknown difference, that difference is a red flag, which must be investigated further. An unexplained difference might be a timing difference, recording a transaction in the wrong ledger, or fraud. Example #1, a bank reconciliation, detects a $100,000 undetermined shortage where deposits involve only checks and clerks regularly scan and electronically deposit checks. Further investigation reveals that an envelope of checks is found in a clerk's desk drawer. It initially appears that the clerk failed to timely deposit customer checks. However, when the checks are scanned and electronically deposited, customers scream that their checks were processed twice. You conduct a second bank reconciliation of another ending date that results in a similar $100,000 undetermined shortage. Interview the clerk involved and those working around the clerk as you might have uncovered some form of lapping. Example #2, a bank reconciliation, detects a $7,000 undetermined shortage where deposits involve both cash and checks and undeposited cash and checks are found in a drawer. Further review of deposit slips reveals little or no cash being deposited or round dollar amounts of cash being deposited on a routine basis. Interview the clerk and those working around the clerk. You might have uncovered some form of cash larceny.

In both examples, ask the following: Who handles deposits? How are the deposits handled? What are the internal controls, if any?

Steps in Performing a Bank Reconciliation

Performing a bank reconciliation is a multistep process. There are several standard formats. Often, the format is located on the back of the monthly bank statement.

Ending Balance on Bank Statement Dated	Step 1	$	-
Adjustments to Bank Statement			
Add: Deposits in Transit (list below)	Step 2		
	Step 2		-
			-
Subtract: Outstanding Checks (list below)	Step 2		
	Step 2		-
	Step 2		-
Adjusted Balance on Bank Statement	**TOTAL**	$	-

Balance per Books and Records as of	**Step 1**	$	-
Adjustments to Books and Records			
Add: Transactions on Bank Statement Not in Books and Records			
Interest Earned from Bank	**Step 3**		-
Other	**Step 3**		-
Other	**Step 3**		-
Subtract: Transaction on Bank Statement Not in Books and Records			
Bank Charges	**Step 3**		-
NSF Checks	**Step 3**		-
NSF Fees	**Step 3**		-
Other	**Step 3**		-
Other	**Step 3**		-
Unexplained Difference (If Any)—Needed to Balance	**Step 4**		
Adjusted Balance on Books and Records		$	-

STEP 1: On the section of the bank reconciliation involving the bank, input the ending balance from the financial institution statement. Similarly, on the section for the books and records (accounting records), insert the ending balance shown in the books of record.

STEP 2: Review the bank statement against the accounting records and determine the deposits in transit and outstanding checks. To identify the deposits in transit (deposits in the accounting records but not listed on the bank statement), vouch the transactions shown in the cash receipts journal against those listed in the bank statement. List the deposits that have yet to clear the financial institution on the reconciliation. To determine the outstanding checks (checks written and reflected in the accounting records but have not cleared the bank), vouch the checks shown in the cash disbursements journal against those listed in the bank statement. List the checks that have not been cashed. If there are too many for the reconciliation, schedule the outstanding checks separately.

Pay special attention to checks that overdraw the account. Occasionally, financial institutions will pay checks that overdraw an account as a courtesy (e.g., pay the monthly mortgage check or the annual real estate taxes). Overdrawn checks clear the bank, but usually result in an insufficient funds (NSF) charge.

Pay close attention to ATM and debit card transactions that have cleared the financial institution but have not been listed in the accounting records. You will have to list them separately under Balance per Books and Records (see **Step 4**) and the company will need to make an adjustment to its accounting records. In the age of ATM and debit cards in the hands of many employees (e.g., company purchasing cards), there may be unrecorded transactions.

STEP 3: On the bank statement, identify transactions that may be on the bank statement but are yet to be entered into the accounting records (e.g., credits not recorded, like interest earned on deposit balances, and debits not recorded, like bank charges for account servicing fees, periodic loan interest payments, and NSF fees). Those often take place on the last day of the month and have not been entered into the accounting records. You also may have debits not recorded like ATM and debit card transactions. On the section of the bank reconciliation involving the books and records, input those transactions and alert the company of the need to make an adjustment to its accounting records.

STEP 4: After making the above adjustments, the adjusted balance on the bank statement and adjusted balance on the Books and Records should agree. If the unexplained difference is large you might have a timing difference, recording a transaction in the wrong ledger, or fraud. You will have to investigate further.

2-3 HOW TO READ CHECKS AND DECODE DEBIT CARD TRANSACTIONS

Learning Objective

After reading this synopsis, you should be able to:

1. Better understand the information on the front and back of canceled checks.
2. Be able to understand debit card transactions found on the bank statement.

Introduction

Essential to spreading canceled checks is the ability to read and decipher the information located on the front and back of checks.

Initially, all the fraud examiner may only have is a quick printout of the front of the check. This will suffice to get the analysis started until the front and back of the cancel checks are obtained. Like the front, the back of a canceled check contains a wealth of information.

How to Read a Canceled Check

Each canceled check contains a number of specific identifiers that describe the check as shown in the following example. The *payee* is the person or company to whom the check is payable. The payee name must agree with the first

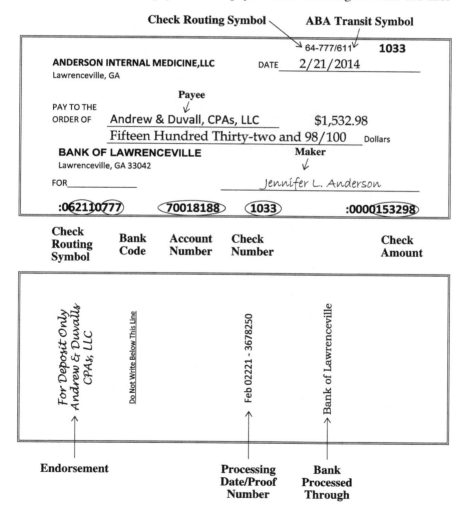

endorsee name on the back of the check. The *check routing symbol* and *American Bankers Association (ABA) bank code* (or *ABA transit symbol*) appears at the upper-right-hand corner and lower-left-hand corner of the check. The *maker* is the person who signs/makes the check. The *account number, check number,* and *check amount* appear at the bottom of the check under the signature. The check amount at the right-hand bottom of the check is entered by the bank proofreaders after matching and agreeing with the customer's handwritten and hand-numbered amounts.

Signatures and Endorsements

The fraud examiner is ***not*** a handwriting expert. However, the fraud examiner can flag maker and endorsee signatures that obviously appear to have been written by another person. These flagged maker and endorsee signatures should be examined and opined by a certified handwriting expert.

Endorsements are signatures on the back of a check. It is suggested that you review a business law textbook on endorsements. There are restricted and unrestricted endorsements that affect the negotiability of the checks. One well-known restricted endorsement is "For Deposit Only" followed by the payee's endorsement. If the payee does not restrict the endorsement, anyone else can sign a second, third, and so on time. As fraud examiners, list all secondary endorsements. Fraudsters use secondary endorsements to convert checks. Although the secondary endorsements may be perfectly legal, you need to track those endorsements for subsequent analysis.

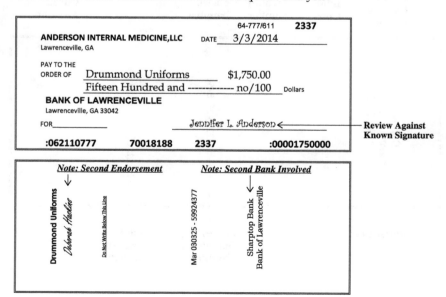

How to Decode a Debit Card Transaction

Each financial institution has its own method of listing debit card transactions. The following are example of coding found on bank statements.

3/28 $398.56 POS DEB 16:53 3/26/16 Grocery-City 21108888 Marietta, GA

This represents a point of service debit at a Grocery City store located in Marietta, Georgia, at 4:53 p.m. on Saturday, March 26, 2016. The transaction cleared the bank on Monday, March 28, 2016.

3/28 Check Crd Purchase 03/26 Chevron 3699 Ellijay GA 5678 473722xxxx xx1269 173064695279267 ?McC=3793

The above point of service debit took place at a Chevron gas station located in Ellijay, Georgia, on Saturday, March 26, 2016, using a MasterCard debit card ending in 3793. The transaction cleared the bank on Monday, March 28, 2016.

03/28 Mach ID 0377D 17622 3/27 Hwy 41 Kennesaw GA 4730 0007207

This debit card coding shows a debit withdrawal using a debit card at a debit machine located in Kennesaw, Georgia, on Sunday, March 27, 2016. The transaction cleared the bank on Monday, March 28, 2016.

NOTE: The actual transaction date and bank statement clearing date may not be the same. The normal bank day, as set by the Federal Reserve System, is from 4:01 p.m. until 4:00 p.m. the following day. Accordingly, a transaction taking place after 6:21 p.m. (e.g., on Wednesday) will be shown as a cleared transaction on the bank statement on the following banking day (e.g., Thursday). Weekends are even longer (i.e., from 4:01 p.m. on Friday through 4:00 p.m. on Monday). When viewing your online bank statement, the debit card transactions are shown as "Pending" until actually cleared.

2-4   HOW TO SPREAD AND ANALYZE CHECK AND DEBIT CARD TRANSACTIONS

Learning Objective

After reading this synopsis, you should be able to:

1. Input data from bank, credit card, or investment accounts.
2. Add categories for subsequent analysis.
3. Sort data based on categories, names, dates, and more.

Introduction

One of the most frequent forensic accounting procedures is analyzing canceled checks, debit card transactions, and deposits to a checking or savings account. The procedure can similarly be applied to analyzing debits and credits to credit card and investment account statements.

When you must input and analyze numerous different accounts or numerous months of the same account, request not only hard copies of the monthly statements, but request the information in .csv (comma separated value) file format, which can be imported into popular programs like Excel, Access, and IDEA. Importing vast data using .csv will save your hands and hours of boring data input.

Steps in Spreading and Analyzing Check and Debit Card Transactions

Performing an analysis of check and debit card transactions is a multistep process.

STEP 1: Input the Data

Schedule the data. *There are a number of formats.* Based on what you want to analyze, determine a format before scheduling the data. This way, you can set column formats (e.g., date format for the dates column, dollar format with decimals for dollars, text format for descriptions, and so on). Keep the check, debit, and deposit columns separate for quick identification.

Depending on the purpose of the analysis (e.g., analyzing all the sources and uses of all transactions, identifying kited funds, or money laundering), you may want to input all transactions or set a threshold (e.g., record only transactions over a limit that you set, say over $500 or $2,500).

On page 43 is an example of a simple checking account analysis. Be sure to clearly label your spreadsheet/analysis so a user knows what you have done.

STEP 2: Add a Category Column

To be able to sort, you may want to add a category column (or some other means of logically sorting the spreadsheet). You are limited only by your lack of imagination. Each time you sort, save the new spreadsheet as a separate tab at the bottom of the spreadsheet. That way you will have numerous, readily available sorts. Each sort is a different analysis.

To get quick totals, use the PivotTable function under the Data tab. See page 44 for an example of adding a category column.

FROM JANUARY 1, 2014 TO JANUARY 31, 2014
ALL TRANSACTIONS—LISTED IN DESCENDING POSTED DATE ORDER
ANDERSON INTERNAL MEDICINE
Norcross, Georgia

LABEL THE SPREADSHEET

Schedule 1

Beginning balance agrees with bank statement
Ending balance agrees with bank statement

Check Number	Check Date	Posted Date	Check/Debit Amount	Deposit Date	Deposit Amount	Bank Balance	Remitter of Deposited Check	Payee Per Check/Debit	Check Endorsement	Check Deposited at	Cashed at	Comments
		01/06/14		01/06/14	3,500.00	3,500.00	Tonya Larsen		Tonya Larsen	BoA		
		01/06/14	300.00			3,200.00		Counter Debit— Official Check Sale Transfer to Chk 3730				
		01/06/14	1,800.00			1,400.00		Woodstock				
		01/06/14	35.00			1,365.00		Check order				
820	01/09/14	01/10/14	180.00			1,185.00		John Johnson	J Stan Johnson		Regions	For Basement
		01/19/14	300.00			885.00		Withdrawal				
		01/21/14	30.00			855.00		MG Sports Grille				
821	01/23/14	01/23/14	35.00			820.00		Publix				
		01/24/14	69.21			750.79		BP				
		01/25/14	21.00			729.79		Zaxby's				
		01/27/14		01/31/14	2,000.00	2,729.79		Anne Taylor				
		01/29/14	201.12			2,528.67		Dos Fajita Mexican				
		01/31/14	32.05			2,496.62		QT				
			3,003.38		5,500.00							

DETAILS OF TRANSACTIONS IN BANK OF LAWRENCEVILLE A/C 123456

FROM JANUARY 1, 2014 TO JANUARY 31, 2014

ALL TRANSACTIONS —LISTED IN DESCENDING POSTED DATE ORDER

ANDERSON INTERNAL MEDICINE

Norcross, Georgia

Schedule 1

Check Number	Check Date	Posted Date	Check/Debit Amount	Deposit Date	Deposit Amount	Bank Balance	Remitter of Deposited Check	Payee Per Check/Debit	Category (IF NEEDED ADD CATEGORIES FOR SORTING)	Check Endorsement	Check Deposited at	Cashed at	Comments
		01/06/14		01/06/14	3,500.00	3,500.00	Tonya Larsen			Tonya Larsen	BoA		
		01/06/14	300.00			3,200.00		Counter Debit—Official Check Sale	Cash				
								Transfer to Chk 3730					
		01/06/14	1,800.00			1,400.00		Woodstock	Cash				
		01/06/14	35.00			1,365.00		Check order	Miscellaneous				
820	01/09/14	01/10/14	180.00			1,185.00		John Johnson	Basement	J Stan Johnson		Regions	For Basement
		01/19/14	300.00			885.00		Withdrawal	Cash				
		01/21/14	30.00			855.00		MG Sports Grille	Restaurant				
821	01/23/14	01/23/14	35.00			820.00		Publix	Grocery				
		01/24/14	69.21			750.79		BP	Automobile				
		01/25/14	21.00			729.79		Zaxby's	Restaurant				
		01/27/14		01/31/14	2,000.00	2,729.79		Anne Taylor	Clothes				
		01/29/14	201.12			2,528.67		Dos Fajita Mexican	Restaurant				
		01/31/14	32.05			2,496.62		QT	Automobile				
			3,003.38		5,500.00								

44

STEP 3: Add a Numbers Column to Re-sort to Original Order and Then Sort

You will almost always have to go back to the original input. So, add another column, add the numbers in chronological order (e.g., 1, 2, 3, and so on), and then perform a custom sort (e.g., on Category, Payee Name, or Remitter). Later, you might want to hide the Number column to avoid confusion by a subsequent readers (you can always unhide that column at a later date). Note that the ending bank balance has not changed—the ending bank balance is your control total. See page 46 for an example of adding a numbers column.

2-5 EXERCISES—CHECK FRAUD, DEBIT CARD FRAUD, AND CASH LARCENY (ANDERSON INTERNAL MEDICINE)

Exercise 1: Individual Assignment

1. Perform a bank reconciliation as of April 1, 2016, using the bank statement for March 2016, cash receipts journal, and cash disbursements journal.
2. Compare the front and back of checks and the deposit slips to the cash receipts and cash disbursement journals and identify:
   a. Checks where payees do not match
   b. Irregular disbursements
   c. Irregular signatures
   d. Irregular endorsements
3. Review the bank statements for disbursements not involving checks and trace to the cash disbursements journal.
   a. What are these transactions?
   b. Where and when (date and day of the week) were these noncheck transactions actually made (not when recorded)?
   c. How far is the distance between the location of these noncheck transactions and Anderson Internal Medicine?
   d. Where does Tonya Larsen live?

FROM JANUARY 1, 2014 TO JANUARY 31, 2014

ALL TRANSACTIONS—SORTED BY CATEGORY ← → CHANGE TITLE TO REFLECT SORT

ANDERSON INTERNAL MEDICINE

Norcross, Georgia

Schedule 1

ADD NUMBERS BEFORE SORTING SO YOU CAN GET BACK TO THE ORIGINAL ORDER
(INCLUDE NUMBERS IN THE SORT AND HIDE WHEN COMPLETED)

No.	Check Number	Check Date	Posted Date	Check/Debit Amount	Deposit Date	Deposit Amount	Bank Balance	Remitter of Deposited Check	Payee Per Check/Debit	Category	Check Endorsement	Check Deposited at	Cashed at	Comments
9			01/24/14	69.21			(69.21)		BP	Automobile				
			01/31/14	32.05			(101.26)		QT	Automobile				
5	820	01/09/14	01/10/14	180.00			(281.26)		John Johnson	Basement	J Stan Johnson		Regions	For Basement
2			01/06/14	300.00			(581.26)		Official Check	Cash				
3			01/06/14	1,800.00			(2,381.26)		3730	Cash				
6			01/19/14	300.00			(2,681.26)		Withdrawal	Cash				
11			01/27/14		01/31/14	2,000.00	(681.26)		Anne Taylor	Clothes				
8	821	01/23/14	01/23/14	35.00			(716.26)		Publix	Grocery				
4			01/06/14	35.00			(751.26)		Check order	Miscellaneous				
7			01/21/14	30.00			(781.26)		Grille	Restaurant				
10			01/25/14	21.00			(802.26)		Zaxby's	Restaurant				
12			01/29/14	201.12			(1,003.38)		Dos Fajita Mexican	Restaurant				
1			01/06/14		01/06/14	3,500.00	2,496.62	Tonya Larsen			Tonya Larsen	BoA		
				3,003.38		3,500.00								
						5,500.00								

    e. What part did Tonya Larsen play in making these noncheck disbursements?

    f. Did Tonya Larsen benefit from these noncheck transactions?

4. Review the deposits.

    a. How often and when were the deposits made?

    b. Is anything missing from the deposits?

    c. How do deposits relate to the bank reconciliation?

Exercise 2: Individual Assignment

1. List the items (e.g., check numbers, transaction dates, and individual amounts) and totals of each category of fraud.

2. What are the alleged frauds (e.g., accounts receivable skimming, disbursement fraud, embezzlement, larceny, payroll fraud, skimming, other)? Discuss each one.

3. How were each of the frauds concealed?

4. What circumstances allowed the frauds to happen (e.g., internal control failures, lack of background checks, missing policies and procedures)? Discuss and be specific.

5. What would you recommend (e.g., controls, monitoring) to deter future frauds from happening? Discuss and be specific.

6. Is there anyone you would like to interview? If so, what do you want to learn from them?

7. Are there any additional steps you would like to take with respect to the fraud examination?

Exercise 3: Group Assignment—Writing Report and Associated Schedules

1. Prepare a final examination report to the attorney for Southern Appalachian Insurance and an accompanying set of schedules

2. Prepare associated audio-visuals (e.g., one-page chart of talking points, summary schedule of the categories of the loss, simplified schedule of the details of each category, bar/pie/or line chart). Note: Do not put the schedules and audiovisuals in a PowerPoint or similar presentation. The schedules and audiovisuals are addendums to the report and MUST be referenced in the report.

2-6 EXERCISE TEMPLATES

Anderson Internal Medicine—Exercise #1

Check Fraud, Debit Card Fraud, Cash Larceny Case, Exercise #1 Template
Bank Reconciliation - Anderson Internal Medicine (4-1-16) (REVISED)

1. Balance per bank   Balance per books

   Add: Deposits in transit   Add: Credits not
                                       recorded

   Less: Outstanding   Subtract: Debits not
   checks   recorded

                      _____   Less: unknown   _____
                                       difference (if any)

   Reconciled balance $ -   Reconciled balance $ -
   Comments (if any):

Compare the front and back of checks and the deposit slips to the cash receipts and cash disbursement journals and identify:

2.a. Check numbers of the checks where payees do not match on check and cash disbursements journal CDJ
2.b. Check numbers of the checks with irregular disbursements—not listed as vendors in CDJ
2.c. Check numbers of the checks with irregular maker signatures—different from known signature
2.d. Check numbers of the checks with irregular endorsements

Review the bank statements for disbursements not involving checks and trace to the cash disbursements journal

3.a. What are these transactions (e.g., cash withdrawals, ewithdrawals, debit card withdrawals)?
3.b. Where and when (date and day of the week) were these noncheck transactions actually made (may not be the same as the date when recorded)?
3.c. What is the distance between the location of these noncheck transactions and Anderson Internal Medicine?

3.d. Where does Tonya Larsen live?

3.e. What part did Tonya Larsen play in making these noncheck disbursements?

3.f. Did Tonya Larsen benefit from these noncheck transactions? If yes, how did she benefit?

Review the deposit slips

4.a. How often and when were the deposits made?

4.b. Is anything missing from the deposits?

4.c. How do the deposits relate to the bank reconciliation?

Anderson Internal Medicine—Exercise #2

Check Fraud, Debit Card Fraud, Cash Larceny Case, Exercise #2 Template

1. List the items (e.g., check numbers, transaction dates, and individual amounts) and totals of each category of fraud.

Check Number	Amount
Total Checks	$ -
Trans. Date	
Total Debit Card Transactions	$ -
Cash - unknown difference	
Total	$ -

2. What are the alleged frauds (e.g., accounts receivable skimming, disbursement fraud, embezzlement, larceny, payroll fraud, skimming, other)? Discuss each one.

3. How were each of the frauds concealed?

4. What circumstances allowed the frauds to happen (e.g., internal control failures, lack of background checks, missing policies and procedures)? Discuss and be specific.

5. What would you recommend (e.g., controls, monitoring) to deter future frauds from happening? Discuss and be specific.

6. Is there anyone you would like to interview? If so, what do you want to learn from them?

7. Are there any additional steps you would like to take with respect to the fraud examination?

2-7 REVIEW QUESTIONS—CHECK FRAUD, DEBIT CARD FRAUD, AND CASH LARCENY (ANDERSON INTERNAL MEDICINE)

1. In the case scenario, it states that when two or more bank reconciliations (e.g., prior and current reconciliation) result in large unaccounted for differences, the differences might be what?
   A. Cash larceny.
   B. Material accounting errors.
   C. Some other type of cash-related fraud.
   D. Any of the above.
2. If a lawyer for the suspect in a fraud examination states that he/she represents the suspect and no one will be allowed to talk with their client, can you interview the suspect or his/her spouse?
   A. Yes, you can interview either the suspect or his/her spouse.
   B. No, you cannot interview either the suspect or his/her spouse.
   C. You cannot interview the suspect, but can interview his/her spouse.
   D. You can subpoena the suspect and compel them to answer your questions under oath.
3. Who is a payee on a check?
   A. The person(s) who signs the front of the check.
   B. The person(s) who signs the back of the check.
   C. The person(s) named on the front of the check who is to receive the funds.
   D. The financial institution that pays the funds specified by the check.
4. In the case, the new office manager found cash, patient and insurance company checks, and two business debit cards in Tonya Larsen's file cabinet. When preparing the bank reconciliation, where do you put the cash and checks—under balance per bank or balance per books?
   A. Balance per bank because the items represent deposits in transit.
   B. Balance per books because the items have not been recorded and an adjustment needs to be made to the books of record.
   C. Neither A nor B.
   D. Both A and B.
5. 3/28 $398.56 POS DEB 16:53 3/26/16 Grocery-City 21108888 Marietta, GA on the bank statement means?
   A. $398.56 was paid by a point-of-sale use of a debit card.
   B. Grocery City in Marietta, Georgia, was the location of the transaction.

   C. The transaction took place on March 26, 2016 (a Saturday), but the financial institution posted the transaction on March 28, 2016 (a Monday).

   D. All of the above.

6. When scheduling checking account transactions for subsequent analysis you perform all of the following except?

   A. Input the dates on the check.

   B. Schedule the dollar amounts, including decimals.

   C. Limit the checks input into the schedule to only those over a certain dollar amount (say, $500.00).

   D. List the payee name as found on each individual check.

7. When you analyze the checking account disbursement paid by a financial institution, what should you do?

   A. Compare the names and dollar amounts on the front and back of the checks to the cash disbursements journal.

   B. Review the bank statements for disbursements not involving checks (e.g., debit card or ATM transactions and cash withdrawals made at the teller window or ATM) and trace those transactions to the cash disbursements journal.

   C. For debit card transactions where you do not recognize the payee (e.g., person or business name), you look the payee up on the Internet to determine the person (e.g., accountant, financial adviser, or lawyer) and/or type of business.

   D. All of the above.

CHAPTER THREE

Case 3: Fraudulent Edits/Adjusting Journal Entries

3-1 ANDERSON INTERNAL MEDICINE (EDITS/AJEs): VOUCHING FROM A SCHEDULE TO SOURCE DOCUMENTS

Learning Objective

After completing and discussing this case, you should be able to examine edits/adjusting journal entries to accounting system records to determine whether any transactions have been altered:

a. Download the accounting record to be examined (e.g., extract edits to cash receipts) for the period you want to examine.

b. Obtain copies of the associated supporting documents (e.g., deposit ticket and bank statement) for the same time period.

c. Schedule the date and amount of the original transaction (e.g., cash before edit) and the date and amount of the edited transactions (e.g., cash after the edit) and differences between the original and edited transactions.

d. Vouch transactions from the accounting record (e.g., data extraction) to the supporting documents (e.g., verify the amount and date of cash actually deposited).

e. Determine whether the edit was justified.
f. If the amounts were not justified, identify the total number and dollars of irregularities.

This case explores the process of vouching from a schedule (e.g., data extraction of edits/adjusting journal entries) to source documents (e.g., deposit slips and bank statements).

HISTORY BEHIND THE FRAUD CASE

The owner of a chain of supply stores was enjoying his morning coffee while reviewing his monthly financial statements for each store. He noticed a month-to-month decline in the sales of one location. Later that day, the owner found the bank statements for the store and examined the last several months of deposits. Like gross receipts, there was a similar month-to-month decline in cash deposits. Overall, sales were down over 25 percent compared to the prior year. He tasked a programmer in the Information Technology (IT) department to extract daily sales, deposits, and edits to both accounts for the last 90 days. The IT programmer came back, concluding that receipts for many deposits appeared to have been decreased several hundred dollars per day.

In the subsequent fraud examination, photocopies of all deposit tickets for the last 90 days were requested from the bank and the IT department extracted daily sales records from the point-of-sale (POS) system for the same period. Tests were undertaken to access the validity of the initial data extraction of daily sales, deposits, and edits: (1) the actual daily sales per the point-of-sale records were vouched to the pre-edit cash receipts in the IT extraction; and (2) the actual daily deposits as shown on the deposit tickets were vouched to the cash receipts on the initial data extraction (i.e., the daily post-edit cash receipts). Then, the amount of the alleged larceny was calculated by subtracting the daily pre- and post-edit totals.

Also common with small businesses, the internal controls over edits/adjusting journal entries were nonexistent. The owner, IT personnel, and store managers at each store could make edits/adjusting journal entries to accounting records, including sales. Of the three, the store managers could make edits without any monitoring.

Introduction

Inexpensive, readily available, accounting packages have edit functions that can be fraudulently used if a company does not have adequate internal controls (i.e., separation of authorization, accounting, and asset custodian duties). After printing checks to the payee listed on the check, a fraudster can use the edit function to change the name of the payee and account. Vouching from the cash disbursements journal and the canceled check and/or bank statement will document the difference. Similarly, a fraudster can use the edit function to reduce the amount of cash receipts and deposit a lower amount (i.e., steal cash).

This case teaches you how to prepare a spreadsheet detailing original and edited transactions listed on an accounting record (e.g., data extraction from the adjustments and/or cash receipts journal). You will learn how to document the edits by vouching to the amount and date of the edited transactions to the supporting documents (e.g., deposit ticket and bank statement).

Background

On April 2, 2016 (the day following the bank's notification of overdrawn checks), Dr. Anderson reviewed the March 2016 details from her practice over breakfast and noted that deposited cash deposits did not match the cash receipts initially recorded in the Medatrix UltraScan Point of Sale (POS) system. She asked Teresa Padgett, an information technology specialist, to look up the original and edited cash receipt transactions recorded in Medatrix UltraScan for March 2016. Teresa found that Tonya Larsen, who has been the office manager since September 2015, had made a number of even-dollar edits to the amount of cash receipts (e.g., $2,197.95 reduced to $1,697.95, a $500.00 reduction) and that the smaller edited amounts of cash were deposited days after actual receipt. Teresa Padgett told Dr. Anderson that she thought Tonya Larsen was stealing—altering deposits with different round dollar amounts (more than $1,000 a week). Time stamps on Tonya Larsen's edits show when she changed the information. Every employee has a distinct ID and password that employees are not to share. Tonya Larsen's ID is "203–Tonya." According to Teresa Padgett, there appears to be a delay of several days between daily sales receipts and actual deposits and there appears to be a pattern of decreased deposits.

Teresa Padgett downloaded the edits to the cash receipts journal for the period September 1, 2015, through March 31, 2016, for further examination.

Summary Requirements

Alexander Z. Boone, Esq., the independent attorney hired by Southern Appalachian Insurance Company, added a review of the edits to the cash receipts journal to your examination of Anderson Internal Medicine's employee dishonesty claim.

Before proceeding, read the documents in Chapter 7, section 7-3, "Fraudulent Edits/Adjusting Journal Entries." As you work the case, you will have to read and reread the documents to fully understand the evidence.

As with the information analyzed and summarized from the bank statements, canceled checks, deposit slips, and so on, the results of this additional assignment will be used by the attorney. Your assignment (in general) is as follows:

1. Schedule the provided data extraction [e.g., date and amount of the original transaction (e.g., cash before adjustment) and the date and amount of the edited transactions (e.g., cash after the adjustment)] and calculate the differences, if any, between the original and edited transactions.
2. Vouch the deposit transactions listed on the schedule to the deposit slips and bank statement to verify the amount and date of cash actually deposited.
3. Identify the individual and total number and dollars of irregularities.

The initial steps (see exercise) are to be completed individually. You may confer online on strategy, but do your own work. In particular, all students are to perform the various fraud examination steps and submit their Excel working papers (e.g., schedules) for grades.

3-2 HOW TO VOUCH/TRACE BETWEEN A SOURCE DOCUMENT AND AN ACCOUNTING LEDGER, JOURNAL, OR ACTIVITY LOG

Learning Objective

After reading this synopsis, you should be able to:

1. Better understand how to verify data extracted from a ledger, journal (e.g., cash receipts journal), or activity log (e.g., edit or audit trail log).
2. Vouch transactions in the ledger, journal, or activity log to the source document or, vice versa, trace the source document to the associated ledger, journal, or activity log.

Introduction

Essential to detecting and documenting fraudulent accounting transactions is vouching/tracing between the applicable accounting ledger, journal, or activity (edit or audit trail) log and the source document.

If you want to determine whether a transaction is valid, you use a process called vouching. *Vouching* follows an item found in the accounting ledger, journal, or activity (edit or audit trail) log back to the source document. *Tracing* is the reverse process, following a source document back to the originating document (ledger, journal, or activity log). In fraud examination, you will use both vouching and tracing.

In Anderson Internal Medicine (Case 2), you traced checks listed in the cash disbursements journal to the canceled checks and bank statements and found that the payee names on several checks did not match the payee names in the cash disbursements journal. You also traced debit card transactions listed on the bank statements back to the cash disbursements journal and found that those transactions were not listed in the accounting records.

Similarly, you can trace numbers and dates on deposit tickets and bank statements to the edit log, which tracks changes to cash deposits. You could also trace to the cash receipts journal; however, that would only show the post-edit numbers—it would miss those deposits that were allegedly stolen. Also, you can trace transactions listed on the edit log (not the cash receipts journal) to the deposit tickets and bank statements. Pay close attention to deposit dates. Good internal controls require deposits to be made daily (as in the same day received) and intact (without withholding any of the deposit). If a company receives cash and checks, both should be deposited on the dates received.

3-3   EXERCISE—FRAUDULENT EDITS (OR AJEs) (ANDERSON INTERNAL MEDICINE)

Exercise 1: Individual Assignment

1. Use the template titled "203-Tonya Edits Template," which is available on the companion website.
2. Data extractions are often difficult to read. So, convert the data extraction to a more understandable Excel schedule. Start with the data contained in the extraction labeled "Data Extraction 203 Tonya Edits (Jan Feb Mar 2016)." Schedule the specific information [e.g., date and amount of the original transaction (e.g., cash before adjustment) and the date and amount of the edited transactions (e.g., cash after the adjustment)] into the template. Calculate the differences, if any, between the original and edited transactions.

3. Then, vouch the edited deposit transactions listed on the schedule to the deposit slips and bank statement provided with the second fraud case to verify the amount and date of cash actually deposited. Insert tick mark "$\sqrt{}$". This will evidence that the edited deposit amounts on the schedule agree with both the deposit slips and bank statement.
4. Identify the individual, monthly total number and dollars, grand total number and dollars of the irregularities. Was there a trend in average irregularity as well as monthly total number and dollars?

3-4 EXERCISE TEMPLATE

Anderson Internal Medicine (Edits/AJEs)

TONYA LARSEN EDITS TO DEPOSITS— JANUARY TO MARCH 2016	V or $\sqrt{}$ = vouched edit total to deposit ticket				
TRANSACTION DESCRIPTION FROM MEDATRIX ULTRASCAN	ORIG.	EDIT	V	DIFF.	MONTHLY TOTALS
					January

TONYA LARSEN EDITS TO DEPOSITS— JANUARY TO MARCH 2016		V or $\sqrt{}$ = vouched edit total to deposit ticket			
TRANSACTION DESCRIPTION FROM MEDATRIX ULTRASCAN	ORIG.	EDIT	V	DIFF.	MONTHLY TOTALS
					February

(*continued*)

TONYA LARSEN EDITS TO DEPOSITS— JANUARY TO MARCH 2016		V or √ = vouched edit total to deposit ticket			
TRANSACTION DESCRIPTION FROM MEDATRIX ULTRASCAN	ORIG.	EDIT	V	DIFF.	MONTHLY TOTALS
					MONTHLY TOTALS
					March
Totals					

4

Case 4: Using Data Analytics: Analyzing and Summarizing Data with Excel Pivot

4-1 ANDERSON INTERNAL MEDICINE (DATA ANALYTICS): USING DATA ANALYTICS— ANALYZING AND SUMMARIZING DATA WITH EXCEL PIVOT

Learning Objective

After completing this case, you should be able to:

1. Use Excel Pivot to analyze a spreadsheet created by, or small database imported into, Excel.
2. Use Excel Pivot to summarize by preparing easy to understand summary schedules for inclusion in examination reports and/or for courtroom presentation.

HISTORY BEHIND THE FRAUD CASE

The president of an unlicensed securities firm was suspected of securities fraud (i.e., selling bogus stock warrants to unsuspecting investors). The contents of 12 monthly bank statements, canceled checks, and deposit tickets of the business were scheduled (over 50 pages of transactions). How could the transactions be easily summarized? What does the schedule of transactions reveal? Were there any significant transactions? Excel Pivot came to the rescue.

In a half hour and several clicks on Excel Pivot, the Pivot tables of deposits and disbursements showed that the president used the business checking account as if it were his personal piggy bank. He primarily used debit cards to pay for two to three meals a day every day, travel and entertainment, an automobile for a girlfriend, and payments for household utilities, cell phones, and "strip clubs." Based on the timing of receipts from customers, he celebrated at "strip clubs." Soon after he was indicted and arrested, he read the fraud examination report and accompanying schedules. Shortly thereafter, he agreed to plead guilty to racketeering. The judge sentenced him to 20 years for racketeering.

Background

Tonya Larsen was the sole person in charge of the practice's finances, including accounting during the period September 1, 2015, to March 31, 2016.

After completing the examination steps in Anderson Internal Medicine cases (Cases 2 and 3), you decided to schedule the bank transactions shown on the bank statements for the six months preceding March 2016 (the month you examined in Cases 2 and 3).

Before proceeding, go to the companion website and download the Excel spreadsheet titled, Anderson Bank Transactions (Sep Oct Nov Dec Jan Feb). It is also available in a lengthy hardcopy format in Chapter 7, section 7-4, "Using Data Analytics: Analyzing and Summarizing Data with Excel Pivot." The downloadable version contains drop down categories, which helps simplify the process of adding categories, whereas the hardcopy version does not. This spreadsheet contains the result of your efforts for September 1, 2015, through February 29, 2016. Based on the initial review of the Excel spreadsheet, you decide that you need to add categories to the withdrawal transactions so you can better summarize the data. You decide to use the following categories commonly used by medical practices:

Answering Service
Automobile
Bank Charges
Basement
Books/Subscriptions
Business
Cash
Cash Deposit
Coding
Contributions
Food
Hardware
Health Insurance
Insurance
Janitorial Services
Legal & Accounting
Linen
Marketing/Promotions
Medical Supplies/Pharmaceuticals
Medical Waste
Miscellaneous
Mortgage
Office Supplies
Parking
Printing
Repairs & Maintenance
Shipping
Taxes
Telephone
Travel
Utilities

In scanning the spreadsheet, you notice unusual names that do not fall under the common categories used by medical practices. Accordingly, you use the following categories for those unusual transactions.

People
Unusual Transactions

To facilitate categorization, a drop-down menu has been provided in the detail of transactions column. To use the menu, select the cell you want to use and click the down arrow that will appear to the right. Then select the category you feel is appropriate for the transaction.

Note: there are intentional spelling errors in the spreadsheet that you will identify and then sanitize (scrub) before completing the Pivot.

Summary Requirements

Your firm has been contracted to perform the fraud examination. The attorney for Southern Appalachian Insurance Company added an additional assignment: conduct an analysis of the bank transactions from September 1, 2015, through February 29, 2016.

Study section 4-2, *How to Use Excel Pivot to Analyze and Summarize Data* before conducting the specific requirements of this case.

The results of your assignment will be used as a summary schedule in your report, a schedule attached to the report, and possibly a courtroom audiovisual should you be called to testify as an expert witness. Your assignment (in general) is, as follows:

1. Assign categories (using the drop-down choices provided) to the disbursement transactions to assist summarizing transactions.
2. Insert a PivotTable in a new worksheet and obtain the total quantities (count) of transactions and total dollars (sum) for each category. Make at least three new PivotTables (Exercises 1, 2, and 3):
   a. Deposits (Amount Deposit and Deposit Category)
   b. Check and Debit Card Disbursements (Check Category, Payee per Check/Debit, Amount Check/Debit) (**un-scrubbed**)
   c. Check and Debit Card Disbursements (Check Category, Payee per Check/Debit, Amount Check/Debit) (**scrubbed**)
3. Sort the total dollars per category in descending order.
4. Enhance the scrubbed PivotTables for report and courtroom presentation purposes: Add an appropriate title and use proper "$" signs, decimal format, etc.

This assignment is to be completed individually. In particular, all students are to perform the various fraud examination steps and submit their Excel PivotTables for grades. NOTE: No Excel template is provided. You are to create your own Excel PivotTables by following the step-by-step instructions.

4-2 HOW TO USE EXCEL PIVOT TO ANALYZE AND SUMMARIZE DATA

Learning Objective

After reading this synopsis, you should be able to:

1. Understand the basics of data analytics.
2. Be able to use Excel Pivot as a data analytic tool to analyze and summarize a simple database (e.g., spread of the details of a bank statement for a 3-, 12-, or 36-month period of time).

Introduction

Data analytics covers a spectrum from relatively simple to extremely complex, depending on the computer program used. Data analysis takes many forms including trends, pattern recognition, relationship analysis, and visual analytics. The data analyzed can be structured (e.g., accounting databases) or unstructured (e.g., cell phone texts). Some highly complex (and very expensive) data analytics packages like ACL, IDEA Data Extraction and Analysis, SAS, and Tableau "data mine" massive quantities of data contained in a single database up to a huge number of disparate databases located throughout the world. These require specially trained persons who regularly use these programs. In a simpler fraud examination, Excel conditional statements and Excel Pivot, which is bundled with Excel, can be used to perform basic data analytics. Older versions of Excel have size limitations (1 Mb of data), while newer cloud-based versions of Excel do not have this size limitation problem, but have the added problems of cloud-based security. Excel conditional statements such as nested IF statements (discussed in this case) are very powerful; however, they require an understanding of basic algebra. Excel Pivot is much easier to use than Excel conditional statements and provides the user the ability to quickly and easily analyze and summarize selected columns and rows of data in an Excel spreadsheet or database that have been imported into Excel. In this case your exercises involve only Excel Pivot.

Most often, fraud examiners can use Excel Pivot to analyze and summarize data:

- Personally input into an Excel spreadsheet (e.g., the details of accounting documents like bank, credit card, investment, and/or trust statements) as well as details contained in accounting ledgers and journals.

▦ Uploaded into Excel databases (e.g., downloads of data from accounting systems, electronic files obtained from third parties by subpoena, and downloads of client emails).

Once fraud examiners create spreadsheets or upload databases, what do the details mean? Fraud examiners can painstakingly examine each and every transaction. Or, they can use the power of Excel Pivot to examine the data to identify patterns and trends, select items/transactions for further review, summarize the data, and/or help draw conclusions.

Be Careful with Data Analytics

1. *Remember: Garbage in, garbage out.* Beware that not only can the data contain intentional fraudulent entries (e.g., bogus payee names), but databases can be corrupted by:
   - ▦ Input errors ($900.00 typed in as $910.00 or Jean typed in as Gene or Jeanne).
   - ▦ Everyday computer activity (e.g., errors in reading, writing, storing, processing).
   - ▦ Conflicting or repetitive information (e.g., when analyzing two or more databases, some of the data fields may have been saved in different formats or contain redundant data).

   Be aware that corrupt data may negatively impact the results when you analyze and summarize the data. Accordingly, it may make the results invalid and subject fraud examiners to cross-examination, which can damage their testimony.

2. *Scrub the data.* Considering the number of persons involved with inputting information, the same data most likely has been entered differently (e.g., errors, typos, text as numbers, capitalization inconsistencies, unneeded spaces before a number or word). If you do not cleanse the data before analyzing and summarizing, you will get multiple totals for each of the names and addresses. Following is an example of the variances that will cause problems.

Company	Street Number	Street Name	City	State
QuikTrip	199	Petit Road	Durango	ILLINOIS
QuickTrip	199	Petit Rd	Durango	Illinois
QT	199	Petit Road	Dorango	IL
QwickTrp	00198	Petit Lane	Durango	IL

To scrub the information, you first save the file (and/or PivotTable) with the data as they exist in the records (i.e., before the scrub). Then, save the file to a new name and cleanse the data. If you go to trial, you will need an audit trail to show how and why you altered the data and, if required, can produce both the original and scrubbed files. You may need the various versions to prove that you made informed alterations of source material.

NOTE: Before scrubbing, take time examining the data. Some of the information with what you think are typos may actually lead to previously unknown fraud. The vendor name might be a typo or an intentional name change to facilitate a fraudulent payment or legitimately obscure the vendor (e.g., strip clubs use names that indicate the transactions were for meals).

An Example of Excel Pivot

The following is a simplified overview designed so you can complete this exercise. For more in-depth information, seek training through any of a number of free online sources like YouTube, paid online sources like Excel Central, academic services like Atomic Learning (available for free to students registered with educational institutions that use Atomic Learning, or equivalent), Excel training manuals, or taking an hour and "playing" with the Excel Pivot. It does not take long to master.

1. Open the spreadsheet or database. See page 68 for an example of a one-page spreadsheet.
2. Save your spreadsheet or database before starting so you can *undo* any changes.
3. Highlight the spreadsheet or database, including the row labels.
4. Click on the Insert tab and then click on PivotTable in the top left corner.
5. A Create PivotTable menu opens and gives you the ability to add the PivotTable to a new worksheet (new tab in the existing Excel Workbook) or existing worksheet (the spreadsheet or database that you are using). In most cases, select "new worksheet" to keep it separate and independent from the source spreadsheet.
6. In the blank PivotTable, a PivotTable Field List pops up on the right-hand side of a blank spreadsheet. It lists the fields (the row labels that you previously highlighted). It also states, "Chose field to add to report" at the top and "Drag fields between areas below" at the bottom. Under the drag fields are four boxes, "Report," "Column," "Row," and "Σ Values."

Posted Date	Check/Debit Amount	Deposit Amount	Bank Balance	Deposit Remitter	Payee Per Check/Debit	Withdrawal Category	Check Endorsement	COMMENTS
10/01/14		BEG. BAL>	88,921.58					
10/01/14	8,575.00		80,346.58		Woodland Ridge	Assisted Living		
10/01/14		20,000.00	100,346.58	Franklin Williamson Investments				
10/02/14	1,900.00		98,446.58		Striptease Sports Grille	Strip Club		
10/06/14	27.00		98,419.58		Check order	Miscellaneous		
10/10/14	5,800.00		92,619.58		Jason Dawson	Basement	JJason Dawson	For Basement
10/16/14	702.00		91,917.58		Withdrawal	Cash		
10/16/14	702.00		91,215.58		Withdrawal	Cash		
10/16/14	8.98		91,206.60		Walgreens	Medical		
10/16/14	12.84		91,193.76		Lance Hotels Sobe Gift	Personal		
10/16/14	88.75		91,105.01		Wings	Restaurant		
10/16/14	71.99		91,033.02		Sushi Rock	Restaurant		
10/16/14	21.99		91,011.03		Wings	Restaurant		
10/16/14	1,299.70		89,711.33		Mansion	Unknown		
10/16/14		20,000.00	109,711.33	Franklin Williamson Investments				
10/17/14	220.00		109,491.33		Withdrawal	Cash		
10/17/14	172.00		109,319.33		Withdrawal	Cash		

7. This is where you play by moving around the fields. For example, using the limited spreadsheet above:

    a. Drag the "Withdrawal Category" to "Row" and you get the names of the Row Labels.

Row Labels
Assisted Living
Basement
Cash
Medical
Miscellaneous
Personal
Restaurant
Strip Club
Unknown
(blank)
Grand Total

    b. Drag the "Check/Debit Amount" to "Σ Values" and you get the Row Labels and a Count of Check/Debit Amount.

Row Labels	Count of Check/Debit Amount
Assisted Living	1
Basement	1
Cash	4
Medical	1
Miscellaneous	1
Personal	1
Restaurant	3
Strip Club	1
Unknown	1
(blank)	
Grand Total	**14**

    c. Drag the "Check/Debit Amount" a second time to "Σ Values" and you get the Row Labels and two Count of Check/Debit Amount.

Row Labels	Count of Check/Debit Amount	Count of Check/Debit Amount2
Assisted Living	1	1
Basement	1	1
Cash	4	4
Medical	1	1
Miscellaneous	1	1
Personal	1	1
Restaurant	3	3
Strip Club	1	1
Unknown	1	1
(blank)		
Grand Total	**14**	**14**

d. Because you do not need two counts, click on the down arrow in the pivot table field list in the second Count inside "Σ Values." At the bottom of the drop-down list is "Value Field Settings" or "Field Settings," depending on Excel version. Click on "Value Field Settings"; click on "Sum"; and click on "Okay." This changes from Count to Sum and looks like:

Row Labels	Count of Check/Debit Amount	Sum of Check/Debit Amount2
Assisted Living	1	8575
Basement	1	5800
Cash	4	1796
Medical	1	8.98
Miscellaneous	1	27
Personal	1	12.84
Restaurant	3	182.73
Strip Club	1	1900
Unknown	1	1299.7
(blank)		
Grand Total	**14**	**19602.25**

e. Highlight and retype the labels at the top of the rows to just "Count" and "Sum." Then, highlight the cells in the sum column and right-click on them. Select format cells and change the number format to an accounting format with and without "$" as seen below:

Row Labels	Count	Sum
Assisted Living	1	$8,575.00
Basement	1	5,800.00
Cash	4	1,796.00
Medical	1	8.98
Miscellaneous	1	27.00
Personal	1	12.84
Restaurant	3	182.73
Strip Club	1	1,900.00
Unknown	1	1,299.70
(blank)		
Grand Total	**14**	**$19,602.25**

f. Simple? Yes and no! If you want a quick summary table, Excel Pivot is simple. If you have a large spreadsheet or uploaded database, you may want much more, but that will require you to explore Excel Pivot (see sources listed above).

g. Below is a PivotTable inserted into the sample Fraud Examination report in Chapter 6. It gives you another example taken from a 12-month spreadsheet.

Category	Number	Dollars	Examples
Restaurant	456	$52,383.76	ARIA Silverstone Bar, Tybee Island Brewing, Hooter's, Roller's Lounge, Eden Forest Country Club, Stoney River, Subway, Wendy's
Strip Club	37	$45,998.00	Strip TZ Sports Grille (aka Striptease Atlanta)

(*continued*)

Category	Number	Dollars	Examples
Entertainment	74	$36,291.50	Will Avants Golf, Sussex Billiards & Beer, West Point Lake, Garland Marine, Shipyard Golf Club, Cloverland Amusement
Automobile	205	$6,799.07	Amoco, BP, Chevron, Exxon, QuikTrip
Grocery	126	$8,101.13	BI-LO, Kroger, Piggly Wiggly, Publix
Wine/Liquor	7	$994.36	Hopkins Warehouse Liquor, Elegant Wine
Sex Items	3	$370.96	Erotic Toys and More

h. Now. **Go and play with the Excel Pivot.** See what it can do for you.

How to Scrub the Data and Refresh the PivotTable

When you prepare a spreadsheet using original documents you should be inputting the information as shown on the document (e.g., "Kinko's—Alpharetta" on the payee line of the check or "Kinko's #213 Canton, GA" for debit card transactions shown in the bank statement). If you testify, expect opposing attorneys to question you on what they perceive as errors. Changing information for analysis (e.g., "Kinko's" for "FedEx Kinko's") might be misconstrued as errors. When you receive a database prepared by someone else, expect multiple inputs of the same data (e.g., Gene, Eugene, Jean) that can corrupt the analysis. The many different versions of the same data make summarization of the data challenging. Accordingly, you will need to scrub (cleanse) the data.

To cleanse the data you need to (1) preserve the original data and (2) cleanse the original data to facilitate analysis. You do this by maintaining an audit trail. Save the original spreadsheet or data file and then rename and save a second spreadsheet or data file. Use names that easily identify the original version (e.g., ORG, version1, v1) and subsequent versions (e.g., WORKING, SCRUB, version2, v2). Note: If subpoenaed or if subsequently testifying as an expert witness you will have to turn over all versions to opposing counsel.

Once you have archived the original spreadsheet (or data file) and saved a copy of the data file, you can start cleansing the data in the new file. For electronic databases with huge amounts of information, you may need the assistance of IT technicians who have programs for cleansing the data. For Excel files, there are several redundant options. One methodology is Search and Replace.

FIND

1. First, find the different versions of the word(s) you want to change.
2. Highlight the Excel column(s) you want to change (e.g., "Payee of Check/Debit") by clicking on the gray bar above the column.
3. On the **Home** tab at the top of the spreadsheet, click on "Find & Select," which is located all the way to the right, and then click on "**Find.**"
4. Next to "Find what:" type in what you want to find (e.g., Kinko's). In the spreadsheet provided for the Data Analytics exercises, you will find "Kinko,'" "FedEx Kinko's," and "Kinko's—Alpharetta." You will not find words that are misspelled (e.g., Kindo's for Kinko's).

SEARCH AND REPLACE

1. Highlight the Excel column(s) or row(s) you want to change (e.g., "Payee of Check/Debit") by clicking on the gray bar above the column or to the left of the row.
2. On the **Home** tab at the top of the spreadsheet, click on "Find & Select," which is located all of the way to the right, and then click on "**Replace.**"
3. Next to "Find what:" type in what you want to find (e.g., Kinko's—Alpharetta) and next to "Replace with:" type in what you want to replace (e.g., Kinko's). *Be very careful* and remember that you have an **Undo** button. If you reversed the find and replace terms (e.g., replace Kinko's with Kinko's—Alpharetta) you may get unintended consequences if there are more than two versions of the words you want to correct (e.g., FedEx Kinko's, would become FedEx Kinko's—Alpharetta). You must think through the search and replace to avoid undoing and starting all over again.
4. Note: Changing the wording in one column will not necessarily change the categories listed in another column. If there are errors in the categories column, especially where you used a drop-down menu, you will have to correct those individually. Do not use search and replace. Either change the category using the drop-down menu or Copy followed by Paste.

REFRESH

The PivotTable summaries can be "refreshed" at any time to include new information that has been subsequently added to the spreadsheet or for changes in existing data like spelling corrections and search and replace. You do not have to start all over again.

1. While inside the PivotTable, click anywhere in the results. Following is an example. In a real PivotTable you can click anywhere, including anywhere inside the names, dollar amounts, or count columns.

Repairs & Maintenance	8,414.21	12
Agbonze Tree Service	170.00	1
Barry's Com'l Repairs	3,821.00	4
Barry's Commercial Repairs	3,288.00	5
Pest USA	1,135.21	2

2. At the top of the Excel spreadsheet on the **Home** tab, two PivotTable Tools appear in the middle: "**Options**" and "**Design**."
3. Click on "**Options**."
4. At the top in the middle of the page is "**Refresh**."
5. Click on the down arrow under "**Refresh**" and you have two choices: "**Refresh**" and "**Refresh All**." Click "**Refresh All**" and all of the PivotTable results are modified.

Nested Conditional Formulas

Data analytics is as broad as it is complex. Rarely are users constricted to just numbers or text or even the same type documents or databases. Having as many tools in your arsenal as possible will become one of the keys to being successful in data analytics.

One of the most powerful tools in Excel data analytics, which will briefly be discussed *only* to provide awareness, is *nested conditional formulas*. Because of its complexity, it is being provided for informative purposes only. You will not be using nested conditional formulas in this course.

Nested conditional formulas are Excel formulas where the Excel user combines more than one function statements to return a desired result (e.g., the disbursements made after a certain deposit that as a group more or less equal to the amount of that deposit—a first-in, first-out (FIFO) analysis to match disbursements to a specific deposit).

Excel offers a large number of function statements, which can be used alone or in groups inside nested conditional formulas. Many are complex and require training and regular use. Others are simple and probably already in use on a regular basis. A few examples of the easier functions are shown below. For comparison purposes only, all of the cells involved in the function statement examples are from A1 through A23. Change the cells included in the analysis (say, to A1:Q234 or B3:D257) and different data are analyzed and result in different outcomes.

- AVERAGE function [=AVERAGE(A1:A23)] gives the average of a set of numbers found in cells A1 through A23.
- COUNT function [=COUNT(A1:A23)] gives the count of the number of cells found in cells A1 through A23.
- IF function [=IF(A1 = "Yes",1,2)] or [=IF(A1 = "Yes",Yes,No)] gives the user the ability to make logical comparisons between a value and what is expected. "1,2" returns 1 if the answer is yes and 2 if the answer is no. Similarly, "Yes,No" returns Yes if the answer is yes and No if the answer is no. It is a proverbial statement asking "IF" something is one thing or another (e.g., is it true or false).
- MIN function [=MIN(A1:A23)] gives the smallest number listed in cells A1 through A23.
- SUM function [=SUM(A1:A23)] adds the values in the range of cells A1 through A23.

To create conditional formulas, you need a logical comparison and the ability to determine whether conditions are true or false.

=IF(logical test functions, value IF true, value IF false)

Nested conditional formulas (a combination of conditional formulas) take the power of Excel further; however, they require more thought than a single function. Nested conditional formulas also require an understanding of basic algebra. Anyone can use a simple Excel "=SUM()" function. If the question you want answered can be limited to a yes (value is true) or no (value is no) question or a series of yes or no questions, then nested conditional formulas can easily perform complex data analysis involving a large database and quickly return the desired answer(s).

Nested conditional formulas may be so complex that users diagram a decision tree to visually see the combination of functions and the order in which the functions interconnect with one another.

For explanatory purposes only, we discuss only one type of nested conditional formulas, daisy-chained (interconnected) "IF" equations, which can do processes such as find, list, and tabulate data. What is meant by a daisy-chained "IF" equation? The equation relies on the first function of the equation to determine the next step(s) by using formulaic variables. The Excel "IF" function is a conditional statement that determines "IF" the condition (variable, formula, constant, etc.) is true or false (e.g., 1 or 2, Yes or No). Basic usage normally leads to a constant value as shown below.

=IF([Condition], [If-True Value1], [If-False Value2])

Using the Anderson Internal Medicine spreadsheet provided with fraud Case 4, an "IF" equation can be used to locate cash deposits:

=IF(K11 = "Cash Deposit", "True", "False")

This "IF" equation results in a single cell containing a formula that returns the constant "True." While this might be useful, a single result is not necessarily meaningful. What would happen if the constant "True" were a variable or another formula? Instead of locating a single bit of data, the IF equation could conceivably take the data analysis farther and return more results. Complicated? Yes. You can have up to 64 levels nested (i.e., consecutive) functions in a single formula. However, it is quicker than spending hours performing potentially inaccurate manual computations and can be far more consistent in its application.

For illustration purposes, following is what a daisy-chain "IF" equation looks like.

=IF(F10 < 499,"G",IF(F10 < 749,"F",IF(F10 < 999,"H",IF(F10 < 1499,"I",
   "A"))))

Column F in the above daisy-chain "IF" equation is Amount Check/Debit in the Anderson Internal Medicine spreadsheet. Here is a decision tree flowchart of the equation:

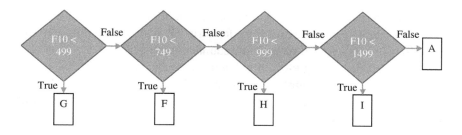

This is powerful. We can use a daisy-chain "IF" equation to perform such tests as analyze the Anderson Internal Medicine spreadsheet and stratify the outgoing flows of money in the account. It can then drag down the analysis column to help Pivot and/or other analysis tools to add further definition to your analysis.

Nested conditional formulas are powerful, particularly when the data are massive. However, they are also complex. After this exposure, those who want to know more will need to take training and then regularly use nested IF statements to attain any degree of proficiency.

4-3   EXERCISES—USING DATA ANALYTICS (ANDERSON INTERNAL MEDICINE)

Exercise 1: Excel Pivot (Checks and Debit Card Disbursements)—Individual Assignment

Using the Excel spreadsheet (small database) titled "Anderson Bank Transactions (Sep Oct Nov Dec Jan)," which is found in the companion website for this course, develop two Excel PivotTables to analyze and summarize the data. *Exercise 1* will involve checks and debit card disbursements and *Exercise 2* will involve deposits. Your starting point is the tab at the bottom of "Anderson Bank Transactions (Sep Oct Nov Dec Jan)" labeled ORG SCH.

NOTE 1: Save frequently to avoid loss of your work!

NOTE 2: Be very careful when assigning categories, as there could be surprises revealed by the names and/or dollar amounts! Not all of the receipts and disbursements may be those of Anderson Internal Medicine—one of the purposes of Excel Pivot (or any other data analysis) is to detect anomalies for further examination. Also, not all names are what they appear to be. In real life, check the names on the Internet to find out more information. For example, Strip TZ Grille is a credit-card/debit-card front for Strip TZ, a strip club that uses the name to hide charges from spouses and significant others.

NOTE 3: When using Pivot, it will automatically create a new tab called "Sheet2," "Sheet3," etc. with each iteration. Use the instructions below to rename the Pivots to something more recognizable, like "DISB" for Checks and Debit Card Disbursement and "DEP" for Deposits.

1. Save the spreadsheet ORG SCH to a copy for analysis and audit trail purposes (this maintains the original file and starts a new file). You do this by putting the cursor over the tab called ORG SCH; right click; and then select "Create a copy" and "(move to end)." That will create a new tab called "ORG SCH (2)." Put your cursor over that new tab; right click; and then rename it something that will reflect it as a working copy, say "Working Sch."

2. Then open "Working Sch" and use the drop-down labels in the column Check Category to assign the checks and debit card transactions to categories for subsequent analysis. These are the disbursement categories provided in the case scenario.

3. Prepare the FIRST of two Excel PivotTables (Checks and Debit Card Disbursements a/k/a DISB) using the steps below.

   For DISB, performing the following steps:

   a. Highlight the entire schedule except Ending Balance (note that the results will include the Opening Balance that will have to be removed from the ultimate results).

   b. Click the "Insert" tab at the top of the spreadsheet, followed by clicking "PivotTable."

   c. The pop up called "Create PivotTable" will give choices. One of the choices is "Select a table or range," which should give the highlighted range in Step b.

   d. Another choice is "Choose where you want the PivotTable to be placed," which should already be marked "New Worksheet." Make sure you put it in a "New Worksheet" to avoid future confusion. This places the PivotTable in a new tab labeled "Sheet5" at the bottom of the worksheet.

   e. On the left side is the blank PivotTable and on the right is the PivotTable Field List, which allows you to click on the boxes in "Choose field to add to report." Start building the PivotTable by experimenting with the "Choose field to add to report." Changes help you to immediately modify the PivotTable.

f. For example, check "Payee of Check/Debit," "Amount Check/Debit," and "Check Category." That gives you all of the individual checks for each payee. Note that the selections are listed under "**Row Labels**" at the bottom of the "PivotTable Field List."

g. Experiment with this example by moving "Amount Check/Debit" from "**Row Labels**" to "**Σ Values**" by dragging and dropping the label. This changes the Pivot results and gives a *Count* of the amount of checks/debits.

h. Experiment further with this example by changing "**Σ Values**" from a *Count* to a *Sum* of the amount of checks/debits. Click on the down arrow for *Count of Amount Checks/Debits* under "**Σ Values**" and select the option "Value Field Setting" and then click on *Sum*. This changes the summary results to *Sum of Amount Check/Debit*. Now you have the sum total of all checks/debits made payable to particular payees.

i. What if you want both the count and sum of checks/debits. Add a second selection to "**Σ Values**." Drop and drag "Amount Check/Debit" from the "Choose field to add to report" down to "**Σ Values**." This adds both *Count of Amount Checks/Debits* and *Sum of Amount Check/Debit* under "**Σ Values**." Now you have the quantity and sum of the checks and debits.

j. Reverse the order "**Row Labels**" from "Payee of Check/Debit" followed by "Check Category" by dragging and dropping "Check Category" to the top of the list.

k. Change the name from Sheet 5 to DISB to provide a better title for future identification.

l. Highlight the rows you want to hide (e.g., Beginning Balance and Blanks that contain no quantities) and then right click and select "Hide."

m. Review the results for the "Check Category" Unusual Transactions and look for anomalies. There are at a minimum seven irregularities. Put those in your memory bank for the next fraud case.

Exercise 2: Excel Pivot (Deposits)—Individual Assignment

Using Working Sch from Exercise 1 prepare the SECOND of two Excel PivotTables (Deposits, or DEP) using the following steps:

1. In short, you will be repeating many of steps a. to j. from Exercise 1.
2. Highlight the entire schedule except Ending Balance (note that the results will include the Opening Balance that will have to be removed from the ultimate results).

3. Click the "Insert" tab at the top of the spreadsheet, followed by clicking "PivotTable."

4. The pop-up called "Create PivotTable" will give choices. One of the choices is "Select a table or range," which should give the highlighted range in Step b.

5. Another choice is "Choose where you want the PivotTable to be placed," which should already be marked "New Worksheet." Make sure you put it in a "New Worksheet" to avoid future confusion. This places the PivotTable in a new tab labeled "Sheet6" at the bottom of the worksheet.

6. On the left side is the blank PivotTable and on the right is the PivotTable Field List, which allows you to click on the boxes in "Choose field to add to report." Start building the PivotTable by experimenting with the "Choose field to add to report." Changes help you to immediately modify the PivotTable.

7. For example, check "Amount Deposit" and "Deposit Category." That gives you all of the individual deposits. Note that the selections are listed under "**Row Labels**" at the bottom of the "PivotTable Field List."

8. Experiment with this example by moving "Amount Deposit" from "**Row Labels**" to "**Σ Values**" by dragging and dropping the label. This changes the Pivot results and gives a *Count* of the amount of checks/debits.

9. Experiment further with this example by changing "**Σ Values**" from a *Count* to a *Sum* of the amount of checks/debits. Click on the down arrow for *Count of Amount Deposit* under "**Σ Values**" and select the option "Value Field Setting" and then click on *Sum*. This changes the summary results to *Sum of Amount Deposit*. Now you have the sum total of all deposits made payable to each category.

10. What if you want both the count and sum of deposit? Add a second selection to "**Σ Values**." Drop and drag "Amount Deposit" from the "Choose field to add to report" down to "**Σ Values**." This adds both *Count of Amount Deposit* and *Sum of Amount Deposit* under "**Σ Values**." Now you have the quantity and sum of the deposits.

11. Change the name from Sheet6 to DEP to provide a better title for future identification.

12. Highlight the rows you want to hide (e.g., Beginning Balance and Blanks that contain no quantities) and then right click and select "Hide."

13. The results should detect one anomaly. If not, repeat and review results until you find the anomaly.

14. What is the anomaly? What is the source of the anomaly? Is the check a normal deposit for Anderson Internal Medicine? If you double-click on the

result you want, it will take you to the details behind the summary number ($36,000 check deposited on December 30, 2015). Put it in your memory bank for the next fraud case.

Exercise 3: Excel Pivot (Scrubbing)—Individual Assignment

You are not done yet. *You have to scrub the data to ensure uniform results.* In the DISB PivotTable for Working Sch, for example, look at the Row Label "Automobile." It has KIA Finance Company and KIA Southwest. Both are the same company. Look at the Row Label "Business." There are three Kinko's.

First, save Working Sch to a new name. You will be using Search and Replace inside Working Sch to scrub the category descriptions. If you do not save Working Sch to a new name, you will lose the results of the PivotTable from Exercise 2 when you click Refresh.

For example, scrub KIA Southwest by changing all of those transactions to KIA Finance Company. Similarly, change the three different sets of Kinko's transactions to a single Kinko's—and so on, until you make all category titles uniform.

Use scrubbing instructions above in the "How-To" section.

Using Working Sch from Exercises 1 and 2, clean up the input errors and refresh the DISB and DEP using the following steps:

1. Save the spreadsheet "Working Sch" to a new name like "Scrub Sch." Now you have the ORG SCH, Working Sch, and Scrub Sch. This maintains your audit trail should you need it in court.
2. Scrub the remaining data.
3. Once the scrub is complete, perform the Pivots again and make sure that the names under the Row Label are uniform. This will ensure your final results.
4. Change the formats of the numbers and totals. Get the Excel Pivot ready for inclusion in the report and/or as a courtroom-ready audiovisual.

4-4 REVIEW QUESTIONS—USING DATA ANALYTICS (ANDERSON INTERNAL MEDICINE)

1. Data can be corrupted by which of the following?
   A. Everyday computer activity (e.g., errors in reading, writing, storing, processing data)
   B. Redundant data stored in more than one location

    C. Intentionally fraudulent entries

    D. Any of the above

2. Examples of input errors that make data analysis challenging include all of the following, except?

    A. QuikTrip, QuickTrip, QT, QwickTrp.

    B. *Johnson*, Johnson, **Johnson**.

    C. Durango, Durango, Dorango.

    D. FedEx Kinko's, Kinko's, Kinko's—Canton.

3. When adding categories to summarize data, you should perform all, except which of the following?

    A. Research payee business names on the Internet to gain a better understanding of what the payee does.

    B. Be aware of similar or duplicate names that may require future cleansing.

    C. Accept the information as is.

    D. Research an individual's name on social media (e.g., Jack Gotti) to gain a better understanding of who the person is.

4. Excel PivotTables can quickly be changed in the PivotTable **Value Field Settings** by:

    A. Clicking on different fields.

    B. Moving fields between **Row Labels** and **Values**.

    C. Clicking the down arrow on **Values** and **Value Field Setting** and selecting Sum, Count, Average, Min, Max.

    D. All of the above.

5. Scrubbing involves which of the following?

    A. Correcting spelling errors.

    B. Collapsing different variations of a name (e.g., Sloppy's, Sloppy's Mid-Town, and Northside Sloppy's) into a single grouping (e.g., Sloppy's).

    C. Removing blanks and extra characters in data fields.

    D. All of the above.

6. When scrubbing Excel data, you perform all, except:

    A. Use "Find what:" to describe what you want to find and type in "Replace with:" what you want to replace.

    B. Change click on what you want to change using the drop-down menu.

    C. Click on "Find & Select" and then click on "Replace."

    D. Highlight the Excel column(s) or row(s) you want to change.

7. To refresh the PivotTable after entering new or corrected data you do all of the following, except:

    A. Use PivotTable Update Tools to "Restore" your original data when you do not get your desired results.

    B. While inside the PivotTable, click anywhere in the results (on the left side of the page) to get "**Options**" and "**Design**" on the menu bar.

    C. You select "**Options**" and then "**Refresh**."

    D. You select "**Refresh All**" to incorporate all new or corrected data.

CHAPTER FIVE

Case 5: Tracing Data Analytics Red Flags Back to Source Documents Using Subpoenas

5-1 ANDERSON INTERNAL MEDICINE AND LARSEN CONVENIENCE STORE (CONSPIRACY AND LOAN FRAUD): TRACE TRANSACTIONS DISCOVERED DURING DATA ANALYTICS BACK TO SOURCE DOCUMENTS USING SUBPOENAS

Learning Objective

After completing this case, you should be able to:

1. Take red flags detected from using data analytics (i.e., suspicious deposit and related disbursements) and trace those transactions back to the source documents (loan documents in this case).
2. Prepare subpoena wording for attorneys to obtain additional bank documents.
3. Review loan documents and determine whether the loan documents (credit applications and supporting documents) contain material misstatements.

HISTORY BEHIND THE FRAUD CASE

Father and son were targets of an arson-for-profit investigation. The father was gambling at a casino at the time an incendiary fire destroyed his business. Data analysis of the primary business bank account detected a large deposit, which was significantly larger than any prior deposits associated with the business. Using first-in, first-out (FIFO) analysis, the recent deposit was matched with funds used to pay a casino, other financial institutions, and a construction company. A second round of subpoenas was served to the source of the large deposit and the entities that received the checks associated with the deposit. It revealed, among other things, that the large deposit was partially used for payment of construction charges in arrears. Another round of subpoenas was serviced to all of the financial institutions in the small town to locate and obtain both the father and son's personal checking accounts. Documents received from the subpoenas revealed payments for gambling debts to several casinos, a host of delinquencies on mortgages owed individually by the father, mortgages owed individually by the son, and vendors that supplied the business as well as a contractor building a commercial structure. This resulted in a fourth round of subpoenas to casinos, mortgage companies, and vendors. Of particular note, the subpoena to the contractor discovered that the proceeds of the commercial loan were not used for new construction, as requested in the credit application. In total, the loan proceeds eventually went through a total of five financial institutions and were a challenge to simplify the sources and uses of loan proceeds during expert testimony.

Father and son were convicted of arson and over 30 fraud counts, including loan application fraud, check kiting, and scheme to defraud a bank. The judge sentenced both to 10 years in prison.

Background

As discussed in the overview of the serial cases, Greg Larsen owned and operated Larsen Convenience Store (case 1) and Tonya Larsen was the office manager for Anderson Internal Medicine (AIM) (cases 2 to 4). Often, the spouse of a fraudster is oblivious to (and innocent of) the alleged fraud(s) being examined. In other instances, the husband and wife are conspirators. Part of a fraud examination involving husband and wife is, among other things, to determine the facts between husband and wife. From cases 1 to 4 we found that Greg's cash flow problems financially impacted his wife, and vice versa.

Recall that the fraud examination of the income tax returns and personal financial statements in case 1 found that Greg Larsen (DBA Larsen

Convenience) had significant cash flow problems: The company's balance in its checking account significantly decreased, the company's credit card balance significantly increased, Greg laid off employees, and all of his vendors made him sign promissory notes and put all of his future shipments during the final two months on cash on delivery (COD) terms. In addition, the income tax returns show that Tonya's salary significantly decreased in 2015 (she had been terminated by her former employer and was unemployed for six months before joining AIM).

In Case 4, you examined documents processed by AIM's bank between September 1, 2015, and February 29, 2016. Through Excel Pivot data analytics, you identified red flags that required additional examination that were posted by the bank in late December 2015. Of particular note, you detected a check dated December 30, 2015, for $36,000.00 that was deposited into the AIM checking account. The $36,000.00 check was made payable to "Cash" and drawn on Greg Larsen's account at Waleska Bank (Waleska, Georgia). A review of all other deposits showed cash deposits that totaled less than $2,000. Larsen Convenience Store burnt down two days later.[1]

In many fraud examinations, evidence is received and examined in helter-skelter order. This case is an example of discovering suspicious activity late in a fraud examination and having to double back and examine new documents. In the current case, a series of subpoenas associated with the red flags returned documents from two financial institutions (Bank of Lawrenceville and Waleska Bank) and an interview was conducted with the lending officer of Waleska Bank.

Innocent Third Parties (Financial Institutions)

Financial institutions often collect their loans or mortgages if they follow good lending policy and file a financing statement (a standard legal form that lenders file with the clerk of court to secure title to various types of non–real-estate property pledged as collateral for a loan) or a deed of trust (mortgage filing similar to financing statements that collateralize the real property). Insurance companies generally pay innocent third parties (like a financial institution) in a casualty loss if the financial institution properly secured the loans or mortgages, respectively.

Although financial institutions suffer no economic loss, the insurance companies who reimburse the financial institutions suffer the loss.

---

[1] Bank of Lawrenceville and Waleska Bank are part of the correspondent bank. Accordingly, all checks, including the $36,000 check, clear overnight.

Conspiracy

The federal government and the various states have criminal statutes regarding conspiracy to commit criminal acts.

According to the U.S. Attorneys' Manual, *Criminal Resource Manual (CRM-923)*, the general conspiracy statue is **18 U.S.C. § 371—Conspiracy to Defraud the United States**. It defines conspiracy as:

> an offense [i]f two or more persons conspire either to commit any offense against the United States, or to defraud the United States, or any agency thereof in any manner or for any purpose… The operative language is the so-called "defraud clause," that prohibits conspiracies to defraud the United States. This clause creates a separate offense from the "offense clause" in Section 371. Both offenses require the traditional elements of Section 371 conspiracy, including an illegal agreement, criminal intent, and proof of an overt act.

In short, a conspiracy is a verbal, written, or unspoken agreement between two or more persons to intentionally commit an apparent criminal act in furtherance of their agreement.

In this fraud case, an argument can be made that Greg and Tonya conspired to obtain loan proceeds for a stated purpose; move that money through a series of federally insured bank accounts; and then disburse that money for other purposes.

Summary Requirements

After conferring with the attorney for Southern Appalachian Insurance Company, you prepared and he edited wording for subpoenas to the Bank of Lawrenceville and Waleska Bank to find out more information concerning the $36,000.00 check. Note: these subpoenas are not provided. Raymond T. Boone, CFE, a special agent with the insurance company's Special Investigative Unit (SIU), subsequently interviews John Grayson, the Senior Vice President and Branch Manager for Waleska Bank in Ball Ground, Georgia.

1. Review the documents returned with the subpoenas and the interview of John Grayson in Chapter 7, section 7-5, "Anderson Internal Medicine and Larsen Convenience (Husband/Wife Loan Fraud and Conspiracy)."
2. Write up the fraud examination analysis for an addendum to the original fraud examination reports for both Larsen Convenience Store and Anderson Internal Medicine that discusses the results of your review.

Be sure to include condition (material error or fraud discovered), criteria (description in the type of material error or fraud and scope of analysis), cause, and effect.

3. Prepare an audiovisual (e.g., flowchart) that shows the flow of money from inception through final checks.

The results of your assignment will be used as an addendum to the original report, schedule(s), and possibly a courtroom audiovisual.

5-2 HOW TO WRITE WORDING TO SUBPOENA DOCUMENTS, INFORMATION, AND/OR OBJECTS

Learning Objective

After reading this section, you should be able to:

1. Prepare wording for a subpoena to obtain financial documents.
2. Be able to review the documents obtained by subpoena and determine whether you need additional documents.

Introduction

Financial and related information most often must be subpoenaed. Entities (corporations, limited liability companies, partnerships, etc.) that maintain financial and other information (e.g., audited and unaudited financial statements; tax returns; and bank, credit card, investment, and/or trust statements) have a fiduciary duty to protect that information, and most often will not provide requested information unless served with a valid subpoena prepared by a civil or criminal attorney associated with an open civil or criminal case (e.g., contract lawsuit, divorce proceedings, or criminal investigation). Individuals (and their unincorporated proprietorships) may invoke their right against self-incrimination and not provide anything in criminal (but not most civil) proceedings. This necessitates obtaining the information from other sources.

There are two basic types of subpoenas. *Subpoena duces tecum* is a court order to a person or entity to attend court (or a grand jury) and bring relevant documents. *Subpoena to testify* is an order for a person to attend a hearing, grand jury, or deposition to testify. Each federal, state, and local court has its own civil and criminal variations. U.S. court samples are provided in the documents section. They illustrate civil and criminal subpoenas to provide documents, information, or objects and criminal subpoenas to testify in a deposition, grand jury, or hearing/trial.

The agents for and attorneys representing the entities receiving the subpoena will limit production to only what they determine has been requested. If the wording in a subpoena is poorly written, you may not get what you want. Even if well written, what is provided is limited to your request (e.g., canceled checks over $499.99), and when you review that information, you may have to prepare another subpoena (e.g., for selected checks, deposit tickets, and offsetting items deposited with the deposit ticket shown in the bank statement). NOTE: Subpoenas are often "fishing expeditions," and wording in the request may be challenged as overly broad. Compliance with a subpoena costs money (e.g., an hourly research fee, plus a set fee per item retrieved). Also, the wording can request ALL information (e.g., bank statements as well as all checks, deposit tickets, and offsetting items); however, subpoenas can be costly and response takes time. If you request too much information, the providing entity may charge an exorbitant amount for research and reproduction and/or take months to produce. What happens if you request all offsets to deposit tickets (checks, debit memorandums, etc.) from a wholesale or retail company? You might get hundreds of checks for customer payments. If you restrict the request to less information, you should get the response quicker and at a lower cost. However, it may necessitate more than one subpoena. Check with your attorney. It is his/her call on how broad or how limited to make the subpoena.

Know your target! In this case, it is Greg Larsen DBA Larsen Convenience, who is a person and/or his alter ego (personally owned proprietorship). He most likely will not respond to a subpoena. If you subpoena Greg Larsen in a criminal case, he can invoke his right against self-incrimination. Records are often available elsewhere. You can, for instance, request Greg Larsen's information from a third party such as a financial institution. With taxing authorities, your attorney will have to request the information through an ex parte order before a judge, who decides whether to sign an order. This is needed particularly when obtaining tax returns from the Internal Revenue Service because of the secret nature of tax information.

Following are samples of subpoena wording associated with requesting bank statements, checks, deposit tickets, and offsetting items. Note that "but not limited to" is added to cover that which you may not have requested:

- ▦ Monthly bank statements and associated documents, including but not limited to, both the front and back of all checks, all deposit tickets, and

offsetting items (checks, debit memorandums, etc.) for XYZ for the period
_____ to _____.

▪ Monthly bank statements for XYZ for the period _____ to
_____.

▪ The demand account documents, including but not limited to, the front and back of all checks, all deposit tickets, and offsetting items (checks, debit memorandums, etc.) for XYZ for the period _____ to _____.

▪ The savings account documents, including but not limited to, the front and back of all checks of $500.00 or more, all deposit tickets, and offsetting items (checks, debit memorandums, etc.) where each offset is $500.00 or more for XYZ for the period _____ to _____.

▪ For XYZ for the period _____ to _____ provide the following to include but not limited to: (this prevents typing in the name of the subpoenaed person or entity and time period over and over).

5-3 EXERCISE—ANDERSON INTERNAL MEDICINE AND LARSEN CONVENIENCE STORE (CONSPIRACY AND LOAN FRAUD)

Exercise 1: Individual Assignment

You find suspicious the $36,000.00 check deposited into the AIM checking account on December 30, 2015. It was made payable to "Cash" and drawn on Greg Larsen's account at Waleska Bank. Why was the $36,000.00 check deposited into AIM, and why were Larsen Convenience Store disbursements made using AIM checks? Accordingly, you want to review the financial information associated with that check:

1. Review the documents returned with the following:
   a. The subpoena to the Bank of Lawrenceville to obtain Anderson Internal Medicine's demand account information for Account 7018188 for the period ending on or around December 31, 2015, including, but not limited to, the deposit ticket and front and back of the canceled check for $36,000.00, and the front and back of all canceled checks over $1,000.00 posted on or after December 30, 2015;
   b. The subpoena to Waleska Bank to obtain the Greg Larsen's demand account information for Account 7011176 for the period ending on or after December 31, 2015, including, but not limited to, the

monthly bank statement, all deposit tickets and off-setting items over $25,000.00, and the front and back of all canceled checks posted on or after the date of the aforementioned deposits over $25,000.00; and

c. The subpoena to Waleska Bank to get the credit application and the front and back of the canceled official checks associated with the $49,000.00 official check deposited into Greg Larsen's demand account on December 28, 2015.

2. Review the SIU interview of John Grayson.

3. Write up the fraud examination analysis for an addendum to the original fraud examination reports for both Larsen Convenience Store and Anderson Internal Medicine that discusses the results of your review. Be sure to briefly discuss what you did or did not do and the findings (condition, criteria, cause, and effect).

4. Prepare an audiovisual (e.g., flowchart) that shows the flow of money from inception through final checks.

The results of your assignment will be used as an addendum to the original report and a courtroom audiovisual should you be called to testify as an expert witness.

This assignment is to be completed individually. In particular, all students are to perform the various fraud examination steps and submit their report narrative and audiovisual(s) for a grade. No Excel templates are provided.

CHAPTER SIX

Reports, Schedules, and Audiovisuals

6-1 WRITING A FRAUD EXAMINATION REPORT

Learning Objective

After reading this summary, you should learn about:

1. The components of a written fraud examination report.
2. How to refer to schedules and audiovisuals in the body of the report.

Fraud Examination Report

Each organization has its own fraud examination report format. Fraud examination report formats often contain the same elements as those found in audit reports.

Following is an outline of common elements. Immediately after the outline is a sample report. The client in the example is a prosecutor; however, the client can easily be a private attorney, corporate attorney, corporate manager, or a person who hired you to determine whether he/she was defrauded.

TO:

FROM:

RE:

DATE:

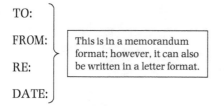

This is in a memorandum format; however, it can also be written in a letter format.

    I. Background

        You need to briefly state why you conducted the fraud examination.

   II. Executive Summary

        Summarize what steps you performed and what you found during the fraud examination. Readers need a quick overview and a reason to "dig" into the details.

  III. Scope

        Explain the scope of the fraud examination (e.g., determine whether predication took place). If need be, discuss any issues that need to be brought to the reader's attention.

  IV. Methodology/Findings

        Give a brief description of what you did and did not do (e.g., the documents reviewed, tests performed, individuals interviewed, assumptions made, and any scope limitations). Findings can be shown immediately after discussing methodology or shown separately. You describe what you found in sufficient detail so the reader understands what happened. However, avoid giving too much detail so the reader does not (1) lose interest or (2) get confused. Providing the right amount of detail is an art form. It is suggested that you have a cold reader read the report to determine whether the cold reader understands it before you issue the report.

        If needed, break the findings down into separate categories. If possible, cover condition (category of fraud), criteria (type of fraud, if applicable),[1] cause (weak or nonexistent internal controls, collusion, etc.), and effect (e.g., estimated loss, bankruptcy, etc.).

        When discussing condition, do not express an opinion of guilt. The ACFE Code of Ethics states, "No opinion shall be expressed regarding the guilt or innocence of any person or party." Guilt is a decision reached by

---

[1]Unless you work for a law enforcement agency, be careful on assigning criteria. Law enforcement fraud examiners may discuss criteria like "theft by taking" or "material misstatements to a financial institution." Non-law enforcement fraud examiners should use general categories like "material misstatements," "misappropriated assets," and "conflicts of interests," which are substantiated by the facts.

the triers of fact, not the fraud examiner. However, based on the facts of the fraud examination, you can draw such general conclusions as "material misstatements," "misappropriated assets," and "conflicts of interests."

V. Summary

Concisely summarize the results of the fraud examination.

VI. Recommendations

If appropriate, provide recommendations to prevent a recurrence of the fraud in the future (e.g., stronger internal controls).

REFER TO SCHEDULES AND AUDIOVISUALS IN THE BODY OF THE REPORT

The report summarizes the fraud examination. While reading the report, the reader will need to review the underlying schedules, exhibits (e.g., documents), and audiovisuals that may be attached to and/or support the report. These help the reader understand the findings. Use a numbering or lettering system to direct the reader to the supporting items. For example, use:

Schedule I/II/III … Schedule A/B/C … Exhibit I/II/III … Exhibit A/B/C … Graph I/II/III … Graph A/B/C … Chart I/II/III … Chart A/B/C …

Consider using *italics* or **bold** fonts to emphasize the numbers or letters, so the reader can easily find the schedules, exhibits, and audiovisuals and toggle between the report and support.

SAMPLE REPORT

December 7, 2016

TO:	**Jason Pickering, Esq.**
	Assistant District Attorney
FROM:	**Henry K. Royston, CFE CPA**
	Forensics Partners, LLC
RE:	**Earl K. Duncan**
CASE:	**16-023**

BACKGROUND

Earl K. Duncan ("the principal") owns and operates Duncan Investment Group, LLC ("DIG"), a small private investment firm located in Cedartown, Georgia, which invests client monies "in emerging growth companies spanning the mid, small, and micro-cap markets."

Between March 1, 2015, and March 12, 2016, the principal deposited approximately $401,000 in funds from a number of individuals and a corporation into the DIG checking account. Some of these individuals said they invested monies with the principal, but did not receive authentic stock certificates. The funds were supposed to have been invested in "Ace Aero-Drones."

ISSUES TO BRING TO YOUR ATTENTION

DIG was organized on May 6, 2014, and terminated on November 3, 2014, and was organized a second time on July 15, 2016, and terminated a second time on November 21, 2016. These organizations and terminations were outside of the deposit period, March 1, 2015 to March 12, 2016.

DIG had only one debit card, which was issued to the principal.

EXECUTIVE SUMMARY

We scheduled and analyzed bank statements, canceled checks, debit card transactions, fees, and deposits. When we did not recognize a payee, we researched the payee on the Internet. As a result, we found:

- None of the client's $401,000 in deposited checks were escrowed, or disbursed, for investments in Ace Aero-Drones Incorporated, or Ace Aero-Drones USA.
- Over $225,000 of the disbursements were personal transactions, including 21 disbursements totaling $23,699 paid to a strip club the day of or day after depositing investor checks.
- The principal and his wife used the DIG checking account as a personal, instead of a business, checking account (e.g., eating at restaurants, buying groceries and gasoline, and entertainment).
- There are no disbursements that indicate the principal withheld taxes from paychecks or made payments to the U.S. Department of the Treasury or Georgia Department of Revenue for income or employment taxes.

Note: According to Secretary of State filing documents, Earl K. Duncan co-managed DIG with Harmon Grunion from around May 6, 2014, until around November 3, 2014, when DIG was terminated. On or around July 15, 2016, DIG was organized again by the principal, Joshua Johnson, and Herschel Pritchard. DIG was terminated again around November 21, 2016.

DOCUMENTS REVIEWED

We reviewed the following documents:

■ Monthly bank statements, canceled checks, and deposit slips drawn on the DIG account with the Bank of Cedartown (#2270 0049 9984) for the months of November 2014 through September 2016 (fraud examiner's note: the account opened on November 6, 2014, and closed on September 20, 2016).

■ The defense attorney's notes of factual content.

■ Organization and termination certificates from the Georgia Secretary of State.

■ We requested income tax returns information for the principal and DIG; however, those have yet to be provided. Accordingly, those were not considered and the report will be modified when received.

FRAUD EXAMINATION APPROACH/FINDINGS

Over $225,000 in Personal Expenses Paid from DIG Checking Account

As summarized in *Schedule 1* and detailed in *Schedule 2*, we examined $445,998.56 in disbursements (e.g., checks, debit card, and debit memorandum transactions). Over $225,000 in disbursements was for personal expenses.

Below is a sample of the personal disbursements that we identified for the 24-month period, which is summarized by category, number of transactions identified, associated total dollars, and examples. Visit *Schedule 1* to view the full listing.

Restaurant	456	$52,383.76	ARIA Silverstone Bar, Tybee Island Brewing, Hooter's, Roller's Lounge, Eden Forest Country Club, Stoney River, Subway, Wendy's
Strip Club	37	$45,998.00	Strip TZ Sports Grille (aka Striptease Atlanta)
Entertainment	74	$36,291.50	Will Avants Golf, Sussex Billiards & Beer, West Point Lake, Garland Marine, Shipyard Golf Club, Cloverland Amusement

(*continued*)

Grocery	126	$ 8,101.13	BI-LO, Kroger, Piggly Wiggly, Publix
Wine/Liquor	7	$ 994.36	Hopkins Warehouse Liquor, Elegant Wine
Sex Items	3	$ 370.96	Erotic Toys and More

Fraud examiner's note: We identified a substantial number of transactions where charges could be of a personal nature (e.g., 73 transactions at Big Lots, BJs, Costco, Home Depot, Lowe's, Target, Value City, and Walmart). However, we could not determine which purchases were business or personal because of the absence of receipts. Accordingly, none of those transactions were listed as personal, albeit many could be personal.

We identified disbursements to Phil Axelrod, a person with whom the principal indicated was associated. We found a March 6, 2016, wire transfer for $75,000 to Phil Axelrod and a debit card disbursement for $7,500 on May 18, 2016 to Axelrod Industries. According to the defense attorney's notes of factual content, Axelrod testified under oath that, "DIG sent $75,000 to repay his personal for consulting services." The $7,500 debit card transaction is the only charge over $5,000 to the principal's (DIG's) debit card.

Investor Checks Show as the Check Purpose Ace Aero-Drones
Schedule 3 lists all $445,998.56 of the deposits from November 6, 2014, through September 20, 2016. *Schedule 4*, however, shows that the principal deposited a net of $401,000 in checks into the DIG checking account from a number of persons during the period March 1, 2015, through March 12, 2016. In the memo section of four checks deposited during this period were the wording "Ace Aero-Drones Stock," "Ace Aero-Drones Plan," and "50 K Stock Ace Aero-Drones."

No Evidence of Escrowing/Disbursing Funds for Ace Aero-Drones
We found that none of the forementioned client deposits were escrowed or disbursed for investments in "Ace Aero-Drones," "Ace Aero-Drones Stock," or "Ace Aero-Drones Plan."

Principal Visited Strip Clubs 21 Times after Depositing Investor Checks
Schedule 5 shows that the principal visited Striptease Club Atlanta (aka Strip TZ Sports Grille) ten (10) times on the day of and day after depositing $35,000 from Marilyn K. Weaver (spending $15,814), eight (8) times after depositing $42,500 from Christopher K. Weaver and $42,500 from Weaver Electronics, Inc. (spending $4,331), and three (3) times after depositing $105,000 from Christopher K. Weaver (spending $3,554). In total, the principal spent $23,699 on the 21 strip club disbursements shortly after depositing investor funds (Fraud examiners note: The principal spent $45,998 on 32 strip club visits over the 24-month period examined).

DIG Checking Account Used as a Personal Checking Account
As shown in organization and termination certificates from the Georgia secretary of state and summarized in *Schedule 6*, DIG operated as a proprietorship (an unincorporated business owned and/or operated by a single person who is responsible for its debts and receives its profits or pays for its losses) from November 4, 2014, through July 14, 2016. Before and after those dates, DIG operated as a limited liability company. The deposits in questions were made during the period March 1, 2015, through March 12, 2016. Accordingly, DIG was a proprietorship operated by the principal during the time when monies were received from investors who wanted to invest in Ace Aero-Drones.

Although titled as a limited liability company, based on the actual disbursements (i.e., over $225,000 in disbursements made for personal purposes by both the principal and his wife), the principal and his wife used the DIG checking account as if it were a personal, instead of a business, checking account. Normally, business checking accounts are kept separate from personal checking accounts and (1) owners remove monies from the business checking account by writing paychecks or draws from their capital accounts and (2) depositing those paychecks or draws from their capital accounts into separate personal checking accounts.

Additionally, there were a number of checks where the memo indicated "paycheck"; but, the paycheck amounts were in rounded numbers (e.g., $3,000.00 made payable to Rena Rodriguez on March 5, 2016, and $1,600.00 made payable to Roger Ferguson on May 16, 2016), and there is no evidence of withholding taxes or payments to the U.S. Department of the Treasury, Internal Revenue Service, or Georgia Department of Revenue taxing authorities. Businesses that employ persons are required to withhold and pay income and social security taxes unless the persons are independent contractors.

SUMMARY REMARKS

We reviewed the documentation associated with $445,998.56 in disbursements and $445,998.56 in deposits. Over $225,000 of the disbursements were personal. The principal spent $23,699 for the 21 strip club disbursements the day of or day after receiving investor funds. DIG received $401,000 in funds from investors and a number of the deposited checks were for "Ace Aero-Drones Stock," and "Ace Aero-Drones Plan" and "50 K Stock Ace Aero-Drones"; however, no authentic stock certificates were provided. Despite the checking account being labeled as an LLC the principal operated it as a personal checking account rather than a business checking account. The principal paid taxable wages; however, we saw no evidence of withholding taxes or payments to the U.S. Department of the Treasury, Internal Revenue Service, or Georgia Department of Revenue taxing authorities.

Should you have any questions or require additional information, please contact me by email at hroyston@forensicpartners.com.

Sincerely,
Henry K. Royston, CFE CPA

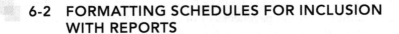

6-2 FORMATTING SCHEDULES FOR INCLUSION WITH REPORTS

Learning Objective

After reading this summary, you should learn how to format schedules for inclusions with fraud examination reports.

Fraud Examination Schedules

As with reports, each organization has its format for schedules and those schedule formats often appear similar to schedule formats used in audit reports.

Below are expected formatting requirements:

I. Numbering/Lettering System

    Prominently show a number or letter at the top of the schedule. This numbering or lettering system directs the reader back to the narrative found in the fraud examination report. For example, use:

    Schedule I/II/III... Schedule A/B/C... Exhibit I/II/III... Exhibit A/B/C... Graph I/II/III... Graph A/B/C... Chart I/II/III... Chart A/B/C...

II. Use a Summary or Lead Schedule to Provide an Overview of the Various Detailed Schedules

    Even in simple fraud examinations, there are often two or more detailed schedules. Use a summary or lead schedule to give a quick simplified overview of the various detailed schedules and refer the reader to the more detailed schedules. Following is a sample summary schedule with references to the detailed schedules.

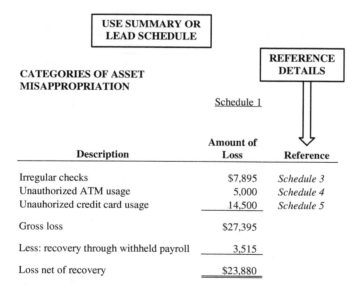

III. Use the Orientation, Margins, and Scaling Functions

    Schedules can be too small or too large or too wide to be effectively reviewed on a single page or pages. The most common problem involves being too wide (i.e., too many columns or too many columns that are set too wide). Use the orientation, margins, and scaling functions in Print Preview to correct these problems.

Below is a schedule that is too wide and if printed requires the reader to use Scotch Tape to piece them together.

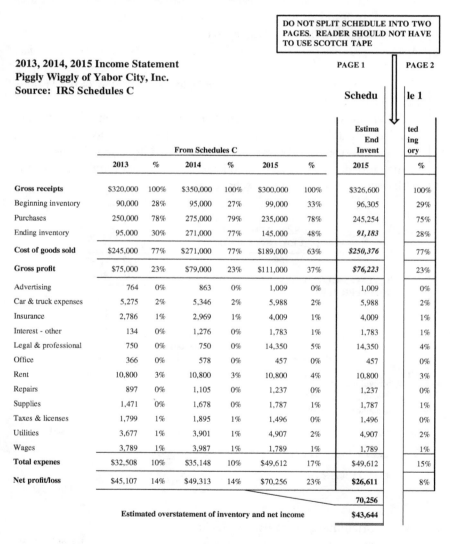

DO NOT SPLIT SCHEDULE INTO TWO PAGES. READER SHOULD NOT HAVE TO USE SCOTCH TAPE

2013, 2014, 2015 Income Statement
Piggly Wiggly of Yabor City, Inc.
Source: IRS Schedules C

PAGE 1   PAGE 2

Schedu | le 1

	2013	%	2014	%	2015	%	Estimated Ending Inventory 2015	%
			From Schedules C					
Gross receipts	$320,000	100%	$350,000	100%	$300,000	100%	$326,600	100%
Beginning inventory	90,000	28%	95,000	27%	99,000	33%	96,305	29%
Purchases	250,000	78%	275,000	79%	235,000	78%	245,254	75%
Ending inventory	95,000	30%	271,000	77%	145,000	48%	*91,183*	28%
Cost of goods sold	$245,000	77%	$271,000	77%	$189,000	63%	*$250,376*	77%
Gross profit	$75,000	23%	$79,000	23%	$111,000	37%	*$76,223*	23%
Advertising	764	0%	863	0%	1,009	0%	1,009	0%
Car & truck expenses	5,275	2%	5,346	2%	5,988	2%	5,988	2%
Insurance	2,786	1%	2,969	1%	4,009	1%	4,009	1%
Interest - other	134	0%	1,276	0%	1,783	1%	1,783	1%
Legal & professional	750	0%	750	0%	14,350	5%	14,350	4%
Office	366	0%	578	0%	457	0%	457	0%
Rent	10,800	3%	10,800	3%	10,800	4%	10,800	3%
Repairs	897	0%	1,105	0%	1,237	0%	1,237	0%
Supplies	1,471	0%	1,678	0%	1,787	1%	1,787	1%
Taxes & licenses	1,799	1%	1,895	1%	1,496	0%	1,496	0%
Utilities	3,677	1%	3,901	1%	4,907	2%	4,907	2%
Wages	3,789	1%	3,987	1%	1,789	1%	1,789	1%
Total expenes	$32,508	10%	$35,148	10%	$49,612	17%	$49,612	15%
Net profit/loss	$45,107	14%	$49,313	14%	$70,256	23%	**$26,611**	8%
							70,256	
Estimated overstatement of inventory and net income							**$43,644**	

Switch the orientation from Portrait to Landscape and then use Custom Scaling Options to adjust the scaling down to a smaller size. Following is the same schedule in Landscape Orientation and 85 percent size. The reader does not have to use tape.

> SWITCH FROM PORTRAIT TO
> LANDSCAPTE ORIENTATION AND
> USE CUSTOM SCALING TO SHRINK

2013, 2014, 2015 Income Statement
Piggly Wiggly of Yabor City, Inc.
Source: IRS Schedules C

Schedule 1

	2013	%	2014	%	2015	%	2015	%
	From Schedules C						Estimated Ending Inventory	
Gross receipts	$320,000	100%	$350,000	100%	$300,000	100%	$326,600	100%
Beginning inventory	90,000	28%	95,000	27%	99,000	33%	96,305	29%
Purchases	250,000	78%	275,000	79%	235,000	78%	245,254	75%
Ending inventory	95,000	30%	271,000	77%	145,000	48%	*91,183*	28%
Cost of goods sold	$245,000	77%	$271,000	77%	$189,000	63%	*$250,376*	77%
Gross profit	$75,000	23%	$79,000	23%	$111,000	37%	*$76,223*	23%
Advertising	764	0%	863	0%	1,009	0%	1,009	0%
Car & truck expenses	5,275	2%	5,346	2%	5,988	2%	5,988	2%
Insurance	2,786	1%	2,969	1%	4,009	1%	4,009	1%
Interest - other	134	0%	1,276	0%	1,783	1%	1,783	1%
Legal & professional	750	0%	750	0%	14,350	5%	14,350	4%
Office	366	0%	578	0%	457	0%	457	0%
Rent	10,800	3%	10,800	3%	10,800	4%	10,800	3%
Repairs	897	0%	1,105	0%	1,237	0%	1,237	0%
Supplies	1,471	0%	1,678	0%	1,787	1%	1,787	1%
Taxes & licenses	1,799	1%	1,895	1%	1,496	0%	1,496	0%
Utilities	3,677	1%	3,901	1%	4,907	2%	4,907	2%
Wages	3,789	1%	3,987	1%	1,789	1%	1,789	1%
Total expenes	$32,508	10%	$35,148	10%	$49,612	17%	$49,612	15%
Net profit/loss	$45,107	14%	$49,313	14%	$70,256	23%	**$26,611**	8%

70,256

Estimated overstatement of in ventory and net income   **$43,644**

The same formatting applies to pictures, charts, graphs, photographs, and so on. Following is a picture of the front and back of a canceled check.

		64-777/611	**7042**
Hoggly Woggly of Jasper, LLC Jasper, GA	DATE	3/31/2016	

PAY TO THE
ORDER OF ___Hoggly Woggly of Georgia___ $1,500.00
___One thousand five hundred and 00/100___   DOLLARS

FIRST BANK OF JASPER

Jasper, GA 30143

FOR_____   Wadeus E. Duncan

R

:062110777   :00988181   7042   :0000150000

Hoggly Woggly of Jasper

Belén Garrett

Do Not Write Below This Line

Mar 0331 - 40924409

Sharptop Bank
First Bank of Jasper

6-3 HOW TO SIMPLIFY THE COMPLEX WITH AUDIOVISUALS

Learning Objective

After reading this synopsis, you should have a better idea about:

1. The types of audiovisuals available to simplify the information found during your fraud examination.
2. How to enhance and script your expert testimony with audiovisuals.

The following is based on an article written by William H. Beecken entitled "Enhance Your Expert Testimony with Audio-Visuals," which appeared in *The White Paper*, the Association of Certified Fraud Examiners (ACFE), January–February 1992.

Introduction

Because fraud examiners work with a multitude of information during their investigations, they have the potential of being among the most important witnesses in an arbitration, hearing, or trial. However, like most expert witnesses, they possess so much information that they also have the potential to confuse or bore the triers of fact (judge, jury, or arbitrator). Unless trained, expert witnesses often resort to using technical jargon, speaking in monotone voices, not effectively controlling their bodies, eyes, and voices during testimony, and wanting to convey voluminous amounts of complex financial information using accounting schedules. All of these have the potential of losing, instead of informing, the triers of fact.

To overcome the pitfalls and be a more effective expert witness, fraud examiners should consider using audiovisuals during their testimony. Through careful preparation of audiovisuals, fraud examiners will:

1. Force themselves to use simplified terminology.
2. Script their direct testimony.
3. Provide prompts for the timing of vocal emphasis and on items that should be highlighted.
4. Focus the eyes of the triers of facts onto the documents that the fraud examiner and his attorney feel are most important.
5. Summarize the most important findings of the fraud examination that the triers of fact will use during deliberations.

A major portion of the population is visual, auditory, or kinesthetic (touch) learners, or some combination thereof. The highest percentage of learners absorbs information best when both see and hear that information. Accordingly, verbal testimony (auditory) augmented by audiovisuals (visual) both increases the absorption of the facts and supports the expert's opinion.

With well-conceived audiovisuals, the triers of fact will pay closer attention, better understand the complexities of the fraud examiner's conclusion, and better remember the fraud examiner's testimony during deliberations.

Confusion is the weapon of the opposing attorney. This is particularly true when the fact finders are juries made up of uneducated peers. In financially oriented cases, opposing attorneys routinely try to exclude persons with financial backgrounds from the jury during the selection process. However, as the adage, goes, "Pictures are worth a thousand words." With today's computers, cameras, and video camcorders, the fraud examiner can quickly enhance and simplify their testimony with simplified audiovisuals that graphically convey the core ideas of their findings.

Using the Correct Chart/Diagram/Visual Analysis

The five most commonly used types of accounting audiovisuals are line charts, bar charts, pie charts, diagrams, and text charts. What many users do not understand is which audiovisual best conveys certain kinds of information.

1. Text charts convey words, phrases, and sentences representing discreet information (e.g., overview of a presentation or demonstration).
2. Line charts best depict changes over time (e.g., increases or decreases in income statement items over several accounting periods).
3. Bar charts best compare differences in size or components at various points in time (e.g., balance sheet totals).
4. Pie charts compare parts of a whole at one point in time (e.g., composition of material misstatements).
5. Diagrams illustrate structures (e.g., organizational charts), procedures (e.g., disbursement cycle flowchart), or movement (e.g., movement of checks in a check kite).

Design Principles for Charts and Graphs

Once the most applicable type of audiovisual is chosen, the following design principles should be observed:

1. *Simplicity.* Follow the KISS (Keep It Simple, Stupid) theory. Focus the viewer's attention on as few attributes, titles, and colors as possible. Provide as much white (open) space as possible. If done properly, the viewer can quickly grasp and readily retain the point being made. Concentrate your presentation on the least common denominator (i.e., the arbitrator, judge, or juror who has trouble balancing his/her checkbook). If needed, use a *series* of simple graphs to convey several related attributes or use consolidating techniques (e.g., averaging data from several time periods) to simplify your presentation.
2. *Balance.* Visually balance the colors and shapes in the audiovisual. Dark, solid, and eye-catching colors should be strategically placed to avoid visually tipping the audiovisual in the wrong direction.

3. *Consistency.* When using a series of related charts or graphs, use the same lettering font and style of audiovisual. Consistency adds an unseen professionalism to the entire expert testimony. Obvious errors or inconsistencies subtract from the information being conveyed.

4. *Lettering.* A combination of upper- and lowercase letters works better than using all uppercase letters. Save the use of all uppercase letters for emphasis. For additional emphasis, use, but do not overuse, italics, shadowing, boldfacing, underlining, or some combination thereof.

5. *Coloring.* AVOID USING OFFENSIVE COLORS! Opposing counsel have persuaded judges that using "red" for net losses or "green" for money is more "prejudicial than probative." As a result, judges have made last-minute decisions precluding experts from using graphs and charts with these "prejudicial" colors. Do not find out that your audiovisual aid is unusable just before or during your testimony. A black and white schedule might suffice and avoid being rejected by the judge.

Examples

Bar Chart

The bar chart is one of the most used audiovisuals. Following is an example of confusing, good, and better bar charts.

Confusing. Too many data points. Use three graphs instead of one graph.

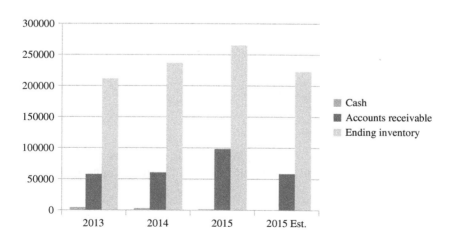

Better. Show a comparison of only one data point (e.g., ending inventory).

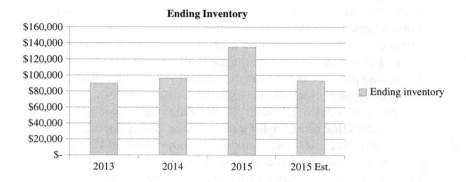

Best. Show a comparison of only one account (e.g., ending inventory); but, enhance the labels; add a comparative bracket and the amount of the difference between what was reported and the estimated actual ending inventory.

Below are a number of examples of good audiovisuals.

Document Audiovisual

A document video shows and highlights material misstatements. Make a screen shot of the document; add a descriptive label; and highlight material misstatements. For example:

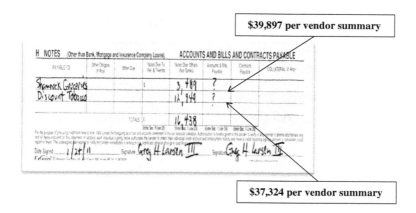

Multiple Document Comparison

Make a screen shot of the two or more related documents; add a descriptive label; and highlight the material misstatements in the two documents.

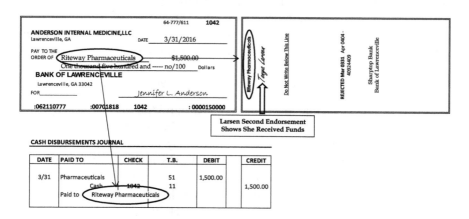

Descriptive Chart

Occasionally you need to explain a process, accounting, or concept. Following is a chart explaining gross profit.

WHAT IS GROSS PROFIT – ONE ITEM?	
Sell Refrigerator (at Retail)	
(GROSS RECEIPTS)	$1,000
Remove Refrigerator from Inventory (at Cost)	
(COST OF GOODS SOLD)	$600
Profit from Sale	
(GROSS PROFIT)	$400

Flowchart—Follow the Money (Loan Proceeds)

Occasionally, you have money that is moved around between accounts at *different* financial institutions, particularly when money is being laundered. Instead of several accounting schedules (one for each institution), which can confuse attorneys, judges, and juries, a single picture quickly provides an overview of the movement of money. Like other audiovisuals, once it is moved into evidence, the audiovisual goes with the judge or jury for deliberations. It represents what you want the triers of fact to remember most. See example on page 111.

Flowchart—Follow the Money (Deposits and Withdrawals)

Similarly, you may track money as it moves around the *same* financial institution but in different cities. If you also have the cell phone records (via consent or using a subpoena), those records may be incorporated into the flowchart. Following is an audiovisual that tracks money inside the same bank over a two-day period. The bank statements record a cash deposit by an accomplice in one city and cash withdrawals in another distance city on the same day, followed by debit card transactions, probably purchasing big-box store stored money cards. The cell phone records the coordination between the accomplice in one state and owner of the bank account in another state. See the flowchart example on page 112.

NOTE: SMITH PERSONAL ACCOUNT

PERSONAL CHECKS - Marietta Bank A/C 7768014

Date	Amount	Payee
01/29/17	$11,959.00	Jobber's Gasoline
01/29/17	1,041.00	Speaker's Bureau
01/29/17	36,000.00	Smith's Self-Storage
	$49,000.00	Total of Deposit and Disbursements

NOTE: SMITH BUSINESS ACCOUNT

BUSINESS CHECKS - Bank of Gilmer County A/C 188144477

Date	Amount	Payee
01/30/17	$ 7,000.00	ABC Construction
01/30/17	10,578.67	Payoff loan on mausoleum
01/30/17	7,324.23	Payoff mortgage arrearage
01/31/17	3,500.00	Cash - Harmon Smith endorsement
01/31/17	3,246.00	Hacker Wholesale
01/31/17	1,440.00	Magnet House of Fun
01/31/17	3,273.00	Carribean Resort
	$36,361.90	Total of Disbursements - FIFO Method

LOAN CHECKS - Marietta Bank A/C 3970188

Date	Amount	Payee
01/28/17	$ 36,000.00	Harmon Smith
01/28/17	1,045.80	North Marietta Escrow
01/28/17	500.00	Loan Fee
01/28/17	430.07	Cobb County Tax Commissioner
	$ 37,975.87	Total Disbursements

111

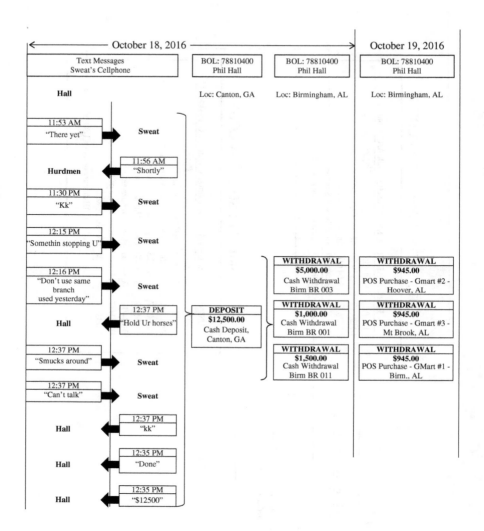

Summary Testimony

Often, a summary listing focuses the expert witness's testimony and provides the attorney a document for your direct examination or the attorney's closing arguments. It represents what you want the triers of fact to remember most.

GOOD SUMMARY	BETTER SUMMARY
DONNIE'S BURGERHUT INDICATORS OF INSOLVENCY	**DONNIE'S BURGERHUT INDICATORS OF INSOLVENCY**
• THREE CONSECUTIVE NET LOSSES FOR YEARS 2013–2015	• *Three consecutive net losses* for the years 2013–2015
• NET LOSS OF $107.183 IN THE FINAL FOUR MONTHS OF OPERATION	• *Net loss of $107,183* in the final four months of operation
• 79 NSF CHARGES IN THE LAST 18 MONTHS	• *79 NSF charges* in the last 18 months
• DEFAULT ON LINE OF CREDIT	• *Default on line of credit*
• THREE REJECTIONS FOR NEW LOANS	• *Three rejections for new loans*
• FREQUENT CHECK KITING BETWEEN BUSINESS AND PERSONAL CHECKING ACCOUNTS	• *Frequent check kiting* between business and personal checking accounts

CHAPTER SEVEN

Documents

7-1 CASE 1: FRAUDULENT FINANCIAL STATEMENTS (LARSEN CONVENIENCE STORE)

Recorded Interview on January 2, 2016
Location: Parking Lot of Larsen Convenience, Canton, Georgia
Participants: Gregory Larsen, owner of Larsen Convenience
SIU Special Agents Collins and Hawkins

Collins	Mr. Larsen, I am Special Agent Tom Collins and this is Special Agent Rodney Hawkins. We are with Southern Appalachian Insurance Company. Here is a copy of my business card.
Larsen	What is this about?
Collins	We are making an inquiry into the fire at your store two days ago. May we ask a few questions and record our conversation?
Larsen	Sure, I've nothing to hide.
Collins	That would be great. We need your assistance in determining the cause of the fire. It will help expedite your claim.
Larsen	Great! I need the money and want to get back into business as soon as possible.
Collins	As I understand it, the fire was called in around midnight on the 31st.

Larsen	That's what I'm told.
Collins	The cause and origin guys ruled out acts of nature and mechanical and electrical causes and sources of the fire. The arson dog alerted on numerous spots inside the store and the Fire Marshal took samples to the GBI State Crime Lab. Do you have any idea of who would have wanted to burn your business?
Larsen	What do you mean, like a customer?
Collins	Customer, relative, neighbor, anyone.
Larsen	A customer came to the store on the 31st. He was drunk and got irate when I wouldn't sell him a case of beer.
Collins	Tell me more. Did you know him? What did he look like? What were you doing?
Larsen	I was getting ready to close for the night. The phone was ringing. The front door was locked. I never saw him before. You know, you try to remember all customers, but sometimes you're busy and just can't remember. I think he was big, about six feet six tall, 350 pounds, and had a beard. The room smelled like alcohol and body odor. He went to the cooler and grabbed a case of beer. All hell broke loose when he couldn't buy beer. No one wants to lose their liquor license. Cops are everywhere. The guy went nuts and threatened to burn down the store. What would you do?
Collins	What kind of car did he drive? Did you get a license plate number?
Larsen	I didn't check. Would you stick your neck out?
Collins	Was your business doing well?
Larsen	Great! Best year ever. I just increased my inventory to cover higher sales. Things were going gangbusters. I was thinking of opening a second store over by the new shopping center. The traffic has quadrupled over there.
Collins	Back to possible suspects. Know anyone else?
Larsen	My wife's family hates me. Her nephew got angry over money. I jumped into my truck, backed up in a hurry, and accidently killed him. The bastards won't let me forget it.
Collins	Anyone mad enough to burn your business.
Larsen	His father is a hothead and a big drinker. He came into the store once and turned over my shelving. Took me hours to get everything straight.
Collins	When did you last see him?
Larsen	I avoid him like the plague. Won't you?
Collins	Do you have his name and address? We will need to visit him.
Larsen	I'll get that for you. I would love it if he was the torch.
Collins	Thanks for your cooperation. We'll be back in touch. Let us know if you think of anything else.

Authorization for Release of Financial Records

TO: Custodian of Records

_____

_____

RE: <u>Fire loss at Larsen Convenience Store, Canton, GA</u>

DATE OF BIRTH:<u>October 26, 1987</u>

SOCIAL SECURITY NUMBER:<u>800-98-1234</u>

You are hereby authorized to furnish to the law firm of <u>Hendrick & Poole</u>, and their duly authorized representatives, copies of any and all information they may request concerning any personal or business financial records, including but not limited to, salaries, bonuses, commissions, allowances, travel expenses, stocks, investments, retirement and pension plans, stock ownership or option plans, pay deferral or provident funds, defined contribution plans, other employee benefit plans, incentive plans, termination benefits, mutual funds, growth funds, life insurance policies, bank accounts, credit union accounts, savings accounts, money market accounts, certificates of deposit, installment loans, mortgage loans, personal loans, signature loans, any other direct indebtedness or obligation incurred by me or on my behalf, any indirect indebtedness or obligation incurred by me or on my behalf (including, but not limited to, any indebtedness or obligation for which I am a co-borrower, guarantor, or surety), savings plans, 401(k) accounts, and Individual Retirement Accounts in which I may have or had an interest, or other information in your possession regarding me, relating to:

<u>Gregory H. Larsen, Tonya V. Larsen, Larsen Convenience Store</u>

_____

This authorization shall constitute valid authorization for the firm <u>of Hendrick & Poole</u> to inspect all such items set forth above, and to copy, and to request and receive copies, including certified copies, thereof from you.

This authorization is valid until you receive written revocation. A copy of this authorization shall be sufficient and as good as the original, and permission is hereby granted to honor a photostatic copy of this authorization.

Signed at <u>Atlanta</u>, Georgia, this <u>18th</u> day of <u>February</u>, 20<u>16.</u>

Gregory H. Larsen
_____
Signature of Insured

Gregory H. Larsen
_____
Typed Name of Insured

POLICY NUMBER: 15-321654-L

___$425,000.00___
POLICY AMT. AT TIME OF LOSS

$__12/28/2015_____
DATE ISSUED

___12/27/2016_____
DATE EXPIRES

Sworn Statement

IN

PROOF OF LOSS

COMPANY CLAIM NUMBER: ATL-2136-BUS

_____Roger Reeves_____
AGENT

1234 Riverstone Pkwy, Canton, GA
AGENCY AT

_____

To the __[INSURANCE COMPANY NAME]__Southern Appalachian Insurance_____

of __Atlanta___[CITY STATE]___Georgia_____
At time of loss, by the above indicated policy of insurance you insured-

_____contents, leasehold improvements, and equipment at store located at 1789 Hwy. 53, Canton, Georgia_____

against loss by _____ to the property described according to the terms and conditions of said policy and of all forms, endorsements, transfers and assignments attached thereto.

TIME AND ORIGIN   A ___fire_____ loss occurred about the hour of __12_o'clock AM/PM., on the __31st day of _December___, 2015__ .
The cause and origin of the said loss were: __unknown_____

OCCUPANCY   The building described, or containing the property described, was occupied at the time of the loss as follows, and for no other purpose whatever: ___convenience store _____ .

TITLE AND CHANGES   At the time of the loss, the interest of your insured in the property described therein was___100%_____ INTEREST __ of the contents, leaseholds improvements, and equipments _ .   No other person or persons had any interest therein or encumbrance thereon, except: ___N/A_____
Since the said policy was issued, there has been no assignment thereof, or change of interest, use, occupancy, possession, location or exposure of the property described, except _____

TOTAL   THE TOTAL AMOUNT OF INSURANCE upon the property described by this policy was, at the time of the loss, $ __425,000_____, as more particularly specified in the apportionment attached, besides which there was no policy or other contract of insurance, written or oral, valid or invalid.

VALUE   THE ACTUAL CASH VALUE of said property at the time of the loss was . . . . $ ____349,925_____

LOSS   THE WHOLE LOSS AND DAMAGE was . contents, leasehold improvements, equipment. $ ___349,925_____

AMT. CLAIMED   THE AMOUNT CLAIMED under the above numbered policy number is...................... $ ____349,925_____

STATEMENTS OF INSURED   The said loss did not originate by any act, design or procurement on the part of your insured, or this affiant; nothing has done by or with the privity or consent of your insured or this affiant, to violate the conditions of the policy, or render it void; no articles are mentioned herein or in annexed schedules but such as were destroyed or damaged at the time of said loss; no property saved has in any manner been concealed, and no attempt to deceive the said company, as to the extent of said loss, has in any manner been made. Any other information that may be required will be furnished and considered a part of this proof.

The furnishing of this blank or the preparation of proofs by a representative of the above insurance company is not a waiver of any of its rights.

State Of___Georgia_____   Insured: _Gregory H. Larsen_____

County Of __Cherokee_____   Insured:_____

Subscribed and sworn to before me this ___18th_____ day of _____March_____, _2016___
Personally Known to Me _____
I.D. _76-123456_____   Notary: _Dorothy Hendrix_____

ANY PERSON WHO KNOWINGLY AND WITH INTENT TO INJURE, DEFRAUD OR DECEIVE ANY INSURANCE COMPANY FILES A STATEMENT OF CLAIM CONTAINING ANY FALSE, INCOMPLETE OR MISLEADING INFORMATION IS GUILTY OF A FELONY OF THE THIRD DEGREE.

Form **1040**	Department of the Treasury—Internal Revenue Service (99) **U.S. Individual Income Tax Return**	20**13**	OMB No. 1545-0074	IRS Use Only—Do not write or staple in this space.

For the year Jan. 1–Dec. 31, 2013, or other tax year beginning _____ , 2013, ending _____ , 20 ___   **See separate instructions.**

Your first name and initial	Last name	Your social security number
Gregory H	Larsen	800-98-1234

If a joint return, spouse's first name and initial	Last name	Spouse's social security number
Tonya V	Larsen	800-76-9876

Home address (number and street). If you have a P.O. box, see instructions.   Apt. no.
213 Underwood Street

▲ Make sure the SSN(s) above and on line 6c are correct.

City, town or post office, state, and ZIP code. If you have a foreign address, also complete spaces below (see instructions).
Canton GA 30115

Presidential Election Campaign
Check here if you, or your spouse if filing jointly, want $3 to go to this fund. Checking a box below will not change your tax or refund. ☐ You ☐ Spouse

Foreign country name	Foreign province/state/county	Foreign postal code

Filing Status

Check only one box.

1 ☐ Single
2 ☒ Married filing jointly (even if only one had income)
3 ☐ Married filing separately. Enter spouse's SSN above and full name here. ▶
4 ☐ Head of household (with qualifying person). (See instructions.) If the qualifying person is a child but not your dependent, enter this child's name here. ▶
5 ☐ Qualifying widow(er) with dependent child

Exemptions

					Boxes checked on 6a and 6b	2
6a	☒ **Yourself.** If someone can claim you as a dependent, **do not** check box 6a					
b	☒ **Spouse**				No. of children on 6c who:	
c	**Dependents:**	(2) Dependent's social security number	(3) Dependent's relationship to you	(4) ✓ If child under age 17 qualifying for child tax credit (see instructions)	• lived with you	
	(1) First name Last name			☐	• did not live with you due to divorce or separation (see instructions)	
				☐		
				☐	Dependents on 6c not entered above	
				☐		

If more than four dependents, see instructions and check here ▶ ☐

d	Total number of exemptions claimed	Add numbers on lines above ▶	2

Income

Attach Form(s) W-2 here. Also attach Forms W-2G and 1099-R if tax was withheld.

If you did not get a W-2, see instructions.

7	Wages, salaries, tips, etc. Attach Form(s) W-2	7	30,000.
8a	Taxable interest. Attach Schedule B if required	8a	173.
b	Tax-exempt interest. **Do not** include on line 8a . . .	8b			
9a	Ordinary dividends. Attach Schedule B if required	9a	
b	Qualified dividends	9b			
10	Taxable refunds, credits, or offsets of state and local income taxes	10	
11	Alimony received	11	
12	Business income or (loss). Attach Schedule C or C-EZ	12	59,570.
13	Capital gain or (loss). Attach Schedule D if required. If not required, check here ▶ ☐	13	
14	Other gains or (losses). Attach Form 4797	14	
15a	IRA distributions .	15a		b Taxable amount . . .	15b	
16a	Pensions and annuities	16a		b Taxable amount . . .	16b	
17	Rental real estate, royalties, partnerships, S corporations, trusts, etc. Attach Schedule E	17	
18	Farm income or (loss). Attach Schedule F	18	
19	Unemployment compensation	19	
20a	Social security benefits	20a		b Taxable amount . . .	20b	
21	Other income. List type and amount _____	21	
22	Combine the amounts in the far right column for lines 7 through 21. This is your **total income** ▶	22	89,743.

Adjusted Gross Income

23	Educator expenses	23			
24	Certain business expenses of reservists, performing artists, and fee-basis government officials. Attach Form 2106 or 2106-EZ	24			
25	Health savings account deduction. Attach Form 8889 .	25			
26	Moving expenses. Attach Form 3903	26			
27	Deductible part of self-employment tax. Attach Schedule SE .	27	4,209.		
28	Self-employed SEP, SIMPLE, and qualified plans . .	28			
29	Self-employed health insurance deduction	29			
30	Penalty on early withdrawal of savings	30			
31a	Alimony paid b Recipient's SSN ▶ _____	31a			
32	IRA deduction	32			
33	Student loan interest deduction	33			
34	Tuition and fees. Attach Form 8917	34			
35	Domestic production activities deduction. Attach Form 8903	35			
36	Add lines 23 through 35	36	4,209.
37	Subtract line 36 from line 22. This is your **adjusted gross income** . . . . . ▶	37	85,534.

For Disclosure, Privacy Act, and Paperwork Reduction Act Notice, see separate instructions. **BAA**   REV 06/04/14 TTW   Form **1040** (2013)

Form 1040 (2013)   Page **2**

Tax and Credits	38	Amount from line 37 (adjusted gross income)		38	85,534.
	39a	Check { ☐ **You** were born before January 2, 1949, ☐ Blind. } **Total boxes** if: { ☐ **Spouse** was born before January 2, 1949, ☐ Blind. } checked ▶ 39a			
Standard Deduction for—	b	If your spouse itemizes on a separate return or you were a dual-status alien, check here▶ 39b☐			
• People who check any box on line 39a or 39b or who can be claimed as a dependent, see instructions.	40	**Itemized deductions** (from Schedule A) **or your standard deduction** (see left margin)		40	12,200.
	41	Subtract line 40 from line 38		41	73,334.
	42	**Exemptions.** If line 38 is $150,000 or less, multiply $3,900 by the number on line 6d. Otherwise, see instructions		42	7,800.
	43	**Taxable income.** Subtract line 42 from line 41. If line 42 is more than line 41, enter -0-		43	65,534.
• All others:	44	**Tax** (see instructions). Check if any from: a ☐ Form(s) 8814 b ☐ Form 4972 c ☐		44	8,936.
Single or Married filing separately, $6,100	45	**Alternative minimum tax** (see instructions). Attach Form 6251		45	
	46	Add lines 44 and 45 ▶		46	8,936.
Married filing jointly or Qualifying widow(er), $12,200	47	Foreign tax credit. Attach Form 1116 if required	47		
	48	Credit for child and dependent care expenses. Attach Form 2441	48		
	49	Education credits from Form 8863, line 19	49		
Head of household, $8,950	50	Retirement savings contributions credit. Attach Form 8880	50		
	51	Child tax credit. Attach Schedule 8812, if required	51		
	52	Residential energy credits. Attach Form 5695	52		
	53	Other credits from Form: a ☐ 3800 b ☐ 8801 c☐	53		
	54	Add lines 47 through 53. These are your **total credits**		54	
	55	Subtract line 54 from line 46. If line 54 is more than line 46, enter -0- ▶		55	8,936.
Other Taxes	56	Self-employment tax. Attach Schedule SE		56	8,417.
	57	Unreported social security and Medicare tax from Form: a ☐ 4137 b ☐ 8919		57	
	58	Additional tax on IRAs, other qualified retirement plans, etc. Attach Form 5329 if required		58	
	59a	Household employment taxes from Schedule H		59a	
	b	First-time homebuyer credit repayment. Attach Form 5405 if required		59b	
	60	Taxes from: a ☐ Form 8959 b ☐ Form 8960 c ☐ Instructions; enter code(s)		60	
	61	Add lines 55 through 60. This is your **total tax** ▶		61	17,353.
Payments	62	Federal income tax withheld from Forms W-2 and 1099	62	3,000.	
	63	2013 estimated tax payments and amount applied from 2012 return	63	14,250.	
If you have a qualifying child, attach Schedule EIC.	64a	**Earned income credit (EIC)**	64a		
	b	Nontaxable combat pay election 64b			
	65	Additional child tax credit. Attach Schedule 8812	65		
	66	American opportunity credit from Form 8863, line 8	66		
	67	Reserved	67		
	68	Amount paid with request for extension to file	68		
	69	Excess social security and tier 1 RRTA tax withheld	69		
	70	Credit for federal tax on fuels. Attach Form 4136	70		
	71	Credits from Form: a ☐ 2439 b ☐ Reserved c ☐ 8885 d ☐	71		
	72	Add lines 62, 63, 64a, and 65 through 71. These are your **total payments** ▶		72	17,250.
Refund	73	If line 72 is more than line 61, subtract line 61 from line 72. This is the amount you **overpaid**		73	
	74a	Amount of line 73 you want **refunded to you.** If Form 8888 is attached, check here ▶☐		74a	
Direct deposit? See instructions.	b	Routing number X X X X X X X X X ▶c Type: ☐ Checking ☐ Savings			
	d	Account number X X X X X X X X X X X X X X X X X			
	75	Amount of line 73 you want applied to your 2014 estimated tax ▶ 75			
Amount You Owe	76	**Amount you owe.** Subtract line 72 from line 61. For details on how to pay, see instructions ▶		76	103.
	77	Estimated tax penalty (see instructions) 77			
Third Party Designee		Do you want to allow another person to discuss this return with the IRS (see instructions)? ☐ **Yes.** Complete below. ☒ **No**			
		Designee's name ▶ Phone no. ▶ Personal identification number (PIN) ▶			

Sign Here

Under penalties of perjury, I declare that I have examined this return and accompanying schedules and statements, and to the best of my knowledge and belief, they are true, correct, and complete. Declaration of preparer (other than taxpayer) is based on all information of which preparer has any knowledge.

Joint return? See instructions. Keep a copy for your records.

Your signature	Date	Your occupation	Daytime phone number
		Store owner	
Spouse's signature. If a joint return, **both** must sign.	Date	Spouse's occupation	If the IRS sent you an Identity Protection PIN, enter it here (see inst.)
		Office Manager	

Paid Preparer Use Only

Print/Type preparer's name	Preparer's signature	Date	Check ☐ if self-employed	PTIN
Firm's name ▶ Self-Prepared		Firm's EIN ▶		
Firm's address ▶		Phone no. ▶		

REV 06/04/14 TTW   Form **1040** (2013)

SCHEDULE C (Form 1040) Department of the Treasury Internal Revenue Service (99)	**Profit or Loss From Business** (Sole Proprietorship) ▶ For information on Schedule C and its instructions, go to *www.irs.gov/schedulec.* ▶ Attach to Form 1040, 1040NR, or 1041; partnerships generally must file Form 1065.	OMB No. 1545-0074 2013 Attachment Sequence No. 09

Name of proprietor	Social security number (SSN)
Gregory H Larsen	800-98-1234

A	Principal business or profession, including product or service (see instructions)	B Enter code from instructions
	Convenience Store	▶ 4 4 7 1 0 0

C	Business name. If no separate business name, leave blank.	D Employer ID number (EIN), (see instr.)
	Larsen's Convenience Store	

E	Business address (including suite or room no.) ▶ 1798 Hwy 53
	City, town or post office, state, and ZIP code Canon, GA 30115

F Accounting method: (1) ☒ Cash (2) ☐ Accrual (3) ☐ Other (specify) ▶ _____

G Did you "materially participate" in the operation of this business during 2013? If "No," see instructions for limit on losses . ☒ Yes ☐ No

H If you started or acquired this business during 2013, check here . . . . ▶ ☐

I Did you make any payments in 2013 that would require you to file Form(s) 1099? (see instructions) . . . . . . ☐ Yes ☒ No

J If "Yes," did you or will you file required Forms 1099? . . . . ☐ Yes ☐ No

Part I Income

1	Gross receipts or sales. See instructions for line 1 and check the box if this income was reported to you on Form W-2 and the "Statutory employee" box on that form was checked . . . . ▶ ☐	1	1,353,558.
2	Returns and allowances	2	
3	Subtract line 2 from line 1	3	1,353,558.
4	Cost of goods sold (from line 42)	4	1,120,046.
5	**Gross profit.** Subtract line 4 from line 3	5	233,512.
6	Other income, including federal and state gasoline or fuel tax credit or refund (see instructions) . . .	6	
7	**Gross income.** Add lines 5 and 6 . . . . ▶	7	233,512.

Part II Expenses   Enter expenses for business use of your home only on line 30.

8	Advertising	8	2,080.	18	Office expense (see instructions)	18	
9	Car and truck expenses (see instructions).	9		19	Pension and profit-sharing plans .	19	
10	Commissions and fees .	10		20	Rent or lease (see instructions):		
11	Contract labor (see instructions)	11		a	Vehicles, machinery, and equipment	20a	
12	Depletion	12		b	Other business property . . .	20b	12,000.
13	Depreciation and section 179 expense deduction (not included in Part III) (see instructions).	13		21	Repairs and maintenance . .	21	10,450.
				22	Supplies (not included in Part III) .	22	
				23	Taxes and licenses	23	2,105.
				24	Travel, meals, and entertainment:		
14	Employee benefit programs (other than on line 19) . .	14		a	Travel	24a	
15	Insurance (other than health)	15	3,666.	b	Deductible meals and entertainment (see instructions) .	24b	
16	Interest:			25	Utilities	25	11,616.
a	Mortgage (paid to banks, etc.)	16a		26	Wages (less employment credits) .	26	84,814.
b	Other	16b		27a	Other expenses (from line 48) .	27a	46,857.
17	Legal and professional services	17	354.	b	**Reserved for future use** . . .	27b	

28	**Total expenses** before expenses for business use of home. Add lines 8 through 27a . . . . . ▶		28	173,942.
29	Tentative profit or (loss). Subtract line 28 from line 7		29	59,570.
30	Expenses for business use of your home. Do not report these expenses elsewhere. Attach Form 8829 unless using the simplified method (see instructions). **Simplified method filers only:** enter the total square footage of: (a) your home: _____ and (b) the part of your home used for business: _____. Use the Simplified Method Worksheet in the instructions to figure the amount to enter on line 30		30	
31	**Net profit or (loss).** Subtract line 30 from line 29. • If a profit, enter on both **Form 1040, line 12** (or **Form 1040NR, line 13**) and on **Schedule SE, line 2.** (If you checked the box on line 1, see instructions). Estates and trusts, enter on **Form 1041, line 3.** • If a loss, you **must** go to line 32.	}	31	59,570.
32	If you have a loss, check the box that describes your investment in this activity (see instructions). • If you checked 32a, enter the loss on both **Form 1040, line 12,** (or **Form 1040NR, line 13**) and on **Schedule SE, line 2.** (If you checked the box on line 1, see the line 31 instructions). Estates and trusts, enter on **Form 1041, line 3.** • If you checked 32b, you **must** attach **Form 6198.** Your loss may be limited.	32a ☐ All investment is at risk. 32b ☐ Some investment is not at risk.		

For Paperwork Reduction Act Notice, see the separate instructions.   BAA   REV 03/03/14 TTW   Schedule C (Form 1040) 2013

122 ▦ Documents

Part III   **Cost of Goods Sold** (see instructions)

33   Method(s) used to value closing inventory: **a** ☒ Cost   **b** ☐ Lower of cost or market   **c** ☐ Other (attach explanation)

34   Was there any change in determining quantities, costs, or valuations between opening and closing inventory?
If "Yes," attach explanation . . . . ☐ **Yes**   ☒ **No**

35	Inventory at beginning of year. If different from last year's closing inventory, attach explanation . . .	**35**	272,960.
36	Purchases less cost of items withdrawn for personal use	**36**	1,119,661.
37	Cost of labor. Do not include any amounts paid to yourself	**37**	
38	Materials and supplies	**38**	
39	Other costs	**39**	
40	Add lines 35 through 39	**40**	1,392,621.
41	Inventory at end of year	**41**	272,575.
42	**Cost of goods sold.** Subtract line 41 from line 40. Enter the result here and on line 4	**42**	1,120,046.

Part IV   **Information on Your Vehicle.** Complete this part **only** if you are claiming car or truck expenses on line 9 and are not required to file Form 4562 for this business. See the instructions for line 13 to find out if you must file Form 4562.

43   When did you place your vehicle in service for business purposes? (month, day, year)   ▶ _____

44   Of the total number of miles you drove your vehicle during 2013, enter the number of miles you used your vehicle for:

   a   Business _____   **b** Commuting (see instructions) _____   **c** Other _____

45   Was your vehicle available for personal use during off-duty hours? . . . . ☐ Yes   ☐ No

46   Do you (or your spouse) have another vehicle available for personal use? . . . . ☐ Yes   ☐ No

47a   Do you have evidence to support your deduction? . . . . ☐ Yes   ☐ No

   b   If "Yes," is the evidence written? . . . . ☐ Yes   ☐ No

Part V   **Other Expenses.** List below business expenses not included on lines 8–26 or line 30.

Administration fee	24,120.
Cash over / short	3,603.
Credit card fees	1,971.
Expense items	10,585.
NSF checks expense	91.
Payroll tax expense	6,487.

48 **Total other expenses.** Enter here and on line 27a	**48**	46,857.

Form **W-2**	**Wage and Tax Statement** ► Keep for your records	**2013**

Name Tonya V Larsen	Social Security Number 800-76-9876

☒ **Spouse's W-2**
☐ **Do not transfer this W-2 to next year**

Military: Complete **Part VI** on Page 2 below

a Employee's social security No . 800-76-9876
b Employer's ID number 12-3456799
c Employer's name, address, and ZIP code
Absolute Orthopedics

Street	3456 South Marietta Parkway
City	Marietta
State	GA ZIP Code 30060
Foreign Country	

d Control number .

☒ **Transfer employee information from the Federal Information Worksheet**

e Employee's name
First Tonya   M.I. V
Last Larsen   Suff.
f Employee's address and ZIP code
Street 213 Underwood Street
City Canton
State GA   ZIP Code 30115
Foreign Country

1	Wages, tips, other compensation 30,000.00	2	Federal income tax withheld 3,000.00
3	Social security wages 30,000.00	4	Social security tax withheld 1,860.00
5	Medicare wages and tips 30,000.00	6	Medicare tax withheld 435.00
7	Social security tips	8	Allocated tips
9		10	Dependent care benefits
11	Nonqualified plans		Distributions from sect. 457 and nonqualified plans *(Important, see Help)*
12	Enter box 12 below		
13	☐ Statutory employee ☐ Retirement plan ☐ Third-party sick pay		

14 Enter box 14 below **after** entering boxes 18, 19, and 20.
NOTE: Enter box 15 **before** entering box 14.

Box 12 Code	Box 12 Amount	If Box 12 code is:	
		A: Enter amount attributable to RRTA Tier 2 tax	
		M: Enter amount attributable to RRTA Tier 2 tax	
		P: Double click to link to Form 3903, line 4. . .	
		R: Enter MSA contribution for Taxpayer . . .	
		Spouse	
		W: Enter HSA contribution for Taxpayer . . .	
		Spouse	
		G: ☐ Employer is **not** a state or local government	

Box 15 State	Employer's state I.D. no.	Box 16 State wages, tips, etc.	Box 17 State income tax
GA		30,000.00	1,800.00

Box 20 Locality name	Box 18 Local wages, tips, etc.	Box 19 Local income tax	Associated State
			—
			—
			—

Box 14 Description or Code on Actual Form W-2	Amount	TurboTax Identification of Description or Code (Identify this item by selecting the identification from the drop down list. If not on the list, select Other).

Supplement: Part III Cost of Goods Sold - Summaries by Product Line

	December 31, 2013
Fuel	$ 882,392
Beginning inventory	15,621
Purchases	781,776
Ending inventory	15,966
Cost of fuel	$ 781,431
Gross profit	$ 100,961
Groceries/food	$ 250,922
Beginning inventory	26,851
Purchases	170,271
Ending inventory	26,633
Cost of groceries	$ 170,489
Gross profit	$ 80,433
Beverages	$ 83,408
Beginning inventory	49,988
Purchases	60,910
Ending inventory	49,521
Cost of beverages	$ 61,377
Gross profit	$ 22,031
Tobacco	$ 133,097
Beginning inventory	179,961
Purchases	104,632
Ending inventory	179,866
Cost of tobacco	$ 104,727
Gross profit	$ 28,370
Print media	2,371
Beginning inventory	539
Purchases	2,072
Ending inventory	589
Cost of print media	$ 2,022
Gross profit	$ 349
Bank ATM Rents	$ 1,368
Beginning inventory	-
Purchases	-
Ending inventory	-
Cost of bank ATM rents	$ -
Gross profit	$ 1,368
Total revenue	$ 1,353,558
Beginning inventory	272,960
Purchases	1,119,661
Ending inventory	272,575
Total cost of goods sold	$ 1,120,046
Total gross profit	$ 233,512

Form 1040
Department of the Treasury—Internal Revenue Service   (99)
U.S. Individual Income Tax Return 2014   OMB No. 1545-0074   IRS Use Only—Do not write or staple in this space.

For the year Jan. 1–Dec. 31, 2014, or other tax year beginning _____, 2014, ending _____, 20 ___   See separate instructions.

Your first name and initial	Last name	Your social security number
Gregory H	Larsen	800-98-1234

If a joint return, spouse's first name and initial	Last name	Spouse's social security number
Tonya V	Larsen	800-76-9876

Home address (number and street). If you have a P.O. box, see instructions.   Apt. no.
213 Underwood Street

▲ Make sure the SSN(s) above and on line 6c are correct.

City, town or post office, state, and ZIP code. If you have a foreign address, also complete spaces below (see instructions).
Canton GA 30115

Foreign country name ____   Foreign province/state/county ____   Foreign postal code ____

Presidential Election Campaign
Check here if you, or your spouse if filing jointly, want $3 to go to this fund. Checking a box below will not change your tax or refund.   ☐ You ☐ Spouse

Filing Status
Check only one box.

1. ☐ Single
2. ☒ Married filing jointly (even if only one had income)
3. ☐ Married filing separately. Enter spouse's SSN above and full name here. ▶
4. ☐ Head of household (with qualifying person). (See instructions.) If the qualifying person is a child but not your dependent, enter this child's name here. ▶
5. ☐ Qualifying widow(er) with dependent child

Exemptions

6a ☒ Yourself. If someone can claim you as a dependent, **do not** check box 6a . . . . .
b ☒ Spouse . . . .

Boxes checked on 6a and 6b   **2**

c Dependents:

(1) First name Last name	(2) Dependent's social security number	(3) Dependent's relationship to you	(4) ✓ If child under age 17 qualifying for child tax credit (see instructions)
			☐
			☐
			☐
			☐

No. of children on 6c who:
• lived with you ____
• did not live with you due to divorce or separation (see instructions) ____
Dependents on 6c not entered above ____

If more than four dependents, see instructions and check here ▶ ☐

d Total number of exemptions claimed . . . .   Add numbers on lines above ▶ **2**

Income

Attach Form(s) W-2 here. Also attach Forms W-2G and 1099-R if tax was withheld.

If you did not get a W-2, see instructions.

7	Wages, salaries, tips, etc. Attach Form(s) W-2	7	36,000.
8a	Taxable interest. Attach Schedule B if required	8a	243.
b	Tax-exempt interest. **Do not** include on line 8a . . .	8b	
9a	Ordinary dividends. Attach Schedule B if required	9a	
b	Qualified dividends	9b	
10	Taxable refunds, credits, or offsets of state and local income taxes	10	
11	Alimony received	11	
12	Business income or (loss). Attach Schedule C or C-EZ	12	64,486.
13	Capital gain or (loss). Attach Schedule D if required. If not required, check here ▶ ☐	13	
14	Other gains or (losses). Attach Form 4797	14	
15a	IRA distributions .	15a		b Taxable amount . . .	15b	
16a	Pensions and annuities	16a		b Taxable amount . . .	16b	
17	Rental real estate, royalties, partnerships, S corporations, trusts, etc. Attach Schedule E	17	
18	Farm income or (loss). Attach Schedule F	18	
19	Unemployment compensation	19	
20a	Social security benefits	20a		b Taxable amount . . .	20b	
21	Other income. List type and amount ____	21	
22	Combine the amounts in the far right column for lines 7 through 21. This is your **total income** ▶	22	100,729.

Adjusted Gross Income

23	Educator expenses	23	
24	Certain business expenses of reservists, performing artists, and fee-basis government officials. Attach Form 2106 or 2106-EZ	24	
25	Health savings account deduction. Attach Form 8889 .	25	
26	Moving expenses. Attach Form 3903	26	
27	Deductible part of self-employment tax. Attach Schedule SE .	27	4,556.
28	Self-employed SEP, SIMPLE, and qualified plans . .	28	
29	Self-employed health insurance deduction	29	
30	Penalty on early withdrawal of savings	30	
31a	Alimony paid b Recipient's SSN ▶ ____	31a	
32	IRA deduction	32	
33	Student loan interest deduction	33	
34	Tuition and fees. Attach Form 8917	34	
35	Domestic production activities deduction. Attach Form 8903	35	
36	Add lines 23 through 35	36	4,556.
37	Subtract line 36 from line 22. This is your **adjusted gross income** . . . . . ▶	37	96,173.

For Disclosure, Privacy Act, and Paperwork Reduction Act Notice, see separate instructions. BAA   REV 05/19/15 TTW   Form **1040** (2014)

Form 1040 (2014)   Page **2**

Tax and Credits	38	Amount from line 37 (adjusted gross income)	38	96,173.
	39a	Check { **You** were born before January 2, 1950, ☐ Blind. } **Total boxes**		
		if: { ☐ **Spouse** was born before January 2, 1950, ☐ Blind. } checked ▶ 39a ☐		
	b	If your spouse itemizes on a separate return or you were a dual-status alien, check here▶ 39b☐		
Standard Deduction for—	40	**Itemized deductions** (from Schedule A) **or** your **standard deduction** (see left margin) . .	40	12,400.
• People who check any box on line 39a or 39b or who can be claimed as a dependent, see instructions.	41	Subtract line 40 from line 38	41	83,773.
	42	**Exemptions.** If line 38 is $152,525 or less, multiply $3,950 by the number on line 6d. Otherwise, see instructions	42	7,900.
	43	**Taxable income.** Subtract line 42 from line 41. If line 42 is more than line 41, enter -0- . .	43	75,873.
	44	**Tax** (see instructions). Check if any from: a ☐ Form(s) 8814 b ☐ Form 4972 c ☐ _____	44	10,681.
• All others:	45	**Alternative minimum tax** (see instructions). Attach Form 6251	45	
Single or Married filing separately, $6,200	46	Excess advance premium tax credit repayment. Attach Form 8962	46	
	47	Add lines 44, 45, and 46 . . . . ▶	47	10,681.
Married filing jointly or Qualifying widow(er), $12,400	48	Foreign tax credit. Attach Form 1116 if required	48		
	49	Credit for child and dependent care expenses. Attach Form 2441	49		
	50	Education credits from Form 8863, line 19	50		
Head of household, $9,100	51	Retirement savings contributions credit. Attach Form 8880	51		
	52	Child tax credit. Attach Schedule 8812, if required. . .	52		
	53	Residential energy credits. Attach Form 5695	53		
	54	Other credits from Form: a ☐ 3800 b ☐ 8801 c ☐ _____	54		
	55	Add lines 48 through 54. These are your **total credits**	55	
	56	Subtract line 55 from line 47. If line 55 is more than line 47, enter -0- . . . . . ▶	56	10,681.
Other Taxes	57	Self-employment tax. Attach Schedule SE	57	9,112.
	58	Unreported social security and Medicare tax from Form: a ☐ 4137 b ☐ 8919 . .	58	
	59	Additional tax on IRAs, other qualified retirement plans, etc. Attach Form 5329 if required . .	59	
	60a	Household employment taxes from Schedule H	60a	
	b	First-time homebuyer credit repayment. Attach Form 5405 if required	60b	
	61	Health care: individual responsibility (see instructions) Full-year coverage ☐	61	
	62	Taxes from: a ☐ Form 8959 b ☐ Form 8960 c ☐ Instructions; enter code(s)	62	
	63	Add lines 56 through 62. This is your **total tax** . . . . ▶	63	19,793.
Payments	64	Federal income tax withheld from Forms W-2 and 1099 . .	64	3,600.	
	65	2014 estimated tax payments and amount applied from 2013 return	65	14,250.	
If you have a qualifying child, attach Schedule EIC.	66a	**Earned income credit (EIC)** . . . . No	66a		
	b	Nontaxable combat pay election	66b			
	67	Additional child tax credit. Attach Schedule 8812	67		
	68	American opportunity credit from Form 8863, line 8	68		
	69	Net premium tax credit. Attach Form 8962	69		
	70	Amount paid with request for extension to file	70		
	71	Excess social security and tier 1 RRTA tax withheld	71		
	72	Credit for federal tax on fuels. Attach Form 4136	72		
	73	Credits from Form: a ☐ 2439 b ☐ Reserved c ☐ Reserved d ☐	73		
	74	Add lines 64, 65, 66a, and 67 through 73. These are your **total payments** . . . . . ▶	74	17,850.
Refund	75	If line 74 is more than line 63, subtract line 63 from line 74. This is the amount you **overpaid**	75	
	76a	Amount of line 75 you want **refunded to you.** If Form 8888 is attached, check here . . ▶☐	76a	
Direct deposit? See instructions.	b	Routing number	X X X X X X X X X	▶c Type: ☐ Checking ☐ Savings	
	d	Account number	X X X X X X X X X X X X X X X X X		
	77	Amount of line 75 you want **applied to your 2015 estimated tax** ▶	77		
Amount You Owe	78	**Amount you owe.** Subtract line 74 from line 63. For details on how to pay, see instructions ▶	78	1,943.
	79	Estimated tax penalty (see instructions)	79		

Third Party Designee	Do you want to allow another person to discuss this return with the IRS (see instructions)? ☐ **Yes.** Complete below. ☒ **No**		
	Designee's name ▶	Phone no. ▶	Personal identification number (PIN) ▶

Sign Here

Under penalties of perjury, I declare that I have examined this return and accompanying schedules and statements, and to the best of my knowledge and belief, they are true, correct, and complete. Declaration of preparer (other than taxpayer) is based on all information of which preparer has any knowledge.

Joint return? See instructions.
Keep a copy for your records.

Your signature	Date	Your occupation	Daytime phone number
		Store owner	
Spouse's signature. If a joint return, **both** must sign.	Date	Spouse's occupation	If the IRS sent you an Identity Protection PIN, enter it here (see inst.)
		Office Manager	

Paid Preparer Use Only	Print/Type preparer's name	Preparer's signature	Date	Check ☐ if self-employed	PTIN
	Firm's name ▶ Self-Prepared			Firm's EIN ▶	
	Firm's address ▶			Phone no.	

www.irs.gov/form1040   REV 05/19/15 TTW   Form **1040** (2014)

SCHEDULE C
(Form 1040)

Department of the Treasury
Internal Revenue Service (99)

Profit or Loss From Business
(Sole Proprietorship)

▶ Information about Schedule C and its separate instructions is at *www.irs.gov/schedulec.*
▶ Attach to Form 1040, 1040NR, or 1041; partnerships generally must file Form 1065.

OMB No. 1545-0074

20**14**

Attachment
Sequence No. **09**

Name of proprietor	Social security number (SSN)
Gregory H Larsen	800-98-1234

A Principal business or profession, including product or service (see instructions)
Convenience Store

B Enter code from instructions
▶ 4 4 7 1 0 0

C Business name. If no separate business name, leave blank.
Larsen's Convenience Store

D Employer ID number (EIN), (see instr.)

E Business address (including suite or room no.) ▶ 1798 Hwy 53
City, town or post office, state, and ZIP code   Canon, GA 30115

F Accounting method: (1) ☒ Cash (2) ☐ Accrual (3) ☐ Other (specify) ▶

G Did you "materially participate" in the operation of this business during 2014? If "No," see instructions for limit on losses . ☒ Yes ☐ No

H If you started or acquired this business during 2014, check here . . . . ▶ ☐

I Did you make any payments in 2014 that would require you to file Form(s) 1099? (see instructions) . . . . ☐ Yes ☒ No

J If "Yes," did you or will you file required Forms 1099? . . . . ☐ Yes ☐ No

Part I   Income

1	Gross receipts or sales. See instructions for line 1 and check the box if this income was reported to you on Form W-2 and the "Statutory employee" box on that form was checked . . . . ▶ ☐	1	1,378,216.
2	Returns and allowances	2	
3	Subtract line 2 from line 1	3	1,378,216.
4	Cost of goods sold (from line 42)	4	1,137,963.
5	**Gross profit.** Subtract line 4 from line 3	5	240,253.
6	Other income, including federal and state gasoline or fuel tax credit or refund (see instructions)	6	
7	**Gross income.** Add lines 5 and 6 . . . . ▶	7	240,253.

Part II   Expenses. Enter expenses for business use of your home **only on line 30.**

8	Advertising	8	2,099.	18	Office expense (see instructions)	18	
9	Car and truck expenses (see instructions).	9		19	Pension and profit-sharing plans .	19	
				20	Rent or lease (see instructions):		
10	Commissions and fees .	10		a	Vehicles, machinery, and equipment	20a	
11	Contract labor (see instructions)	11		b	Other business property . . .	20b	12,000.
12	Depletion	12		21	Repairs and maintenance . . .	21	9,869.
13	Depreciation and section 179 expense deduction (not included in Part III) (see instructions).	13		22	Supplies (not included in Part III) .	22	
				23	Taxes and licenses	23	2,179.
				24	Travel, meals, and entertainment:		
14	Employee benefit programs (other than on line 19) . .	14		a	Travel	24a	
15	Insurance (other than health)	15	3,698.	b	Deductible meals and entertainment (see instructions) .	24b	
16	Interest:			25	Utilities	25	12,301.
a	Mortgage (paid to banks, etc.)	16a		26	Wages (less employment credits) .	26	85,995.
b	Other	16b		27a	Other expenses (from line 48) . .	27a	47,274.
17	Legal and professional services	17	352.	b	**Reserved for future use . . .**	27b	

28	**Total expenses** before expenses for business use of home. Add lines 8 through 27a . . . . . . ▶	28	175,767.
29	Tentative profit or (loss). Subtract line 28 from line 7	29	64,486.
30	Expenses for business use of your home. Do not report these expenses elsewhere. Attach Form 8829 unless using the simplified method (see instructions). **Simplified method filers only:** enter the total square footage of: (a) your home: _____ and (b) the part of your home used for business: _____ . Use the Simplified Method Worksheet in the instructions to figure the amount to enter on line 30	30	
31	**Net profit or (loss).** Subtract line 30 from line 29. • If a profit, enter on both **Form 1040, line 12** (or **Form 1040NR, line 13**) and on **Schedule SE, line 2.** (If you checked the box on line 1, see instructions). Estates and trusts, enter on **Form 1041, line 3.** • If a loss, you **must** go to line 32.	31	64,486.
32	If you have a loss, check the box that describes your investment in this activity (see instructions). • If you checked 32a, enter the loss on both **Form 1040, line 12,** (or **Form 1040NR, line 13**) and on **Schedule SE, line 2.** (If you checked the box on line 1, see the line 31 instructions). Estates and trusts, enter on **Form 1041, line 3.** • If you checked 32b, you **must** attach **Form 6198.** Your loss may be limited.	32a ☐ All investment is at risk. 32b ☐ Some investment is not at risk.	

For Paperwork Reduction Act Notice, see the separate instructions.   **BAA**   REV 01/08/15 TTW   Schedule C (Form 1040) 2014

Part III Cost of Goods Sold (see instructions)

33	Method(s) used to value closing inventory: **a** ☒ Cost **b** ☐ Lower of cost or market **c** ☐ Other (attach explanation)		
34	Was there any change in determining quantities, costs, or valuations between opening and closing inventory? If "Yes," attach explanation	☐ Yes	☒ No
35	Inventory at beginning of year. If different from last year's closing inventory, attach explanation SEE STMT	35	272,575.
36	Purchases less cost of items withdrawn for personal use	36	1,139,824.
37	Cost of labor. Do not include any amounts paid to yourself	37	
38	Materials and supplies	38	
39	Other costs	39	
40	Add lines 35 through 39	40	1,412,399.
41	Inventory at end of year	41	274,436.
42	**Cost of goods sold.** Subtract line 41 from line 40. Enter the result here and on line 4	42	1,137,963.

Part IV Information on Your Vehicle. Complete this part **only** if you are claiming car or truck expenses on line 9 and are not required to file Form 4562 for this business. See the instructions for line 13 to find out if you must file Form 4562.

43 When did you place your vehicle in service for business purposes? (month, day, year) ▶

44 Of the total number of miles you drove your vehicle during 2014, enter the number of miles you used your vehicle for:

a Business _____ **b** Commuting (see instructions) _____ **c** Other _____

45	Was your vehicle available for personal use during off-duty hours?	☐ Yes ☐ No
46	Do you (or your spouse) have another vehicle available for personal use?	☐ Yes ☐ No
47a	Do you have evidence to support your deduction?	☐ Yes ☐ No
b	If "Yes," is the evidence written?	☐ Yes ☐ No

Part V Other Expenses. List below business expenses not included on lines 8–26 or line 30.

Administration fee	24,120.
Cash over / short	2,765.
Credit card fees	2,031.
Expense items	11,521.
NSF checks expense	50.
Payroll tax expense	6,787.
48 Total other expenses. Enter here and on line 27a	**48** 47,274.

| Form **W-2** | **Wage and Tax Statement**
► Keep for your records | **2014** |

Name
Tonya V Larsen

Social Security Number
800-76-9876

[X] **Spouse's W-2**
[ ] **Do not transfer this W-2 to next year**

Military: Complete **Part VI** on Page 2 below

a Employee's social security No . 800-76-9876
b Employer's ID number 12-3456799
c Employer's name, address, and ZIP code
Absolute Orthopedics

Street   3456 South Marietta Parkway
City   Marietta
State   GA   ZIP Code   30060
Foreign Country

d Control number .

[X] **Transfer employee information from**
the Federal Information Worksheet
e Employee's name
First Tonya   M.I. V
Last Larsen   Suff.
f Employee's address and ZIP code
Street 213 Underwood Street
City Canton
State GA   ZIP Code 30115
Foreign Country

1 Wages, tips, other compensation   36,000.00
2 Federal income tax withheld   3,600.00
3 Social security wages   36,000.00
4 Social security tax withheld   2,232.00
5 Medicare wages and tips   36,000.00
6 Medicare tax withheld   522.00
7 Social security tips
8 Allocated tips
9
10 Dependent care benefits
11 Nonqualified plans
Distributions from sect. 457 and nonqualified plans *(Important, see Help)*
12 Enter box 12 below
13 [ ] Statutory employee [ ] Retirement plan [ ] Third-party sick pay
14 Enter box 14 below **after** entering boxes 18, 19, and 20.
NOTE: Enter box 15 **before** entering box 14.

Box 12 Code	Box 12 Amount	If Box 12 code is:
		A: Enter amount attributable to RRTA Tier 2 tax
		M: Enter amount attributable to RRTA Tier 2 tax
		P: Double click to link to Form 3903, line 4. . .
		R: Enter MSA contribution for Taxpayer . . .
		Spouse . . . .
		W: Enter HSA contribution for Taxpayer . . .
		Spouse . . . .
		G: [ ] Employer is **not** a state or local government

Box 15 State	Employer's state I.D. no.	Box 16 State wages, tips, etc.	Box 17 State income tax
GA		36,000.00	2,160.00

Box 20 Locality name	Box 18 Local wages, tips, etc.	Box 19 Local income tax	Associated State

Box 14 Description or Code on Actual Form W-2	Amount	TurboTax Identification of Description or Code (Identify this item by selecting the identification from the drop down list. If not on the list, select Other).

Supplement: Part III Cost of Goods Sold - Summaries by Product Line

		December 31, 2014
Fuel	$	901,968
Beginning inventory		15,966
Purchases		798,756
Ending inventory		16,764
Cost of fuel	$	797,958
Gross profit	$	104,010
Groceries/food	$	252,897
Beginning inventory		26,633
Purchases		171,988
Ending inventory		27,965
Cost of groceries	$	170,656
Gross profit	$	82,241
Beverages	$	83,978
Beginning inventory		49,521
Purchases		61,560
Ending inventory		50,511
Cost of beverages	$	60,570
Gross profit	$	23,408
Tobacco	$	135,199
Beginning inventory		179,866
Purchases		105,122
Ending inventory		178,679
Cost of tobacco	$	106,309
Gross profit	$	28,890
Print media		2,749
Beginning inventory		589
Purchases		2,398
Ending inventory		517
Cost of print media	$	2,470
Gross profit	$	279
Bank ATM Rents	$	1,425
Beginning inventory		-
Purchases		-
Ending inventory		-
Cost of bank ATM rents	$	-
Gross profit	$	1,425
Total revenue	$	1,378,216
Beginning inventory		272,575
Purchases		1,139,824
Ending inventory		274,436
Total cost of goods sold	$	1,137,963
Total gross profit	$	240,253

Form **1040** Department of the Treasury—Internal Revenue Service   (99)
U.S. Individual Income Tax Return **2015** OMB No. 1545-0074 IRS Use Only—Do not write or staple in this space.

For the year Jan. 1–Dec. 31, 2015, or other tax year beginning ____, 2015, ending ____, 20 ___   See separate instructions.

Your first name and initial	Last name	Your social security number
Gregory H	Larsen	800-98-1234
If a joint return, spouse's first name and initial	Last name	Spouse's social security number
Tonya V	Larsen	800-76-9876

Home address (number and street). If you have a P.O. box, see instructions.   Apt. no.
176 Rook Heights   102

▲ Make sure the SSN(s) above and on line 6c are correct.

City, town or post office, state, and ZIP code. If you have a foreign address, also complete spaces below (see instructions).
Woodstock GA 30189

Presidential Election Campaign
Check here if you, or your spouse if filing jointly, want $3 to go to this fund. Checking a box below will not change your tax or refund.   ☐ You ☐ Spouse

Foreign country name ____   Foreign province/state/county ____   Foreign postal code ____

Filing Status
Check only one box.

1 ☐ Single
2 ☒ Married filing jointly (even if only one had income)
3 ☐ Married filing separately. Enter spouse's SSN above and full name here. ▶
4 ☐ Head of household (with qualifying person). (See instructions.) If the qualifying person is a child but not your dependent, enter this child's name here. ▶
5 ☐ Qualifying widow(er) with dependent child

Exemptions

6a ☒ **Yourself.** If someone can claim you as a dependent, **do not** check box 6a . . . . .
b ☒ **Spouse** . . . .

c **Dependents:**

(1) First name Last name	(2) Dependent's social security number	(3) Dependent's relationship to you	(4) ✓ If child under age 17 qualifying for child tax credit (see instructions)
			☐
			☐
			☐
			☐

If more than four dependents, see instructions and check here ▶ ☐

Boxes checked on 6a and 6b   2
No. of children on 6c who:
• lived with you
• did not live with you due to divorce or separation (see instructions)
Dependents on 6c not entered above
Add numbers on lines above ▶   2

d Total number of exemptions claimed . . . .

Income

Attach Form(s) W-2 here. Also attach Forms W-2G and 1099-R if tax was withheld.

If you did not get a W-2, see instructions.

7	Wages, salaries, tips, etc. Attach Form(s) W-2	**7**	21,375.
8a	Taxable interest. Attach Schedule B if required	**8a**	12.
b	Tax-exempt interest. **Do not** include on line 8a . . .	**8b**	
9a	Ordinary dividends. Attach Schedule B if required	**9a**	
b	Qualified dividends	**9b**	
10	Taxable refunds, credits, or offsets of state and local income taxes	**10**	
11	Alimony received	**11**	
12	Business income or (loss). Attach Schedule C or C-EZ	**12**	130,458.
13	Capital gain or (loss). Attach Schedule D if required. If not required, check here ▶ ☐	**13**	
14	Other gains or (losses). Attach Form 4797	**14**	
15a	IRA distributions .	**15a**		b Taxable amount . . .	**15b**	
16a	Pensions and annuities	**16a**		b Taxable amount . . .	**16b**	
17	Rental real estate, royalties, partnerships, S corporations, trusts, etc. Attach Schedule E	**17**	
18	Farm income or (loss). Attach Schedule F	**18**	
19	Unemployment compensation	**19**	
20a	Social security benefits	**20a**		b Taxable amount . . .	**20b**	
21	Other income. List type and amount _____	**21**	
22	Combine the amounts in the far right column for lines 7 through 21. This is your **total income** ▶	**22**	151,845.

Adjusted Gross Income

23	Educator expenses	**23**	
24	Certain business expenses of reservists, performing artists, and fee-basis government officials. Attach Form 2106 or 2106-EZ	**24**	
25	Health savings account deduction. Attach Form 8889 .	**25**	
26	Moving expenses. Attach Form 3903	**26**	
27	Deductible part of self-employment tax. Attach Schedule SE .	**27**	9,094.
28	Self-employed SEP, SIMPLE, and qualified plans . .	**28**	
29	Self-employed health insurance deduction	**29**	
30	Penalty on early withdrawal of savings	**30**	
31a	Alimony paid b Recipient's SSN ▶	**31a**	
32	IRA deduction	**32**	
33	Student loan interest deduction	**33**	
34	Tuition and fees. Attach Form 8917	**34**	
35	Domestic production activities deduction. Attach Form 8903	**35**	
36	Add lines 23 through 35	**36**	9,094.
37	Subtract line 36 from line 22. This is your **adjusted gross income** . . . . . ▶	**37**	142,751.

For Disclosure, Privacy Act, and Paperwork Reduction Act Notice, see separate instructions. **BAA**   REV 12/30/15 TTW   Form **1040** (2015)

Form 1040 (2015)   Page **2**

Tax and Credits	38	Amount from line 37 (adjusted gross income)		38	142,751.
	39a	Check { □ **You** were born before January 2, 1951, □ Blind. } **Total boxes** if: { □ **Spouse** was born before January 2, 1951, □ Blind. } **checked ▶ 39a**			
	b	If your spouse itemizes on a separate return or you were a dual-status alien, check here ▶ 39b□			
Standard Deduction for—	40	**Itemized deductions** (from Schedule A) **or** your **standard deduction** (see left margin) . .		40	12,600.
	41	Subtract line 40 from line 38		41	130,151.
• People who check any box on line 39a or 39b **or** who can be claimed as a dependent, see instructions.	42	**Exemptions.** If line 38 is $154,950 or less, multiply $4,000 by the number on line 6d. Otherwise, see instructions		42	8,000.
	43	**Taxable income.** Subtract line 42 from line 41. If line 42 is more than line 41, enter -0- . .		43	122,151.
	44	**Tax** (see instructions). Check if any from: a □ Form(s) 8814　b □ Form 4972　c □		44	22,125.
	45	**Alternative minimum tax** (see instructions). Attach Form 6251		45	
• All others:	46	Excess advance premium tax credit repayment. Attach Form 8962		46	
Single or Married filing separately, $6,300	47	Add lines 44, 45, and 46 . . . . ▶		47	22,125.
	48	Foreign tax credit. Attach Form 1116 if required	48		
Married filing jointly or Qualifying widow(er), $12,600	49	Credit for child and dependent care expenses. Attach Form 2441	49		
	50	Education credits from Form 8863, line 19	50		
	51	Retirement savings contributions credit. Attach Form 8880	51		
Head of household, $9,250	52	Child tax credit. Attach Schedule 8812, if required . . .	52		
	53	Residential energy credits. Attach Form 5695	53		
	54	Other credits from Form: a □ 3800 b □ 8801　c □ ___	54		
	55	Add lines 48 through 54. These are your **total credits**		55	
	56	Subtract line 55 from line 47. If line 55 is more than line 47, enter -0- . . . . . . ▶		56	22,125.
Other Taxes	57	Self-employment tax. Attach Schedule SE		57	18,188.
	58	Unreported social security and Medicare tax from Form: a □ 4137　b □ 8919 . .		58	
	59	Additional tax on IRAs, other qualified retirement plans, etc. Attach Form 5329 if required . .		59	
	60a	Household employment taxes from Schedule H		60a	
	b	First-time homebuyer credit repayment. Attach Form 5405 if required		60b	
	61	Health care: individual responsibility (see instructions)　Full-year coverage □		61	
	62	Taxes from:　a □ Form 8959　b □ Form 8960　c □ Instructions; enter code(s)		62	
	63	Add lines 56 through 62. This is your **total tax** . . . . ▶		63	40,313.
Payments	64	Federal income tax withheld from Forms W-2 and 1099 . .	64	2,565.	
	65	2015 estimated tax payments and amount applied from 2014 return	65	10,500.	
If you have a qualifying child, attach Schedule EIC.	66a	**Earned income credit (EIC)** . . . . . NO . . .	66a		
	b	Nontaxable combat pay election	66b			
	67	Additional child tax credit. Attach Schedule 8812	67		
	68	American opportunity credit from Form 8863, line 8	68		
	69	Net premium tax credit. Attach Form 8962	69		
	70	Amount paid with request for extension to file	70		
	71	Excess social security and tier 1 RRTA tax withheld	71		
	72	Credit for federal tax on fuels. Attach Form 4136	72		
	73	Credits from Form: a □ 2439 b □ Reserved c □ 8885 d □	73		
	74	Add lines 64, 65, 66a, and 67 through 73. These are your **total payments** . . . . . ▶		74	13,065.
Refund	75	If line 74 is more than line 63, subtract line 63 from line 74. This is the amount you **overpaid**		75	
	76a	Amount of line 75 you want **refunded to you.** If Form 8888 is attached, check here . . ▶ □		76a	
Direct deposit? ▶ See Instructions.	b	Routing number　X X X X X X X X X　▶ c Type: □ Checking □ Savings			
	d	Account number　X X X X X X X X X X X X X X X X X			
	77	Amount of line 75 you want **applied to your 2016 estimated tax** ▶	77		
Amount You Owe	78	**Amount you owe.** Subtract line 74 from line 63. For details on how to pay, see instructions ▶		78	27,248.
	79	Estimated tax penalty (see instructions)	79		

Third Party Designee	Do you want to allow another person to discuss this return with the IRS (see instructions)?　□ **Yes. Complete below.**　☒ **No**			
	Designee's name ▶	Phone no. ▶	Personal identification number (PIN) ▶	

Sign Here

Joint return? See Instructions. Keep a copy for your records.

Under penalties of perjury, I declare that I have examined this return and accompanying schedules and statements, and to the best of my knowledge and belief, they are true, correct, and complete. Declaration of preparer (other than taxpayer) is based on all information of which preparer has any knowledge.

Your signature	Date	Your occupation Store owner	Daytime phone number
▶ Spouse's signature. If a joint return, **both** must sign.	Date	Spouse's occupation Office Manager	If the IRS sent you an Identity Protection PIN, enter it here (see inst.)

Paid Preparer Use Only	Print/Type preparer's name	Preparer's signature	Date	Check □ if self-employed	PTIN
	Firm's name　▶　Self-Prepared			Firm's EIN ▶	
	Firm's address ▶			Phone no.	

www.irs.gov/form1040　　　　　　　　　　　　　　　　　　　　　　　　REV 12/30/15 TTW　Form **1040** (2015)

SCHEDULE C (Form 1040)	**Profit or Loss From Business** (Sole Proprietorship)	OMB No. 1545-0074
Department of the Treasury Internal Revenue Service (99)	▶ Information about Schedule C and its separate instructions is at *www.irs.gov/schedulec.* ▶ Attach to Form 1040, 1040NR, or 1041; partnerships generally must file Form 1065.	20**15** Attachment Sequence No. **09**

Name of proprietor	Social security number (SSN)
Gregory H Larsen	800-98-1234

A	Principal business or profession, including product or service (see instructions)	B Enter code from instructions
	Convenience Store	▶ 4 4 7 1 0 0

C	Business name. If no separate business name, leave blank.	D Employer ID number (EIN), (see instr.)
	Larsen's Convenience Store	

E Business address (including suite or room no.) ▶ 1798 Hwy 53

City, town or post office, state, and ZIP code   Canon, GA 30115

F Accounting method: (1) ☒ Cash (2) ☐ Accrual (3) ☐ Other (specify) ▶ _____

G Did you "materially participate" in the operation of this business during 2015? If "No," see instructions for limit on losses . ☒ Yes ☐ No

H If you started or acquired this business during 2015, check here . . . . ▶ ☐

I Did you make any payments in 2015 that would require you to file Form(s) 1099? (see instructions) . . . . . . ☐ Yes ☒ No

J If "Yes," did you or will you file required Forms 1099? . . . . ☐ Yes ☐ No

Part I Income

1	Gross receipts or sales. See instructions for line 1 and check the box if this income was reported to you on Form W-2 and the "Statutory employee" box on that form was checked . . . . ▶ ☐	1	1,405,780.
2	Returns and allowances	2	
3	Subtract line 2 from line 1	3	1,405,780.
4	Cost of goods sold (from line 42)	4	1,102,056.
5	**Gross profit.** Subtract line 4 from line 3	5	303,724.
6	Other income, including federal and state gasoline or fuel tax credit or refund (see instructions)	6	
7	**Gross income.** Add lines 5 and 6 . . . . ▶	7	303,724.

Part II Expenses. Enter expenses for business use of your home **only** on line 30.

8	Advertising	8	2,414.	18	Office expense (see instructions)	18	
9	Car and truck expenses (see instructions)	9		19	Pension and profit-sharing plans .	19	
				20	Rent or lease (see instructions):		
10	Commissions and fees .	10		a	Vehicles, machinery, and equipment	20a	
11	Contract labor (see instructions)	11		b	Other business property . . .	20b	12,000.
12	Depletion	12		21	Repairs and maintenance . . .	21	10,066.
13	Depreciation and section 179 expense deduction (not included in Part III) (see instructions). . . .	13		22	Supplies (not included in Part III) .	22	
				23	Taxes and licenses	23	2,223.
				24	Travel, meals, and entertainment:		
14	Employee benefit programs (other than on line 19) . .	14		a	Travel	24a	
				b	Deductible meals and entertainment (see instructions) .	24b	
15	Insurance (other than health)	15	5,698.	25	Utilities	25	12,547.
16	Interest:			26	Wages (less employment credits) .	26	70,495.
a	Mortgage (paid to banks, etc.)	16a		27a	Other expenses (from line 48) . .	27a	46,971.
b	Other	16b		b	**Reserved for future use** . . .	27b	
17	Legal and professional services	17	10,852.				

28	**Total expenses** before expenses for business use of home. Add lines 8 through 27a . . . . . . ▶	28	173,266.
29	Tentative profit or (loss). Subtract line 28 from line 7	29	130,458.
30	Expenses for business use of your home. Do not report these expenses elsewhere. Attach Form 8829 unless using the simplified method (see instructions). **Simplified method filers only:** enter the total square footage of: (a) your home: _____ and (b) the part of your home used for business: _____ . Use the Simplified Method Worksheet in the instructions to figure the amount to enter on line 30	30	
31	**Net profit or (loss).** Subtract line 30 from line 29. • If a profit, enter on both **Form 1040, line 12** (or **Form 1040NR, line 13**) and on **Schedule SE, line 2.** (If you checked the box on line 1, see instructions). Estates and trusts, enter on **Form 1041, line 3.** • If a loss, you **must** go to line 32.	31	130,458.
32	If you have a loss, check the box that describes your investment in this activity (see instructions). • If you checked 32a, enter the loss on both **Form 1040, line 12,** (or **Form 1040NR, line 13**) and on **Schedule SE, line 2.** (If you checked the box on line 1, see the line 31 instructions). Estates and trusts, enter on **Form 1041, line 3.** • If you checked 32b, you **must** attach **Form 6198.** Your loss may be limited.	32a ☐ All investment is at risk. 32b ☐ Some investment is not at risk.	

For Paperwork Reduction Act Notice, see the separate instructions.   **BAA**   REV 12/07/15 TTW   Schedule C (Form 1040) 2015

Part III **Cost of Goods Sold** (see instructions)

33	Method(s) used to value closing inventory:	**a** ☒ Cost	**b** ☐ Lower of cost or market	**c** ☐ Other (attach explanation)

34 Was there any change in determining quantities, costs, or valuations between opening and closing inventory?
If "Yes," attach explanation . . . . ☐ Yes ☒ No

35	Inventory at beginning of year. If different from last year's closing inventory, attach explanation . . . SEE STMT	**35**	274,436.
36	Purchases less cost of items withdrawn for personal use	**36**	1,167,545.
37	Cost of labor. Do not include any amounts paid to yourself	**37**	
38	Materials and supplies	**38**	
39	Other costs	**39**	
40	Add lines 35 through 39	**40**	1,441,981.
41	Inventory at end of year	**41**	339,925.
42	**Cost of goods sold.** Subtract line 41 from line 40. Enter the result here and on line 4	**42**	1,102,056.

Part IV **Information on Your Vehicle.** Complete this part **only** if you are claiming car or truck expenses on line 9 and are not required to file Form 4562 for this business. See the instructions for line 13 to find out if you must file Form 4562.

43 When did you place your vehicle in service for business purposes? (month, day, year) ▶ _____

44 Of the total number of miles you drove your vehicle during 2015, enter the number of miles you used your vehicle for:

a Business _____ **b** Commuting (see instructions) _____ **c** Other _____

45 Was your vehicle available for personal use during off-duty hours? . . . . ☐ Yes ☐ No

46 Do you (or your spouse) have another vehicle available for personal use?. . . . . ☐ Yes ☐ No

47a Do you have evidence to support your deduction? . . . . ☐ Yes ☐ No

b If "Yes," is the evidence written? . . . . ☐ Yes ☐ No

Part V **Other Expenses.** List below business expenses not included on lines 8–26 or line 30.

Administration fee	24,602.
Cash over / short	2,820.
Credit card fees	2,072.
Expense items	11,751.
NSF checks expense	51.
Payroll tax expense	5,675.

48	**Total other expenses.** Enter here and on line 27a **48**	46,971.

Form **W-2**	**Wage and Tax Statement** ► Keep for your records	**2015**

Name	Social Security Number
Tonya V Larsen	800-76-9876

[X] **Spouse's W-2**
[ ] **Do not transfer this W-2 to next year**

Military: Complete **Part VI** on Page 2 below

a Employee's social security No . 800-76-9876	**1** Wages, tips, other compensation 12,000.00	**2** Federal income tax withheld 1,440.00
b Employer's ID number 12-3456799		
c Employer's name, address, and ZIP code Absolute Orthopedics	**3** Social security wages 12,000.00	**4** Social security tax withheld 744.00
Street 3456 South Marietta Parkway	**5** Medicare wages and tips 12,000.00	**6** Medicare tax withheld 174.00
City Marietta	**7** Social security tips	**8** Allocated tips
State GA ZIP Code 30060		
Foreign Country	Verification Code	**10** Dependent care benefits
d Control number .	**11** Nonqualified plans	Distributions from sect. 457 and nonqualified plans *(Important, see Help)*
[X] **Transfer employee information from the Federal Information Worksheet**		
e Employee's name	**12** Enter box 12 below	
First Tonya M.I. V		
Last Larsen Suff.	**13** [ ] Statutory employee	
f Employee's address and ZIP code	[ ] Retirement plan	
Street 176 Rook Heights, Apt. 102	[ ] Third-party sick pay	
City Woodstock		
State GA ZIP Code 30189	**14** Enter box 14 below **after** entering boxes 18, 19, and 20.	
Foreign Country	**NOTE:** Enter box 15 **before** entering box 14.	

Box 12 Code	Box 12 Amount	If Box 12 code is:
		A: Enter amount attributable to RRTA Tier 2 tax
		M: Enter amount attributable to RRTA Tier 2 tax
		P: Double click to link to Form 3903, line 4 . . .
		R: Enter MSA contribution for Taxpayer . . .
		Spouse . . . .
		W: Enter HSA contribution for Taxpayer . . .
		Spouse . . . .
		G: [ ] Employer is **not** a state or local government

Box 15 State	Employer's state I.D. no.	Box 16 State wages, tips, etc.	Box 17 State income tax
GA		12,000.00	720.00

Box 20 Locality name	Box 18 Local wages, tips, etc.	Box 19 Local income tax	Associated State
			—
			—
			—

Box 14 Description or Code on Actual Form W-2	Amount	TurboTax Identification of Description or Code (Identify this item by selecting the identification from the drop down list. If not on the list, select Other).

Form **W-2**	**Wage and Tax Statement** ► Keep for your records	**2015**

Name Tonya V Larsen	Social Security Number 800-76-9876

[X] **Spouse's W-2**
[ ] **Do not transfer this W-2 to next year**

Military: Complete **Part VI** on Page 2 below

a Employee's social security No . 800-76-9876
b Employer's ID number 12-3456789
c Employer's name, address, and ZIP code
Andersen Internal Medicine

Street _____
City _____
State _____ ZIP Code _____
Foreign Country _____

d Control number . _____

[X] **Transfer employee information from the Federal Information Worksheet**
e Employee's name
First Tonya M.I. V
Last Larsen Suff. ___
f Employee's address and ZIP code
Street 176 Rook Heights, Apt. 102
City Woodstock
State GA ZIP Code 30189
Foreign Country _____

1 Wages, tips, other compensation 9,375.00	2 Federal income tax withheld 1,125.00
3 Social security wages 9,375.00	4 Social security tax withheld 351.28
5 Medicare wages and tips 9,375.00	6 Medicare tax withheld 135.93
7 Social security tips	8 Allocated tips
Verification Code	10 Dependent care benefits
11 Nonqualified plans	Distributions from sect. 457 and nonqualified plans *(Important, see Help)*
12 Enter box 12 below	
13 [ ] Statutory employee [ ] Retirement plan [ ] Third-party sick pay	
14 Enter box 14 below **after** entering boxes 18, 19, and 20. NOTE: Enter box 15 **before** entering box 14.	

Box 12 Code	Box 12 Amount	If Box 12 code is: A: Enter amount attributable to RRTA Tier 2 tax _____ M: Enter amount attributable to RRTA Tier 2 tax _____ P: Double click to link to Form 3903, line 4. . . _____ R: Enter MSA contribution for Taxpayer . . . _____ Spouse . . . . _____ W: Enter HSA contribution for Taxpayer . . . _____ Spouse . . . . _____ G: [ ] Employer is **not** a state or local government

Box 15 State	Employer's state I.D. no.	Box 16 State wages, tips, etc.	Box 17 State income tax
GA		9,375.00	432.75

Box 20 Locality name	Box 18 Local wages, tips, etc.	Box 19 Local income tax	Associated State

Box 14 Description or Code on Actual Form W-2	Amount	TurboTax Identification of Description or Code (Identify this item by selecting the identification from the drop down list. If not on the list, select Other).

Supplement: Part III Cost of Goods Sold - Summaries by Product Line

		December 31, 2015
Fuel	$	920,007
Beginning inventory		16,764
Purchases		814,731
Ending inventory		17,100
Cost of fuel	$	814,395
Gross profit	$	105,612
Groceries/food	$	257,955
Beginning inventory		27,965
Purchases		175,428
Ending inventory		43,524
Cost of groceries	$	159,868
Gross profit	$	98,086
Beverages	$	85,658
Beginning inventory		50,511
Purchases		67,716
Ending inventory		66,522
Cost of beverages	$	51,706
Gross profit	$	33,952
Tobacco	$	137,903
Beginning inventory		178,679
Purchases		107,224
Ending inventory		212,253
Cost of tobacco	$	73,651
Gross profit	$	64,252
Print media		2,804
Beginning inventory		517
Purchases		2,446
Ending inventory		527
Cost of print media	$	2,436
Gross profit	$	368
Bank ATM Rents	$	1,454
Beginning inventory		-
Purchases		-
Ending inventory		-
Cost of bank ATM rents	$	-
Gross profit	$	1,454
Total revenue	$	1,405,780
Beginning inventory		274,436
Purchases		1,167,545
Ending inventory		339,925
Total cost of goods sold	$	1,102,057
Total gross profit	$	303,724

PERSONAL FINANCIAL STATEMENT
7(a) / 504 LOANS AND SURETY BONDS

U.S. SMALL BUSINESS ADMINISTRATION   As of January 7 , 2014

SBA uses the information required by this Form 413 as one of a number of data sources in analyzing the repayment ability and creditworthiness of an application for an SBA guaranteed 7(a) or 504 loan or a guaranteed surety.

Complete this form for: (1) each proprietor; (2) general partner; (3) managing member of a limited liability company (LLC); (4) each owner of 20% or more of the equity of the Applicant (including the assets of the owner's spouse and any minor children); and (5) any person providing a guaranty on the loan

Return completed form to:
For 7(a) loans: the lender processing the application for SBA guaranty
For 504 loans: the Certified Development Company (CDC) processing the application for SBA guaranty
For Surety Bonds: the Surety Company or Agent processing the application for surety bond guaranty

Name Gregory H. Larsen   **Business Phone** 770-735-1234

Home Address 213 Underwood Street   **Home Phone** 770-735-9876

City, State, & Zip Code Canton, GA 30115

Business Name of Applicant Gregory H. Larsen dba Larsen's Convenience Store

ASSETS	(Omit Cents)	LIABILITIES	(Omit Cents)
Cash on Hand & in banks	$ 3896	Accounts Payable	$ 95069
Savings Accounts	$ 2314	Notes Payable to Banks and Others	$ 50000
IRA or Other Retirement Account	$ 0	(Describe in Section 2)	
(Describe in Section 5)		Installment Account (Auto)	$ 36349
Accounts & Notes Receivable	$ 0	Mo. Payments $ 1081	
(Describe in Section 5)		Installment Account (Other)	$ 789
Life Insurance – Cash Surrender Value Only	$ 0	Mo. Payments $	
(Describe in Section 8)		Loan(s) Against Life Insurance	$ 0
Stocks and Bonds	$ 0	Mortgages on Real Estate	$ 222500
(Describe in Section 3)		(Describe in Section 4)	
Real Estate	$ 250000	Unpaid Taxes	$ 7936
(Describe in Section 4)		(Describe in Section 6)	
Automobiles	$ 48466	Other Liabilities	$ 0
(Describe in Section 5, and include Year/Make/Model)		(Describe in Section 7)	
Other Personal Property	$ 35000	Total Liabilities	$ 412643
(Describe in Section 5)		Net Worth	$ 209608
Other Assets	$ 272575		
(Describe in Section 5)		**Total Liabilities & Net Worth** $ 622251	
Total Assets $ 622251		*Must equal total in assets column.	

Section 1. Source of Income.   **Contingent Liabilities**

Salary	$ 30000	As Endorser or Co-Maker	$ 0
Net Investment Income	$ 173	Legal Claims & Judgments	$ 0
Real Estate Income	$ 0	Provision for Federal Income Tax	$ 0
Other Income (Describe below)*	$ 0	Other Special Debt	$ 0

Description of Other Income in Section 1.

Wife's salary and interest on savings account

*Alimony or child support payments should not be disclosed in "Other Income" unless it is desired to have such payments counted toward total income.

Section 2. Notes Payable to Banks and Others. (Use attachments if necessary. Each attachment must be identified as part of this statement and signed.)

Names and Addresses of Noteholder(s)	Original Balance	Current Balance	Payment Amount	Frequency (monthly, etc.)	How Secured or Endorsed Type of Collateral
SBA - S&B Trust Company	75000	50000	573.74	Monthly	Inventory & leasehold Improvements

Section 3. Stocks and Bonds. (Use attachments if necessary. Each attachment must be identified as part of this statement and signed.)

Number of Shares	Name of Securities	Cost	Market Value Quotation/Exchange	Date of Quotation/Exchange	Total Value

Section 4. Real Estate Owned. (List each parcel separately. Use attachment if necessary. Each attachment must be identified as a part of this statement and signed.)

	Property A	Property B	Property C
Type of Real Estate (e.g. Primary Residence, Other Residence, Rental Property, Land, etc.)	Primary residence		
Address	213 Underwood Street, Canton, GA		
Date Purchased	July 14, 2011		
Original Cost	300,000		
Present Market Value	250,000		
Name & Address of Mortgage Holder	Appalachian Mtg, Ellijay, GA		
Mortgage Account Number	12-6399699		
Mortgage Balance	222,500		
Amount of Payment per Month/Year	1,393		
Status of Mortgage	Current		

Section 5. Other Personal Property and Other Assets. (Describe, and, if any is pledged as security, state name and address of lien holder, amount of lien, terms of payment and, if delinquent, describe delinquency.)

2011 Jeep Grand Cherokee (13,899), 2014 Ford F-150 Crew Cab (34,567), household goods (35,000), leasehold improvements (store) (10,000), inventory (store) 272,575)

Section 6. Unpaid Taxes. (Describe in detail as to type, to whom payable, when due, amount, and to what property, if any, a tax lien attaches.)

7,963 (state sales and use taxes)

Section 7. Other Liabilities. (Describe in detail.)

Credit card (789), 2011 Jeep Grand Cherokee (10,424), 2014 Ford F-150 (25,925), accounts payable for store: Shamrock Groceries (13,898), Discount Tobacco (9,079), Marietta Bev. (4,893), GA-TN Fuel (66,998), Jenkins Media (201)

Section 8. Life Insurance Held. (Give face amount and cash surrender value of policies – name of insurance company and Beneficiaries.)

I authorize the SBA/Lender/Surety Company to make inquiries as necessary to verify the accuracy of the statements made and to determine my creditworthiness.

CERTIFICATION: (to be completed by each person submitting the information requested on this form)

By signing this form, I certify under penalty of criminal prosecution that all information on this form and any additional supporting information submitted with this form is true and complete to the best of my knowledge. I understand that SBA or its participating Lenders or Certified Development Companies or Surety Companies will rely on this information when making decisions regarding an application for a loan or a surety bond. I further certify that I have read the attached statements required by law and executive order.

Signature *Gregory H. Larsen*	Date	01/07/2014 _
Print Name Gregory H. Larsen	Social Security No. _	800-98-1234
Signature	Date	_
Print Name	Social Security No. _	

NOTICE TO LOAN AND SURETY BOND APPLICANTS: CRIMINAL PENALITIES AND ADMINISTRATIVE REMEDIES FOR FALSE STATEMENTS:

Knowingly making a false statement on this form is a violation of Federal law and could result in criminal prosecution, significant civil penalties, and a denial of your loan or surety bond application. A false statement is punishable under 18 U.S.C. §§ 1001 and 3571 by imprisonment of not more than five years and/or a fine of up to $250,000; under 15 U.S.C. § 645 by imprisonment of not more than two years and/or a fine of not more than $5,000; and, if submitted to a Federally-insured institution, a false statement is punishable under 18 U.S.C. § 1014 by imprisonment of not more than thirty years and/or a fine of not more than $1,000,000. Additionally, false statements can lead to treble damages and civil penalties under the False Claims Act, 31 U.S.C. § 3729, and other administrative remedies including suspension and debarment.

PLEASE NOTE: The estimated average burden hours for the completion of this form is 1.5 hours per response. If you have questions or comments concerning this estimate or any other aspect of this information, please contact Chief, Administrative Branch, U.S. Small Business Administration, Washington, D.C. 20416, and Clearance officer, paper Reduction Project (3245-0188), Office of Management and Budget, Washington, D.C. 20503. PLEASE DO NOT SEND FORMS TO OMB.

OMB APPROVAL NO.: 3245-0188
EXPIRATION DATE: 01/31/2018

PERSONAL FINANCIAL STATEMENT
7(a) / 504 LOANS AND SURETY BONDS

U.S. SMALL BUSINESS ADMINISTRATION   **As of** January 7 , 2015

SBA uses the information required by this Form 413 as one of a number of data sources in analyzing the repayment ability and creditworthiness of an application for an SBA guaranteed 7(a) or 504 loan or a guaranteed surety.

Complete this form for: (1) each proprietor; (2) general partner; (3) managing member of a limited liability company (LLC); (4) each owner of 20% or more of the equity of the Applicant (including the assets of the owner's spouse and any minor children); and (5) any person providing a guaranty on the loan

Return completed form to:
For 7(a) loans: the lender processing the application for SBA guaranty
For 504 loans: the Certified Development Company (CDC) processing the application for SBA guaranty
For Surety Bonds: the Surety Company or Agent processing the application for surety bond guaranty

Name Gregory H. Larsen   **Business Phone** 770-735-1234

Home Address 213 Underwood Street   **Home Phone** 770-735-9876

City, State, & Zip Code Canton, GA 30115

Business Name of Applicant Gregory H. Larsen dba Larsen's Convenience Store

ASSETS	(Omit Cents)	LIABILITIES	(Omit Cents)
Cash on Hand & in banks..............$	4122	Accounts Payable..........................$	97032
Savings Accounts.........................$	1789	Notes Payable to Banks and Others... ... ...$	47500
IRA or Other Retirement Account...........$	0	(Describe in Section 2)	
(Describe in Section 5)		Installment Account (Auto)..............$	30445
Accounts & Notes Receivable................$	0	Mo. Payments $ 1081	
(Describe in Section 5)		Installment Account (Other)...............$	2167
Life Insurance – Cash Surrender Value Only... ..$	0	Mo. Payments $	
(Describe in Section 8)		Loan(s) Against Life Insurance.............$	0
Stocks and Bonds............................$	0	Mortgages on Real Estate...............$	211375
(Describe in Section 3)		(Describe in Section 4)	
Real Estate..................................$	260000	Unpaid Taxes................................$	7987
(Describe in Section 4)		(Describe in Section 6)	
Automobiles..................................$	35985	Other Liabilities.............................$	0
(Describe in Section 5, and include		(Describe in Section 7)	
Year/Make/Model)		Total Liabilities............................$	396506
Other Personal Property.....................$	35000	Net Worth......................................$	224826
(Describe in Section 5)			
Other Assets................................$	274436	**Total Liabilities & Net Worth** $	621332
(Describe in Section 5)		***Must equal total in assets column.**	
Total Assets $	621332		

Section 1. Source of Income.		Contingent Liabilities	
Salary...$	36000	As Endorser or Co-Maker.....................$	0
Net Investment Income...........................$	243	Legal Claims & Judgments...................$	0
Real Estate Income...............................$	0	Provision for Federal Income Tax.............$	0
Other Income (Describe below)*.......................$	0	Other Special Debt...............................$	0

Description of Other Income in Section 1.

Wife's salary and interest on savings account

*Alimony or child support payments should not be disclosed in "Other Income" unless it is desired to have such payments counted toward total income.

SBA Form 413 (7a/504/SBG) (09-14) **Previous Editions Obsolete**   Page 1

Section 2. Notes Payable to Banks and Others. (Use attachments if necessary. Each attachment must be identified as part of this statement and signed.)

Names and Addresses of Noteholder(s)	Original Balance	Current Balance	Payment Amount	Frequency (monthly, etc.)	How Secured or Endorsed Type of Collateral
SBA - S&B Trust Company	75000	47500	573.74	Monthly	Inventory & leasehold improvements

Section 3. Stocks and Bonds. (Use attachments if necessary. Each attachment must be identified as part of this statement and signed.)

Number of Shares	Name of Securities	Cost	Market Value Quotation/Exchange	Date of Quotation/Exchange	Total Value

Section 4. Real Estate Owned. (List each parcel separately. Use attachment if necessary. Each attachment must be identified as a part of this statement and signed.)

	Property A	Property B	Property C
Type of Real Estate (e.g. Primary Residence, Other Residence, Rental Property, Land, etc.)	Primary residence		
Address	213 Underwood Street, Canton, GA		
Date Purchased	July 14, 2011		
Original Cost	300,000		
Present Market Value	260,000		
Name & Address of Mortgage Holder	Appalachian Mtg, Ellijay, GA		
Mortgage Account Number	12-6399699		
Mortgage Balance	222,500		
Amount of Payment per Month/Year	1,393		
Status of Mortgage	Current		

Section 5. Other Personal Property and Other Assets. (Describe, and, if any is pledged as security, state name and address of lien holder, amount of lien, terms of payment and, if delinquent, describe delinquency.)

2011 Jeep Grand Cherokee (11,788), 2014 Ford F-150 Crew Cab (24,197), household goods (25,000), leasehold improvements (store) (10,000), inventory (store) (274,436)

Section 6. Unpaid Taxes. (Describe in detail as to type, to whom payable, when due, amount, and to what property, if any, a tax lien attaches.)

7,987 (state sales and use taxes)

Section 7. Other Liabilities. (Describe in detail.)

Credit card (2,167), 2011 Jeep Grand Cherokee (8,841), 2014 Ford F-150 (21,604), accounts payable for store: Shamrock Groceries (14,877), Discount Tobacco (9,877), Marietta Bev. (5,079), GA-TN Fuel (67,001), Jenkins Media (198)

Section 8. Life Insurance Held. (Give face amount and cash surrender value of policies – name of insurance company and Beneficiaries.)

I authorize the SBA/Lender/Surety Company to make inquiries as necessary to verify the accuracy of the statements made and to determine my creditworthiness.

CERTIFICATION: (to be completed by each person submitting the information requested on this form)

By signing this form, I certify under penalty of criminal prosecution that all information on this form and any additional supporting information submitted with this form is true and complete to the best of my knowledge. I understand that SBA or its participating Lenders or Certified Development Companies or Surety Companies will rely on this information when making decisions regarding an application for a loan or a surety bond. I further certify that I have read the attached statements required by law and executive order.

Signature   *Gregory H. Larsen*   Date   01/07/2015   _

Print Name   Gregory H. Larsen   Social Security No.   800-98-1234   _

Signature   Date   _

Print Name   Social Security No.   _

NOTICE TO LOAN AND SURETY BOND APPLICANTS: CRIMINAL PENALITIES AND ADMINISTRATIVE REMEDIES FOR FALSE STATEMENTS:

Knowingly making a false statement on this form is a violation of Federal law and could result in criminal prosecution, significant civil penalties, and a denial of your loan or surety bond application. A false statement is punishable under 18 U.S.C. §§ 1001 and 3571 by imprisonment of not more than five years and/or a fine of up to $250,000; under 15 U.S.C. § 645 by imprisonment of not more than two years and/or a fine of not more than $5,000; and, if submitted to a Federally-insured institution, a false statement is punishable under 18 U.S.C. § 1014 by imprisonment of not more than thirty years and/or a fine of not more than $1,000,000. Additionally, false statements can lead to treble damages and civil penalties under the False Claims Act, 31 U.S.C. § 3729, and other administrative remedies including suspension and debarment.

PLEASE NOTE: The estimated average burden hours for the completion of this form is 1.5 hours per response. If you have questions or comments concerning this estimate or any other aspect of this information, please contact Chief, Administrative Branch, U.S. Small Business Administration, Washington, D.C. 20416, and Clearance officer, paper Reduction Project (3245-0188), Office of Management and Budget, Washington, D.C. 20503. PLEASE DO NOT SEND FORMS TO OMB.

OMB APPROVAL NO.: 3245-0188
EXPIRATION DATE: 01/31/2018

PERSONAL FINANCIAL STATEMENT
7(a) / 504 LOANS AND SURETY BONDS

U.S. SMALL BUSINESS ADMINISTRATION   As of January 7 , 2016

SBA uses the information required by this Form 413 as one of a number of data sources in analyzing the repayment ability and creditworthiness of an application for an SBA guaranteed 7(a) or 504 loan or a guaranteed surety.

Complete this form for: (1) each proprietor; (2) general partner; (3) managing member of a limited liability company (LLC); (4) each owner of 20% or more of the equity of the Applicant (including the assets of the owner's spouse and any minor children); and (5) any person providing a guaranty on the loan

Return completed form to:
For 7(a) loans: the lender processing the application for SBA guaranty
For 504 loans: the Certified Development Company (CDC) processing the application for SBA guaranty
For Surety Bonds: the Surety Company or Agent processing the application for surety bond guaranty

Name Gregory H. Larsen   **Business Phone** 770-735-1234

Home Address 213 Underwood Street   **Home Phone** 770-735-9876

City, State, & Zip Code Canton, GA 30115

Business Name of Applicant Gregory H. Larsen dba Larsen's Convenience Store

ASSETS	(Omit Cents)	LIABILITIES	(Omit Cents)
Cash on Hand & in banks	$ 127	Accounts Payable	$ 95915
Savings Accounts	$ 617	Notes Payable to Banks and Others	$ 45125
IRA or Other Retirement Account	$ 0	(Describe in Section 2)	
(Describe in Section 5)		Installment Account (Auto)	$ 24358
Accounts & Notes Receivable	$ 0	Mo. Payments $ 1081	
(Describe in Section 5)		Installment Account (Other)	$ 7864
Life Insurance – Cash Surrender Value Only	$ 0	Mo. Payments $	
(Describe in Section 8)		Loan(s) Against Life Insurance	$ 0
Stocks and Bonds	$ 0	Mortgages on Real Estate	$ 200806
(Describe in Section 3)		(Describe in Section 4)	
Real Estate	$ 267800	Unpaid Taxes	$ 8042
(Describe in Section 4)		(Describe in Section 6)	
Automobiles	$ 31209	Other Liabilities	$ 0
(Describe in Section 5, and include Year/Make/Model)		(Describe in Section 7)	
Other Personal Property	$ 35000	Total Liabilities	$ 382110
(Describe in Section 5)		Net Worth	$ 302568
Other Assets	$ 339925		
(Describe in Section 5)		**Total Liabilities & Net Worth**	**$ 684678**
Total Assets	**$ 684678**	*Must equal total in assets column.	

Section 1.   Source of Income.

		Contingent Liabilities	
Salary	$ 21375	As Endorser or Co-Maker	$ 0
Net Investment Income	$ 12	Legal Claims & Judgments	$ 0
Real Estate Income	$ 0	Provision for Federal Income Tax	$ 0
Other Income (Describe below)*	$ 0	Other Special Debt	$ 0

Description of Other Income in Section 1.

Wife's salary and interest on savings account

*Alimony or child support payments should not be disclosed in "Other Income" unless it is desired to have such payments counted toward total income.

SBA Form 413 (7a/504/SBG) (09-14) **Previous Editions Obsolete**   Page 1

Section 2. Notes Payable to Banks and Others. (Use attachments if necessary. Each attachment must be identified as part of this statement and signed.)

Names and Addresses of Noteholder(s)	Original Balance	Current Balance	Payment Amount	Frequency (monthly, etc.)	How Secured or Endorsed Type of Collateral
SBA - S&B Trust Company	75000	45125	573.74	Monthly	Inventory & leasehold improvements

Section 3. Stocks and Bonds. (Use attachments if necessary. Each attachment must be identified as part of this statement and signed.)

Number of Shares	Name of Securities	Cost	Market Value Quotation/Exchange	Date of Quotation/Exchange	Total Value

Section 4. Real Estate Owned. (List each parcel separately. Use attachment if necessary. Each attachment must be identified as a part of this statement and signed.)

	Property A	Property B	Property C
Type of Real Estate (e.g. Primary Residence, Other Residence, Rental Property, Land, etc.)	Primary residence		
Address	213 Underwood Street, Canton, GA		
Date Purchased	July 14, 2011		
Original Cost	300,000		
Present Market Value	267800		
Name & Address of Mortgage Holder	Appalachian Mtg, Ellijay, GA		
Mortgage Account Number	12-6399699		
Mortgage Balance	222,500		
Amount of Payment per Month/Year	1,393		
Status of Mortgage	Current		

Section 5. Other Personal Property and Other Assets. (Describe, and, if any is pledged as security, state name and address of lien holder, amount of lien, terms of payment and, if delinquent, describe delinquency.)

2011 Jeep Grand Cherokee (9,432), 2014 Ford F-150 Crew Cab (21,777), household goods (25,000), leasehold improvements (store) (10,000), inventory (store) (339,925)

Section 6. Unpaid Taxes. (Describe in detail as to type, to whom payable, when due, amount, and to what property, if any, a tax lien attaches.)

7,987 (state sales and use taxes)

Section 7. Other Liabilities. (Describe in detail.)

Credit card (7,864), 2011 Jeep Grand Cherokee (7,074), 2014 Ford F-150 (17,284), accounts payable for store: Shamrock Groceries (14,380), Discount Tobacco (9,123), Marietta Bev. (5,144), GA-TN Fuel (67,058), Jenkins Media (210)

Section 8. Life Insurance Held. (Give face amount and cash surrender value of policies – name of insurance company and Beneficiaries.)

I authorize the SBA/Lender/Surety Company to make inquiries as necessary to verify the accuracy of the statements made and to determine my creditworthiness.

CERTIFICATION: (to be completed by each person submitting the information requested on this form)

By signing this form, I certify under penalty of criminal prosecution that all information on this form and any additional supporting information submitted with this form is true and complete to the best of my knowledge. I understand that SBA or its participating Lenders or Certified Development Companies or Surety Companies will rely on this information when making decisions regarding an application for a loan or a surety bond. I further certify that I have read the attached statements required by law and executive order.

Signature   *Gregory H. Larsen*   Date   01/07/2016   _

Print Name   Gregory H. Larsen   Social Security No.   800-98-1234   _

Signature   Date   _

Print Name   Social Security No.   _

NOTICE TO LOAN AND SURETY BOND APPLICANTS: CRIMINAL PENALITIES AND ADMINISTRATIVE REMEDIES FOR FALSE STATEMENTS:

Knowingly making a false statement on this form is a violation of Federal law and could result in criminal prosecution, significant civil penalties, and a denial of your loan or surety bond application. A false statement is punishable under 18 U.S.C. §§ 1001 and 3571 by imprisonment of not more than five years and/or a fine of up to $250,000; under 15 U.S.C. § 645 by imprisonment of not more than two years and/or a fine of not more than $5,000; and, if submitted to a Federally-insured institution, a false statement is punishable under 18 U.S.C. § 1014 by imprisonment of not more than thirty years and/or a fine of not more than $1,000,000. Additionally, false statements can lead to treble damages and civil penalties under the False Claims Act, 31 U.S.C. § 3729, and other administrative remedies including suspension and debarment.

PLEASE NOTE: The estimated average burden hours for the completion of this form is 1.5 hours per response. If you have questions or comments concerning this estimate or any other aspect of this information, please contact Chief, Administrative Branch, U.S. Small Business Administration, Washington, D.C. 20416, and Clearance officer, paper Reduction Project (3245-0188), Office of Management and Budget, Washington, D.C. 20503. PLEASE DO NOT SEND FORMS TO OMB.

Georgia Department of Revenue

Greg H. Larsen, III dba Larsen's Convenience
Transcript Totals
2015 Sales and Use Taxes per Form ST-3

Month	Total State Sales	Exempt State Sales	Taxable State Sales	Total Sales Tax
January	$ 116,839	$ -	$ 116,839	$ 8,179
February	117,841	-	117,841	8,249
March	117,236	-	117,236	8,207
April	117,589	-	117,589	8,231
May	117,710	7	117,703	8,239
June	117,935	-	117,935	8,255
July	116,153	-	116,153	8,131
August	116,669	-	116,669	8,167
September	117,233	-	117,233	8,206
October	116,967	109	116,858	8,180
November	116,725	-	116,725	8,171
December	116,883	-	116,883	8,182
	$ 1,405,780	$ 116	$ 1,405,664	$ 98,396

SHAMROCK GROCERIES
171 HAMPTON COURT, DORAVILLE, GA 30340

Greg H. Larsen, III dba Larsen's Convenience
2015 Purchases by Month

Month	Total State Sales	Accounts Payable
January	$ 14,332	$ 14,332
February	14,569	14,569
March	14,231	14,231
April	14,313	14,313
May	15,893	15,893
June	13,722	13,722
July	14,177	14,177
August	13,798	13,798
September	13,651	27,449
October	14,433	41,882
November	14,489	41,882
December	14,380	41,882
	$ 171,988	$ 41,882

Georgia-Tennessee Fuel Partners
4279 Fulton Industrial Blvd SW 30336

**Greg H. Larsen, III dba Larsen's Convenience
2015 Purchases by Month**

Month	Total State Sales	Accounts Payable
January	$ 66,563	$ 66,563
February	66,501	66,501
March	63,798	63,798
April	64,899	64,899
May	67,899	67,899
June	67,563	67,563
July	67,523	67,523
August	66,998	66,998
September	66,789	133,787
October	66,521	200,308
November	66,634	200,308
December	67,058	200,308
	$ 798,746	**$ 200,308**

Marietta Beverage Company
613 Twelfth Street, Marietta GA 30060

Greg H. Larsen, III dba Larsen's Convenience
2015 Purchases by Month

Month	Total State Sales	Accounts Payable
January	$ 5,130	$ 5,130
February	5,031	5,031
March	5,079	5,079
April	5,139	5,139
May	5,201	5,201
June	5,223	5,223
July	5,127	5,127
August	5,137	5,137
September	5,148	10,285
October	5,099	15,384
November	5,102	15,384
December	5,144	15,384
	$ 61,560	$ 15,384

DISCOUNT TOBACCO SUPPLY
877 Dubai Circle, Marietta, GA 30006

Greg H. Larsen, III dba Larsen's Convenience
2015 Purchases by Month

Month	Total State Sales	Accounts Payable (EOM)
January	8,981	$ 8,981
February	8,793	8,793
March	8,564	8,564
April	8,692	8,692
May	8,379	8,379
June	8,913	8,913
July	8,799	8,799
August	8,968	8,968
September	8,963	17,931
October	9,103	27,034
November	8,844	27,034
December	9,123	27,034
	$ 106,122	$ 27,034

JENKINS MEDIA SERVICES
6313 Hwy 92, Woodstock GA 30188

Greg H. Larsen, III dba Larsen's Convenience
2015 Purchases by Month

Month	Total State Sales	Accounts Payable (EOM)
January	201	$ 201
February	211	211
March	198	198
April	197	197
May	206	206
June	189	189
July	185	185
August	194	194
September	196	196
October	204	400
November	207	400
December	210	400
	$ 2,398	$ 400

10/30/2015

Unleaded	10,846.00	Coors	9,114.00
Premium	4,523.00	Coors Light	7,568.00
Diesel	3,394.00	Budweizer	9,650.00
TOTAL FUEL	18,763.00	Budweizer Light	8,921.00
		Warsteiner	463.00
Basic	11,185.00	Miller	2,996.00
Benson & Hedges	1,026.00	Miller Light	1,666.00
Camel	11,730.00	Schlitz	357.00
Chesterfield	2,650.00	Red Dog	101.00
Kent	7,951.00	Rolling Rcok	213.00
Kool	21,354.00	Samuel Adams	269.00
Marlboro	21,607.00	Colt 45	277.00
Max	9,882.00	Pabst Blue Ribbon	399.00
Newport	9,745.00	Dos Equis	1,377.00
Winston	20,216.00	Corona	1,652.00
Winston Lights	21,724.00	Diet Dr. Pepper	321.00
Swisher Sweets	998.00	Fanta	225.00
Dutch Masters	917.00	Diet Mountain Dew	299.00
Palma	938.00	Diet Pepsi	369.00
Iguana Little Cigars	1,091.00	Sprite	273.00
Hoyo de Monterrey Exclaibur	762.00	Dr. Pepper	169.00
Griffins	1,089.00	Pepsi	370.00
Rembrandts	1,145.00	Mountain Dew	297.00
Remington Filtered	560.00	Diet Coke	349.00
Redman	891.00	Coke	379.00
Beechnut	963.00	Snapple	226.00
Levi Garret	1,642.00	Snapple Red	179.00
Southern Pride	909.00	A&W Root Beer	267.00
Grizzly FC Wintergreen	1,438.00	Cheerwine	189.00
Copenhagen Straigt	5,990.00	Crush	197.00
Skoal LC Spearmint	6,987.00	Nehi	237.00
Timberwolf LC Straight	6,017.00	Pibb Xtra	301.00
Grizzly Snuff	5,909.00	Sunkist	159.00
TOTAL TOBACCO	177,316.00	Sun Drop	137.00
		TOTAL BEVERAGE	49,966.00

Lays	3,101.00
Doritos	3,121.00
Fritos	2,697.00
Sun Chips	1,289.00
Baked	1,707.00
Rold Gold	655.00
Sabra	437.00
Tostitos	1,137.00
Lance Crackers	997.00
Chips Ahoy	969.00
Newtons	737.00
Oreo	1,065.00
Teddy Grahams	703.00
Wheat Thins	716.00
Ding Dong	936.00
Ho Hos	899.00
Twinkie	1,069.00
Zingers	1,104.00
Hot dogs	1,897.00
Burittos	798.00
Hamburgers	2,156.00
TOTAL GROCERIES	28,190.00
Magazines	317.00
Maps	165.00
TOTAL PRINT MEDIA	482.00
TOTAL INVENTORY	274,717.00

7-2   CASE 2: CHECK FRAUD, DEBIT CARD FRAUD, CASH LARCENY (ANDERSON INTERNAL MEDICINE)

Bank Reconciliation—Anderson Internal Medicine
Prepared by Tonya Larsen on April 1, 2016

Balance per bank	$	(5,945.43)	Balance per books	$	751.78
Add: Deposit(s) in transit		2,219.02	Less: NSF check		(140.00)
		2,163.19			
		2,175.00			
Less: Checks in transit		-	Add: interest earned		-
Reconciled balance	$	611.78	Reconciled balance	$	611.78

Bank of Lawrenceville
Lawrenceville GA 33042
www.bkoflville.com

ANDERSON INTERNAL MEDICINE, LLC
199 SHORTER DRIVE, STE 201
LAWRENCEVILLE, GA 30043

********************* **BANK OF LAWRENCEVILLE CHECKING - SUMMARY** **************

Balance as of February 29, 2016		$	526.21
Total Deposits and Credits:	26	+	37,139.68
Total Checks and Debits:	30	-	43,331.32
Service Charges:	8	-	280.00
Interest Earned:	0	+	-
Ending Balance as of March 31, 2016		$	(5,945.43)

** **CHECKS** **

Date	Number	Amount	Date	Number	Amount
3/2	1019	1,239.59	3/21	1031	256.00
3/2	1020	768.00	3/21	1032	149.00
3/2	1021	127.00	3/25	1033	1,532.98
3/8	1022	2,991.63	3/28	1034	1,266.45
3/9	1023	1,913.13	3/28	1035	256.00
3/14	1024	3,234.12	3/28	1036	125.00
3/14	1025	1,234.59	3/28	1037	7,050.28
3/15	1026	768.00	3/29	1038*	2,339.50
3/16	1027	135.00	3/28	2023	3,123.55
3/17	1028	1,847.63	3/24	2024	4,039.30
3/18	1029	1,455.53	3/29	2025	2,501.66
3/21	1030	1,179.89	3/29	2026	2,497.89

* Skip in check number sequence

** **OTHER DEBITS** *************************************

3/3	110.00	ATM Withdrawal - 987 Hwy 5, Canton, GA 0007534
3/11	100.00	ATM Withdrawal - 987 Hwy 5, Canton, GA 0007735
3/14	147.00	POS DEB 22:37 3/13/16 Strip TZ Sports Grill 31977 Athens, GA
3/14	277.98	POS DEB 8:58 3/12/16 Food-Mart 21408741 Canton, GA
3/21	294.65	POS DEB 14:56 3/19/16 Food-Mart 21408741 Canton, GA
3/28	369.97	POS DEB 14:38 3/27/16 Food-Mart 21408741 Canton, GA

** **CREDITS** *************************************

Date	Amount	Description
3/1	1,734.40	DDR REGULAR DEPOSIT
3/3	1,298.30	DDR REGULAR DEPOSIT
3/3	2,307.43	DDR REGULAR DEPOSIT

FDIC

Bank of Lawrenceville
Lawrenceville GA 33042
www.bkoflville.com

Statement Period:
03/01/16 to 03/31/16
Account 20018877

ANDERSON INTERNAL MEDICINE, LLC
199 SHORTER DRIVE, STE 201
LAWRENCEVILLE, GA 30043

3/3	1,782.53	DDR REGULAR DEPOSIT
3/4	1,587.53	DDR REGULAR DEPOSIT
3/4	1,241.61	DDR REGULAR DEPOSIT
3/8	1,139.63	DDR REGULAR DEPOSIT
3/9	1,503.27	DDR REGULAR DEPOSIT
3/9	1,763.82	DDR REGULAR DEPOSIT
3/10	1,477.74	DDR REGULAR DEPOSIT
3/10	1,313.93	DDR REGULAR DEPOSIT
3/11	1,551.82	DDR REGULAR DEPOSIT
3/11	1,273.16	DDR REGULAR DEPOSIT
3/11	1,219.92	DDR REGULAR DEPOSIT
3/11	1,399.92	DDR REGULAR DEPOSIT
3/15	1,783.23	DDR REGULAR DEPOSIT
3/15	1,098.49	DDR REGULAR DEPOSIT
3/17	1,467.13	DDR REGULAR DEPOSIT
3/17	1,142.96	DDR REGULAR DEPOSIT
3/18	1,121.06	DDR REGULAR DEPOSIT
3/18	1,887.37	DDR REGULAR DEPOSIT
3/22	1,703.45	DDR REGULAR DEPOSIT
3/24	1,140.92	DDR REGULAR DEPOSIT
3/25	1,068.76	DDR REGULAR DEPOSIT
3/28	1,126.09	DDR REGULAR DEPOSIT
3/29	1,005.21	DDR REGULAR DEPOSIT

*** **DAILY BALANCE** ***

Date	Balance	Date	Balance	Date	Balance
3/1	2,260.61	3/11	15,871.87	3/23	15,096.17
3/2	126.02	3/14	10,210.18	3/24	12,197.79
3/3	5,404.28	3/15	13,091.90	3/25	11,733.57
3/4	8,233.42	3/16	12,956.90	3/28	668.41
3/7	8,233.42	3/17	13,719.36	3/29	668.41
3/8	6,381.42	3/18	15,272.26	3/30	1,673.62
3/9	7,735.38	3/21	13,392.72	3/31	(5,945.43)
3/10	10,527.05	3/22	15,096.17		

*********************** **OVERDRAFT AND RETURN ITEM FEES** ***********************************

Date	Amount	Description
3/31	140.00	Overdraft fees
3/31	140.00	Returned check fees

FDIC

Check 1019

ANDERSON INTERNAL MEDICINE,LLC
Lawrenceville, GA

64-777/611
1019

PAY TO THE ORDER OF ___ Linens to You ___

DATE ___ 3/1/2016 ___

$1,239.59

One thousand two hundred thirty-nine and 59/100 ___ Dollars

BANK OF LAWRENCEVILLE
Lawrenceville, GA 33042

FOR ___

Jennifer L. Anderson

:062110777   :007018188   1019   :0000123959

Check 00001020

Account: 7018188

PLEASE POST THIS PAYMENT FOR OUT MUTUAL
CUSTOMER
987-3239
Payment Processing Center
(800) 987:
Online Bill
84-777/811

$768.00
00001020

Pay   Seven hundred sixty-eight and 00/100 ___   DOLLARS

*********$768.00

TO THE ORDER OF   PHYSICIANS CENTRAL
PO BOX 987 COMMERCE, GA 30528

:062110777

BANK OF LAWRENCEVILLE

March 1, 2016

Check 1021

ANDERSON INTERNAL MEDICINE,LLC
Lawrenceville, GA

64-777/611
1021

PAY TO THE ORDER OF ___ Johnson Medical Coding ___

DATE ___ 3/1/2016 ___

$127.00

One hundred twenty-seven and ___ 00/100 ___ Dollars

BANK OF LAWRENCEVILLE
Lawrenceville, GA 33042

FOR ___

Jennifer L. Anderson

:062110777   :007018188   1021   :000000012700

Check 00001031

Account: 7018188

PLEASE POST THIS PAYMENT FOR OUT MUTUAL
CUSTOMER
3239
Processing Center
(800) 987:
Online Bill Payment
84-777/811

$256.00
00001031

Pay   Two hundred fifty-six and 00/100 ___   DOLLARS

*********$256.00

TO THE ORDER OF   PHYSICIANS CENTRAL
PO BOX 987 COMMERCE, GA 30528

:062110777

BANK OF LAWRENCEVILLE

March 18, 2016

Check 1032

ANDERSON INTERNAL MEDICINE,LLC
Lawrenceville, GA

64-777/611
1032

PAY TO THE ORDER OF ___ Johnson Medical Coding ___

DATE ___ 3/18/2016 ___

$149.00

One thousand five hundred forty-nine and ___ 00/100 ___ Dollars

BANK OF LAWRENCEVILLE
Lawrenceville, GA 33042

FOR ___

Jennifer L. Anderson

:062110777   :007018188   1032   :0000014900

Check 1033

ANDERSON INTERNAL MEDICINE,LLC
Lawrenceville, GA

64-777/611
1033

PAY TO THE ORDER OF ___ Andrew & Duvall, CPAs, LLC ___

DATE ___ 3/21/2016 ___

$1,532.98

One thousand five hundred thirty-two and -- 98/100 ___ Dollars

BANK OF LAWRENCEVILLE
Lawrenceville, GA 33042

FOR ___

Jennifer L. Anderson

:062110777   :007018188   1033   :0000153298

158

For Deposit Only **Johnson Medical Coding** Do Not Write Below This Line Mar 0301 - 8537922 Bank of Lawrenceville	**For Deposit Only** **Physicians Central Insurance** Do Not Write Below This Line Mar 0301 - 8537315 Bank of Lawrenceville	For Deposit Only Linens to You Do Not Write Below This Line Mar 0301 - 8536211 Bank of Lawrenceville
For Deposit Only *Andrew & Duvall, CPAs,* *LLC* Do Not Write Below This Line Mar 03221 - 3678250 Bank of Lawrenceville	**For Deposit Only** **Johnson Medical Coding** Do Not Write Below This Line Mar 0321- 3678250 Bank of Lawrenceville	**For Deposit Only** **Physicians Central Insurance** Do Not Write Below This Line Mar 0318 - 3678892 Bank of Lawrenceville

159

Check 1022

ANDERSON INTERNAL MEDICINE,LLC
Lawrenceville, GA
64-777/611
1022
DATE 3/7/2016
PAY TO THE ORDER OF: Atlanta Medical Supply $2,991.63
Two thousand nine hundred ninety-one and 99/100 Dollars
BANK OF LAWRENCEVILLE
Lawrenceville, GA 33042
FOR
Jennifer L. Anderson
:062110777 :007018188 1022 :0000299163

Check 1023

ANDERSON INTERNAL MEDICINE,LLC
Lawrenceville, GA
64-777/611
1023
DATE 3/7/2016
PAY TO THE ORDER OF: Central Office Supply $1,913.13
One thousand nine hundred thirteen and 13/100 Dollars
BANK OF LAWRENCEVILLE
Lawrenceville, GA 33042
FOR
Jennifer L. Anderson
:062110777 :007018188 1023 :0000191313

Check 1024

ANDERSON INTERNAL MEDICINE,LLC
Lawrenceville, GA
64-777/611
1024
DATE 3/9/2016
PAY TO THE ORDER OF: Georgia Power Company $3,234.12
Three thousand two hundred thirty-four & 12/100 Dollars
BANK OF LAWRENCEVILLE
Lawrenceville, GA 33042
FOR
Jennifer L. Anderson
:062110777 :007018188 1024 :0000323412

Check 1034

ANDERSON INTERNAL MEDICINE,LLC
Lawrenceville, GA
64-777/611
1034
DATE 3/25/2016
PAY TO THE ORDER OF: Linens to You $1,266.45
One thousand two hundred sixty-six and 45/100 Dollars
BANK OF LAWRENCEVILLE
Lawrenceville, GA 33042
FOR
Jennifer L. Anderson
:062110777 :007018188 1034 :0000126645

Check 1035

Account: 7018188 $256.00
PLEASE POST THIS PAYMENT FOR OUT MUTUAL CUSTOMER
Please Direct Any Question To: (800) 882-
3299
Processing Center
Debes III Payment
64-777/611
ANDERSON INTERNAL MEDICINE, LLC
Lawrenceville, GA
Pay Two hundred fifty-six and 00/100 ------------- DOLLARS
March 25, 2016
BANK OF LAWRENCEVILLE
TO THE ORDER OF: PHYSICIANS CENTRAL
PO BOX 987 COMMERCE, GA 30528
**********$256.00
:062110777
00001035

Check 1036

ANDERSON INTERNAL MEDICINE,LLC
Lawrenceville, GA
64-777/611
1036
DATE 3/25/2016
PAY TO THE ORDER OF: Johnson Medical Coding $125.00
One hundred twenty-five and ---------00/100 Dollars
BANK OF LAWRENCEVILLE
Lawrenceville, GA 33042
FOR
Jennifer L. Anderson
:062110777 :007018188 1036 :0000012500

For Deposit Only Georgia Power Company	**For Deposit Only Central Office Supply**	**For Deposit Only Atlanta Medical Supply**
<u>Do Not Write Below This Line</u>	<u>Do Not Write Below This Line</u>	<u>Do Not Write Below This Line</u>
Mar 0311 - 8539997	Mar 0308 - 8539997	Mar 0307 - 8539997
DeKalb Bank and Trust Bank of Lawrenceville	First Atlanta Bank and Trust Bank of Lawrenceville	Atlanta Central Bank and Trust Bank of Lawrenceville

For Deposit Only Johnson Medical Coding	**For Deposit Only Physicians Central Insurance**	For Deposit Only Linens to You
<u>Do Not Write Below This Line</u>	<u>Do Not Write Below This Line</u>	<u>Do Not Write Below This Line</u>
Mar 0328 - 12136247	Mar 0328 - 12136223	Mar 0325 - 12136212
Bank of Lawrenceville	Bank of Lawrenceville	Bank of Lawrenceville

Check 00001025

Account: 7018188 PLEASE POST THIS PAYMENT FOR OUT MUTUAL CUSTOMER $1,234.59

ANDERSON INTERNAL MEDICINE, LLC
Lawrenceville, GA

Please Direct Any Question To:
987-3239 (888) Online Bill 64-777/611
Payment Processing Center

BANK OF LAWRENCEVILLE
Lawrenceville, GA

March 11, 2016

Pay One thousand two hundred thirty-four and 59/100 ———————— DOLLARS

TO THE ORDER OF LINENS TO YOU, 1577
MAIN ST, WOODSTOCK, GA 30189

**************$1,234.59

:062110777

00001025

Check 00001026

Account: 7018188 PLEASE POST THIS PAYMENT FOR OUT MUTUAL CUSTOMER $768.00

ANDERSON INTERNAL MEDICINE, LLC
Lawrenceville, GA

Please Direct Any Question To:
987-3239 (888) Online Bill 64-777/611
Payment Processing Center

BANK OF LAWRENCEVILLE
Lawrenceville, GA

March 11, 2016

Pay Seven hundred sixty-eight and 00/100 ———————— DOLLARS

TO THE ORDER OF PHYSICIANS CENTRAL
PO BOX 987 COMMERCE, GA 30528

**********$768.00

:062110777

00001026

Check 1027

ANDERSON INTERNAL MEDICINE,LLC
Lawrenceville, GA

64-777/611 1027

DATE 3/14/2016

PAY TO THE ORDER OF Johnson Medical Coding $135.00

One hundred thirty-five and ———————00/100 Dollars

BANK OF LAWRENCEVILLE
Lawrenceville, GA 33042

FOR _____ Jennifer L. Anderson

:062110777 :007018188 1027 : 000013500

Check 00001037

Account: 7018188 PLEASE POST THIS PAYMENT FOR OUT MUTUAL CUSTOMER $7,050.29

ANDERSON INTERNAL MEDICINE, LLC
Lawrenceville, GA

Please Direct Any Question To:
3239 (888) 987- Online Bill Payment 64-777/611
Processing Center

BANK OF LAWRENCEVILLE
Lawrenceville, GA

March 27, 2016

Pay Seven thousand fifty and 29/100 ———————— DOLLARS

TO THE ORDER OF STANDARD MORTGAGE COMPANY,
569 HWY 92, WOODSTOCK, GA 30188

**********$7,050.29

:062110777

00001037

Check 1038

ANDERSON INTERNAL MEDICINE,LLC
Lawrenceville, GA

64-777/611 1038

DATE 3/25/2016

PAY TO THE ORDER OF Sharptop Bank $2,339.50

Two thousand three hundred thirty-nine and 50/100 Dollars

BANK OF LAWRENCEVILLE
Lawrenceville, GA 33042

FOR _____ Jennifer L. Anderson

:062110777 :007018188 1038 : 000233950

Check 2023

ANDERSON INTERNAL MEDICINE,LLC
Lawrenceville, GA

64-777/611 2023

DATE 3/22/2016

PAY TO THE ORDER OF KIA Finance Company $3,123.55

Three thousand one hundred twenty-three & 55/100 Dollars

BANK OF LAWRENCEVILLE
Lawrenceville, GA 33042

FOR _____ Jennifer L. Anderson

:062110777 :007018188 2023 : 000312355

For Deposit Only **Johnson Medical Coding** Do Not Write Below This Line Mar 0314 - 8637822 Bank of Lawrenceville	**For Deposit Only** **Physicians Central Insurance** Do Not Write Below This Line Mar 0314 - 8637999 Bank of Lawrenceville	For Deposit Only Linens to You Do Not Write Below This Line Mar 0311 - 8638922 Bank of Lawrenceville
For Deposit Only *HKH Finance Company* Do Not Write Below This Line Mar 0325 - 123937374 Orlando Banking Company Bank of Lawrenceville	For Deposit Only Sharptop Bank Do Not Write Below This Line Mar 0329 - 123936554 Sharptop Bank Bank of Lawrenceville	For Deposit Only Standard Mortgage Company Do Not Write Below This Line Mar 0325 - 12356887 Cleveland Bank & Trust Bank of Lawrenceville

163

ANDERSON INTERNAL MEDICINE,LLC
Lawrenceville, GA

64-777/611 1028

DATE _3/14/2016_

PAY TO THE ORDER OF _Gwinnett County Tax Office_ **$1,847.63**

One thousand eight hundred forty-seven & 63/100 _____ Dollars

BANK OF LAWRENCEVILLE
Lawrenceville, GA 33042

FOR _____

Jennifer L. Anderson

:062110777 :007018188 1028 :0000184763

ANDERSON INTERNAL MEDICINE,LLC
Lawrenceville, GA

64-777/611 1029

PAY TO THE ORDER OF _Horizon Telephone Company_ **$1,455.53**

DATE _3/14/2016_

One thousand four hundred fifty-five and 53/100 _____ Dollars

BANK OF LAWRENCEVILLE
Lawrenceville, GA 33042

FOR _____

Jennifer L. Anderson

:062110777 :007018188 1029 :0000145553

ANDERSON INTERNAL MEDICINE,LLC
Lawrenceville, GA

64-777/611 1030

PAY TO THE ORDER OF _Linens to You_ **$1,179.89**

DATE _3/18/2016_

One thousand one hundred seventy-nine & — 89/100 _____ Dollars

BANK OF LAWRENCEVILLE
Lawrenceville, GA 33042

FOR _____

Jennifer L. Anderson

:062110777 :007018188 1030 :0000117918

ANDERSON INTERNAL MEDICINE,LLC
Lawrenceville, GA

64-777/611 2024

DATE _3/22/2016_

PAY TO THE ORDER OF _S&B Trust Company_ **$4,039.30**

Four thousand thirty-nine and — 30/100 _____ Dollars

BANK OF LAWRENCEVILLE
Lawrenceville, GA 33042

FOR _Delinquent Amt_

Jennifer X. Anderson

:062110777 :007018188 2024 :0000403930

ANDERSON INTERNAL MEDICINE,LLC
Lawrenceville, GA

64-777/611 2025

PAY TO THE ORDER OF _Southeast Medical Center_ **$2,501.66**

DATE _3/25/2016_

Two thousand five hundred one and — 66/100 _____ Dollars

BANK OF LAWRENCEVILLE
Lawrenceville, GA 33042

FOR _Delinquent Balance_

Jennifer X. Anderson

:062110777 :007018188 2025 :0000250166

ANDERSON INTERNAL MEDICINE,LLC
Lawrenceville, GA

64-777/611 2026

PAY TO THE ORDER OF _Tonya Larsen_ **$2,497.89**

DATE _3/25/2016_

Two thousand four hundred ninety-seven & 89/100 _____ Dollars

BANK OF LAWRENCEVILLE
Lawrenceville, GA 33042

FOR _____

Jennifer X. Anderson

:062110777 :007018188 2026 :0000249789

164

For Deposit Only **Linens to You** Do Not Write Below This Line Mar 0321 - 3732665 Bank of Lawrenceville	**For Deposit Only** Horizon Telephone Company Do Not Write Below This Line Mar 0316 - 9966325 Forsyeth State Bank Bank of Lawrenceville	**For Deposit Only** Gwinnett County Tax Office Do Not Write Below This Line Mar 0316 - 8996325 Bank of Gwinnett Bank of Lawrenceville
Tonya Larsen Do Not Write Below This Line Mar 0328 - 123999987 Sharptop Bank Bank of Lawrenceville	**For Deposit Only** **Southeast Medical Center** Do Not Write Below This Line Mar 0325 - 123938777 Bank of Gwinnett Bank of Lawrenceville	**For Deposit Only** **S&B Trust Company** Do Not Write Below This Line Mar 0325 - 123931245 Southeast National Bank Bank of Lawrenceville

Check 1039

ANDERSON INTERNAL MEDICINE, LLC
Lawrenceville, GA

64-777/611

1039

PAY TO THE ORDER OF __Atlanta Medical Supply__   DATE __3/29/2016__ $1,534.73

One thousand five hundred thirty-four and 73/100 _____ Dollars

BANK OF LAWRENCEVILLE
Lawrenceville, GA 33042

FOR _____   _Jennifer L. Anderson_

:062110777   :007018188   1039   :0000153473

Check 1040

ANDERSON INTERNAL MEDICINE, LLC
Lawrenceville, GA

64-777/611

1040

PAY TO THE ORDER OF __Reliance Property & Casualty__   DATE __3/29/2016__ $1,783.83

One thousand seven hundred eighty-three & 83/100 _____ Dollars

BANK OF LAWRENCEVILLE
Lawrenceville, GA 33042

FOR _____   _Jennifer L. Anderson_

:062110777   :007018188   1040   :0000178383

Check 1041

ANDERSON INTERNAL MEDICINE, LLC
Lawrenceville, GA

64-777/611

1041

PAY TO THE ORDER OF __Axix Life Insurance__   DATE __3/30/2016__ $1,341.19

One thousand three hundred forty-one and 19/100 _____ Dollars

BANK OF LAWRENCEVILLE
Lawrenceville, GA 33042

FOR _____   _Jennifer L. Anderson_

:062110777   :007018188   1041   :0000134119

Check 1042

ANDERSON INTERNAL MEDICINE, LLC
Lawrenceville, GA

64-777/611

1042

PAY TO THE ORDER OF __Riteway Pharmaceuticals__   DATE __3/31/2016__ $1,500.00

One thousand five hundred and ——no/100 _____ Dollars

BANK OF LAWRENCEVILLE
Lawrenceville, GA 33042

FOR _____   _Jennifer L. Anderson_

:062110777   :007018188   1042   :0000150000

166

**For Deposit Only
Reliance Property &
Casualty**

Do Not Write Below This Line

REJECTED Mar 0331 Apr
0404 - 39920745

Atlanta Central Bank &
Trust Bank of
Lawrenceville

**For Deposit Only
Atlanta Medical Supply**

Do Not Write Below This Line

REJECTED Mar 0331 Apr
0404 - 39920037

Atlanta Central Bank and
Trust Bank of
Lawrenceville

Riteway Pharmaceuticals

Tonya Larsen

Do Not Write Below This Line

REJECTED Mar 0331 Apr
0404 - 40924409

Sharptop Bank
Bank of Lawrenceville

**For Deposit Only
Axix Life Insurance**

Do Not Write Below This Line

REJECTED Mar 0331 Apr
0404 - 39924507

First Bank of Athens
Bank of Lawrenceville

DEPOSIT TICKET
64-777/611

ANDERSON INTERNAL MEDICINE
Lawrenceville, GA

DATE 3/3/2016

CASH	CURRENCY	500.00
	COIN	
LIST CHECKS SINGLY		798.30
TOTAL FROM OTHER SIDE		
TOTAL		1,298.30
LESS CASH RECEIVED		
NET CASH RECEIVED		1,298.30

BANK OF LAWRENCEVILLE

:062110777: 70018188

DEPOSIT TICKET
64-777/611

ANDERSON INTERNAL MEDICINE
Lawrenceville, GA

DATE 3/3/2016

CASH	CURRENCY	500.00
	COIN	
LIST CHECKS SINGLY		1,282.53
TOTAL FROM OTHER SIDE		
TOTAL		1,782.53
LESS CASH RECEIVED		
NET CASH RECEIVED		1,782.53

BANK OF LAWRENCEVILLE

:062110777: 70018188

DEPOSIT TICKET
64-777/611

ANDERSON INTERNAL MEDICINE
Lawrenceville, GA

DATE 3/4/2016

CASH	CURRENCY	500.00
	COIN	
LIST CHECKS SINGLY		741.67
TOTAL FROM OTHER SIDE		
TOTAL		1,241.67
LESS CASH RECEIVED		
NET CASH RECEIVED		1,241.67

BANK OF LAWRENCEVILLE

:062110777: 70018188

DEPOSIT TICKET
64-777/611

ANDERSON INTERNAL MEDICINE
Lawrenceville, GA

DATE 3/1/2016

CASH	CURRENCY	500.00
	COIN	
LIST CHECKS SINGLY		1,234.40
TOTAL FROM OTHER SIDE		
TOTAL		1,734.40
LESS CASH RECEIVED		
NET CASH RECEIVED		1,734.40

BANK OF LAWRENCEVILLE

:062110777: 70018188

DEPOSIT TICKET
64-777/611

ANDERSON INTERNAL MEDICINE
Lawrenceville, GA

DATE 3/3/2016

CASH	CURRENCY	500.00
	COIN	
LIST CHECKS SINGLY		1,807.43
TOTAL FROM OTHER SIDE		
TOTAL		2,307.43
LESS CASH RECEIVED		
NET CASH RECEIVED		2,307.43

BANK OF LAWRENCEVILLE

:062110777: 70018188

DEPOSIT TICKET
64-777/611

ANDERSON INTERNAL MEDICINE
Lawrenceville, GA

DATE 3/4/2016

CASH	CURRENCY	500.00
	COIN	
LIST CHECKS SINGLY		1,087.53
TOTAL FROM OTHER SIDE		
TOTAL		1,587.53
LESS CASH RECEIVED		
NET CASH RECEIVED		1,587.53

BANK OF LAWRENCEVILLE

:062110777: 70018188

DEPOSIT TICKET

64-777/611

ANDERSON INTERNAL MEDICINE
Lawrenceville, GA

DATE 3/8/2016

DEPOSITS MADE MAY NOT BE AVAILABLE FOR IMMEDIATE WITHDRAWAL

SIGN HERE FOR CASH RECEIVED (IF REQUIRED)

BANK OF LAWRENCEVILLE

:062110777: 70018188

CASH	CURRENCY	500.00
	COIN	
LIST CHECKS SINGLY		639.63
TOTAL FROM OTHER SIDE		
TOTAL		1,139.63
LESS CASH RECEIVED		
NET CASH RECEIVED		1,139.63

DEPOSIT TICKET

64-777/611

ANDERSON INTERNAL MEDICINE
Lawrenceville, GA

DATE 3/9/2016

DEPOSITS MADE MAY NOT BE AVAILABLE FOR IMMEDIATE WITHDRAWAL

SIGN HERE FOR CASH RECEIVED (IF REQUIRED)

BANK OF LAWRENCEVILLE

:062110777: 70018188

CASH	CURRENCY	500.00
	COIN	
LIST CHECKS SINGLY		1,263.82
TOTAL FROM OTHER SIDE		
TOTAL		1,763.82
LESS CASH RECEIVED		
NET CASH RECEIVED		1,763.82

DEPOSIT TICKET

64-777/611

ANDERSON INTERNAL MEDICINE
Lawrenceville, GA

DATE 3/10/2016

DEPOSITS MADE MAY NOT BE AVAILABLE FOR IMMEDIATE WITHDRAWAL

SIGN HERE FOR CASH RECEIVED (IF REQUIRED)

BANK OF LAWRENCEVILLE

:062110777: 70018188

CASH	CURRENCY	500.00
	COIN	
LIST CHECKS SINGLY		813.93
TOTAL FROM OTHER SIDE		
TOTAL		1,313.93
LESS CASH RECEIVED		
NET CASH RECEIVED		1,313.93

DEPOSIT TICKET

64-777/611

ANDERSON INTERNAL MEDICINE
Lawrenceville, GA

DATE 3/9/2016

DEPOSITS MADE MAY NOT BE AVAILABLE FOR IMMEDIATE WITHDRAWAL

SIGN HERE FOR CASH RECEIVED (IF REQUIRED)

BANK OF LAWRENCEVILLE

:062110777: 70018188

CASH	CURRENCY	500.00
	COIN	
LIST CHECKS SINGLY		1,003.27
TOTAL FROM OTHER SIDE		
TOTAL		1,503.27
LESS CASH RECEIVED		
NET CASH RECEIVED		1,503.27

DEPOSIT TICKET

64-777/611

ANDERSON INTERNAL MEDICINE
Lawrenceville, GA

DATE 3/10/2016

DEPOSITS MADE MAY NOT BE AVAILABLE FOR IMMEDIATE WITHDRAWAL

SIGN HERE FOR CASH RECEIVED (IF REQUIRED)

BANK OF LAWRENCEVILLE

:062110777: 70018188

CASH	CURRENCY	500.00
	COIN	
LIST CHECKS SINGLY		977.74
TOTAL FROM OTHER SIDE		
TOTAL		1,477.74
LESS CASH RECEIVED		
NET CASH RECEIVED		1,477.74

DEPOSIT TICKET

64-777/611

ANDERSON INTERNAL MEDICINE
Lawrenceville, GA

DATE 3/11/2016

DEPOSITS MADE MAY NOT BE AVAILABLE FOR IMMEDIATE WITHDRAWAL

SIGN HERE FOR CASH RECEIVED (IF REQUIRED)

BANK OF LAWRENCEVILLE

:062110777: 70018188

CASH	CURRENCY	500.00
	COIN	
LIST CHECKS SINGLY		1,061.82
TOTAL FROM OTHER SIDE		
TOTAL		1,561.82
LESS CASH RECEIVED		
NET CASH RECEIVED		1,561.82

DEPOSIT TICKET 64-777/611

ANDERSON INTERNAL MEDICINE
Lawrenceville, GA

DATE 3/11/2016

CASH	CURRENCY	500.00
	COIN	
LIST CHECKS SINGLY		773.16
TOTAL FROM OTHER SIDE		
TOTAL		1,273.16
LESS CASH RECEIVED		
NET CASH RECEIVED		1,273.16

DEPOSITS MADE MAY NOT BE AVAILABLE FOR IMMEDIATE WITHDRAWAL

SIGN HERE FOR CASH RECEIVED (IF REQUIRED)

BANK OF LAWRENCEVILLE

:062110777: 70018188

DEPOSIT TICKET 64-777/611

ANDERSON INTERNAL MEDICINE
Lawrenceville, GA

DATE 3/11/2016

CASH	CURRENCY	500.00
	COIN	
LIST CHECKS SINGLY		779.92
TOTAL FROM OTHER SIDE		
TOTAL		1,279.92
LESS CASH RECEIVED		
NET CASH RECEIVED		1,279.92

DEPOSITS MADE MAY NOT BE AVAILABLE FOR IMMEDIATE WITHDRAWAL

SIGN HERE FOR CASH RECEIVED (IF REQUIRED)

BANK OF LAWRENCEVILLE

:062110777: 70018188

DEPOSIT TICKET 64-777/611

ANDERSON INTERNAL MEDICINE
Lawrenceville, GA

DATE 3/11/2016

CASH	CURRENCY	500.00
	COIN	
LIST CHECKS SINGLY		899.92
TOTAL FROM OTHER SIDE		
TOTAL		1,399.92
LESS CASH RECEIVED		
NET CASH RECEIVED		1,399.92

DEPOSITS MADE MAY NOT BE AVAILABLE FOR IMMEDIATE WITHDRAWAL

SIGN HERE FOR CASH RECEIVED (IF REQUIRED)

BANK OF LAWRENCEVILLE

:062110777: 70018188

DEPOSIT TICKET 64-777/611

ANDERSON INTERNAL MEDICINE
Lawrenceville, GA

DATE 3/15/2016

CASH	CURRENCY	500.00
	COIN	
LIST CHECKS SINGLY		1,283.23
TOTAL FROM OTHER SIDE		
TOTAL		1,783.23
LESS CASH RECEIVED		
NET CASH RECEIVED		1,783.23

DEPOSITS MADE MAY NOT BE AVAILABLE FOR IMMEDIATE WITHDRAWAL

SIGN HERE FOR CASH RECEIVED (IF REQUIRED)

BANK OF LAWRENCEVILLE

:062110777: 70018188

DEPOSIT TICKET 64-777/611

ANDERSON INTERNAL MEDICINE
Lawrenceville, GA

DATE 3/15/2016

CASH	CURRENCY	500.00
	COIN	
LIST CHECKS SINGLY		598.49
TOTAL FROM OTHER SIDE		
TOTAL		1,098.49
LESS CASH RECEIVED		
NET CASH RECEIVED		1,098.49

DEPOSITS MADE MAY NOT BE AVAILABLE FOR IMMEDIATE WITHDRAWAL

SIGN HERE FOR CASH RECEIVED (IF REQUIRED)

BANK OF LAWRENCEVILLE

:062110777: 70018188

DEPOSIT TICKET 64-777/611

ANDERSON INTERNAL MEDICINE
Lawrenceville, GA

DATE 3/17/2016

CASH	CURRENCY	500.00
	COIN	
LIST CHECKS SINGLY		967.73
TOTAL FROM OTHER SIDE		
TOTAL		1,467.13
LESS CASH RECEIVED		
NET CASH RECEIVED		1,467.13

DEPOSITS MADE MAY NOT BE AVAILABLE FOR IMMEDIATE WITHDRAWAL

SIGN HERE FOR CASH RECEIVED (IF REQUIRED)

BANK OF LAWRENCEVILLE

:062110777: 70018188

DEPOSIT TICKET — 3/17/2016

ANDERSON INTERNAL MEDICINE
Lawrenceville, GA

DATE 3/17/2016

64-777/611

CASH	CURRENCY	
	COIN	
LIST CHECKS SINGLY		1,142.96
TOTAL FROM OTHER SIDE		
TOTAL		1,142.96
LESS CASH RECEIVED		
NET CASH RECEIVED		1,142.96

BANK OF LAWRENCEVILLE

:062110777: 70018188

DEPOSIT TICKET — 3/18/2016

ANDERSON INTERNAL MEDICINE
Lawrenceville, GA

DATE 3/18/2016

64-777/611

CASH	CURRENCY	
	COIN	
LIST CHECKS SINGLY		1,887.37
TOTAL FROM OTHER SIDE		
TOTAL		1,887.37
LESS CASH RECEIVED		
NET CASH RECEIVED		1,887.37

BANK OF LAWRENCEVILLE

:062110777: 70018188

DEPOSIT TICKET — 3/24/2016

ANDERSON INTERNAL MEDICINE
Lawrenceville, GA

DATE 3/24/2016

64-777/611

CASH	CURRENCY	
	COIN	
LIST CHECKS SINGLY		1,140.92
TOTAL FROM OTHER SIDE		
TOTAL		1,140.92
LESS CASH RECEIVED		
NET CASH RECEIVED		1,140.92

BANK OF LAWRENCEVILLE

:062110777: 70018188

DEPOSIT TICKET — 3/18/2016

ANDERSON INTERNAL MEDICINE
Lawrenceville, GA

3/18/2016

64-777/611

CASH	CURRENCY	
	COIN	
LIST CHECKS SINGLY		1,121.06
TOTAL FROM OTHER SIDE		
TOTAL		1,121.06
LESS CASH RECEIVED		
NET CASH RECEIVED		1,121.06

BANK OF LAWRENCEVILLE

:062110777: 70018188

DEPOSIT TICKET — 3/22/2016

ANDERSON INTERNAL MEDICINE
Lawrenceville, GA

DATE 3/22/2016

64-777/611

CASH	CURRENCY	
	COIN	
LIST CHECKS SINGLY		1,703.45
TOTAL FROM OTHER SIDE		
TOTAL		1,703.45
LESS CASH RECEIVED		
NET CASH RECEIVED		1,703.45

BANK OF LAWRENCEVILLE

:062110777: 70018188

DEPOSIT TICKET — 3/25/2016

ANDERSON INTERNAL MEDICINE
Lawrenceville, GA

DATE 3/25/2016

64-777/611

CASH	CURRENCY	
	COIN	
LIST CHECKS SINGLY		1,068.76
TOTAL FROM OTHER SIDE		
TOTAL		1,068.76
LESS CASH RECEIVED		
NET CASH RECEIVED		1,068.76

BANK OF LAWRENCEVILLE

:062110777: 70018188

DEPOSIT TICKET

64-777/611

ANDERSON INTERNAL MEDICINE
Lawrenceville, GA

DATE   3/28/2016

DEPOSITS MADE MAY NOT BE AVAILABLE FOR IMMEDIATE WITHDRAWAL.

SIGN HERE FOR CASH RECEIVED (IF REQUIRED)

BANK OF LAWRENCEVILLE

:062110777: 70018188

CASH	CURRENCY	
	COIN	
LIST CHECKS SINGLY		1,126.09
TOTAL FROM OTHER SIDE		
	TOTAL	1,126.09
LESS CASH RECEIVED		
	NET CASH RECEIVED	1,126.09

DEPOSIT TICKET

64-777/611

ANDERSON INTERNAL MEDICINE
Lawrenceville, GA

DATE   3/29/2016

DEPOSITS MADE MAY NOT BE AVAILABLE FOR IMMEDIATE WITHDRAWAL.

SIGN HERE FOR CASH RECEIVED (IF REQUIRED)

BANK OF LAWRENCEVILLE

:062110777: 70018188

CASH	CURRENCY	
	COIN	
LIST CHECKS SINGLY		1,005.21
TOTAL FROM OTHER SIDE		
	TOTAL	1,005.21
LESS CASH RECEIVED		
	NET CASH RECEIVED	1,005.21

172

Anderson Internal Medicine
Lawrenceville, GA 30043

CASH RECEIPTS JOURNAL

DATE	PAID TO	T.B.	DEBIT	CREDIT
3/1	Cash	11	1,734.40	
	Fees	30		1,734.40
	Record patient cash receipts			
3/3	Cash	11	1,298.30	
	Fees	30		1,298.30
	Record patient cash receipts			
3/3	Cash	11	2,307.43	
	Fees	30		2,307.43
	Record patient cash receipts			
3/3	Cash	11	1,782.53	
	Fees	30		1,782.53
	Record patient cash receipts			
3/4	Cash	11	1,587.53	
	Fees	30		1,587.53
	Record patient cash receipts			
3/4	Cash	11	1,241.61	
	Fees	30		1,241.61
	Record patient cash receipts			
3/8	Cash	11	1,139.63	
	Fees	30		1,139.63
	Record patient cash receipts			
3/9	Cash	11	1,503.27	
	Fees	30		1,503.27
	Record patient cash receipts			
3/9	Cash	11	1,763.82	
	Fees	30		1,763.82
	Record patient cash receipts			
3/10	Cash	11	1,477.74	
	Fees	30		1,477.74
	Record patient cash receipts			
3/10	Cash	11	1,313.93	
	Fees	30		1,313.93
	Record patient cash receipts			
3/11	Cash	11	1,551.82	
	Fees	30		1,551.82

Anderson Internal Medicine
Lawrenceville, GA 30043

CASH RECEIPTS JOURNAL

DATE	PAID TO	T.B.	DEBIT	CREDIT
	Record patient cash receipts			
3/11	Cash	11	1,273.16	
	Fees	30		1,273.16
	Record patient receipts			
3/11	Cash	11	1,219.92	
	Fees	30		1,219.92
	Record patient receipts			
3/11	Cash	11	1,399.92	
	Fees	30		1,399.92
	Record patient receipts			
3/15	Cash	11	1,783.23	
	Fees	30		1,783.23
	Record patient receipts			
3/15	Cash	11	1,098.49	
	Fees	30		1,098.49
	Record patient receipts			
3/17	Cash	11	1,467.13	
	Fees	30		1,467.13
	Record patient receipts			
3/17	Cash	11	1,142.96	
	Fees	30		1,142.96
	Record patient receipts			
3/18	Cash	11	1,121.06	
	Fees	30		1,121.06
	Record patient receipts			
3/18	Cash	11	1,887.37	
	Fees	30		1,887.37
	Record patient receipts			
3/22	Cash	11	1,703.45	
	Fees	30		1,703.45
	Record patient receipts			
3/24	Cash	11	1,140.92	
	Fees	30		1,140.92
	Record patient receipts			

Anderson Internal Medicine
Lawrenceville, GA 30043

CASH RECEIPTS JOURNAL

DATE	PAID TO	T.B.	DEBIT	CREDIT
3/25	Cash	11	1,068.76	
	Fees	30		1,068.76
	Record patient receipts			
3/28	Cash	11	1,126.09	
	Fees	30		1,126.09
	Record patient receipts			
3/29	Cash	11	1,005.21	
	Fees	30		1,005.21
	Record patient receipts			

Anderson Internal Medicine
Lawrenceville, GA 30043

CASH DISBURSEMENTS JOURNAL

DATE	PAID TO	CHECK	T.B.	DEBIT	CREDIT
3/1	Linens		47	1,239.59	
	Cash	1019	11		1,239.59
	Paid to Linens to You				
3/1	Malpractice Insurance - Physicians		41	768.00	
	Cash	1020	11		768.00
	Paid to Physicians Central				
3/1	Coding		43	127.00	
	Cash	1021	11		127.00
	Paid to Johnson Medical Coding				
3/7	Medical supplies		50	2,991.63	
	Cash	1022	11		2,991.63
	Paid to Atlanta Medical Supply				
3/7	Office supplies		60	1,913.13	
	Cash	1023	11		1,913.13
	Paid to Central Office Supply				
3/9	Utilities		80	3,234.12	
	Cash	1024	11		3,234.12
	Paid to Georgia Power Company				
3/11	Linens		47	1,234.59	
	Cash	1025	11		1,234.59
	Paid to Linens to You				
3/11	Malpractice Insurance - Physicians		41	768.00	
	Cash	1026	11		768.00
	Paid to Physicians Central				
3/14	Coding		43	135.00	
	Cash	1027	11		135.00
	Paid to Johnson Medical Coding				
3/14	Taxes & licenses		90	1,847.63	
	Cash	1028	11		1,847.63
	Paid to Gwinnett County Tax Office				
3/14	Telephone Expense		85	1,455.53	
	Cash	1029	11		1,455.53
	Paid to Horizon Telephone Company				

Anderson Internal Medicine
Lawrenceville, GA 30043

CASH DISBURSEMENTS JOURNAL

DATE	PAID TO		CHECK	T.B.	DEBIT	CREDIT
3/18	Linens			47	1,179.89	
		Cash	1030	11		1,179.89
	Paid to Linens to You					
3/18	Malpractice Insurance - Nurses			42	256.00	
		Cash	1031	11		256.00
	Paid to Physicians Central					
3/18	Coding			43	149.00	
		Cash	1032	11		149.00
	Paid to Johnson Medical Coding					
3/21	Legal and professional			70	1,532.98	
		Cash	1033	11		1,532.98
	Paid to Andrew & Duvall, CPAs, LLC					
3/22	Pharmaceuticals			51	3,123.55	
		Cash	2023	11		3,123.55
	Paid to Astro-Bitford Pharmaceuticals					
3/22	Medical supplies			50	4,039.30	
		Cash	2024	11		4,039.30
	Paid to Atlanta Medical Supply					
3/25	Linens			47	1,266.45	
		Cash	1034	11		1,266.45
	Paid to Linens to You					
3/25	Malpractice Insurance - Nurses			44	256.00	
		Cash	1035	11		256.00
	Paid to Physicians Central					
3/25	Uniform expense			95	2,501.66	
		Cash	2025	11		2,501.66
	Paid to Standard Textile					
3/25	Advertising			30	2,497.89	
		Cash	2026	11		2,497.89
	Paid to Zumbro & Fleck Concepts					
3/25	Coding			43	125.00	
		Cash	1036	11		125.00
	Paid to Johnson Medical Coding					

Anderson Internal Medicine
Lawrenceville, GA 30043

CASH DISBURSEMENTS JOURNAL

DATE	PAID TO	CHECK	T.B.	DEBIT	CREDIT
3/25	Interest expense		80	6,914.11	
	Mortgage		25	136.17	
	Cash	1037	11		7,050.28
	Paid to Standard Mortgage Co				
3/25	Car & truck expenses		35	2,339.50	
	Cash	1038	11		2,339.50
	Paid to Sharptop Bank				
3/29	Medical supplies		50	1,534.73	
	Cash	1039	11		1,534.73
	Paid to Atlanta Medical Supply				
3/29	Insurance - Property & Casualty		44	1,783.83	
	Cash	1040	11		1,783.83
	Paid to Reliance Property & Casualty				
3/30	Insurance - Life		75	1,341.19	
	Cash	1041	11		1,341.19
	Paid to Axix Life Insurance				
3/31	Pharmaceuticals		51	1,500.00	
	Cash	1042	11		1,500.00
	Paid to Riteway Pharmaceuticals				

7-3   CASE 3: FRAUDULENT EDITS/ADJUSTED JOURNAL ENTRIES [ANDERSON INTERNAL MEDICINE (EDITS/AJES)]

Report of Interview

Interviewee: Jennifer Anderson, MD (insured)
Interviewer: Jason R. Walsh, CFE, Special Agent
Date: April 21, 2016

Jennifer Anderson said that she owns and operates Anderson Internal Medicine, PC (AIM) in Lawrenceville, Georgia. AIM has been in business since September 2007. Dr. Anderson said that AIM uses a point-of-sale (POS) computer program called Medatrix UltraScan to record the cash receipts (cash and checks), debit card, credit card (AMEX, Discover, MasterCard, VISA), and insurance charges (Insurance Companies, Medicare, Medicaid, etc.) for patient services. The credit card (AMEX, Discover, MasterCard, and VISA) settlement amounts (received one to three days after charge) and insurance charges (received one to four months after charge) are deposited in a separate bank monitored checking account.

She reviewed the March 2016 UltraScan details from her practice over breakfast on April 2, 2016 (the day following the bank's notification of overdrawn checks), and noted that deposited cash deposits did not match the cash receipts initially recorded in UltraScan. She requires her front end personnel to daily deposit all cash receipts. She asked Teresa Padgett, an information technology specialist, to look up the cash receipt transactions recorded in Medatrix UltraScan for March 2016. Teresa found that Tonya Larsen, who has been the office manager since September 2015, had made a number of even-dollar edits to the amount of cash receipts (e.g., $2,197.95 reduced to $1,697.95, a $500.00 reduction) and that the smaller edited amounts of cash were deposited days after actual receipt. Teresa Padgett told Dr. Anderson that she thought Tonya Larsen was stealing—altering deposits with different round dollar amounts (approximately $1,000 a week off on average). Time stamps on Tonya Larsen's edits show when she changed the information. Every employee has a distinct ID and password that they are not to share. Tonya Larsen's ID is "203—Tonya." According to Teresa Padgett, there appears to be a several day time delay between daily sales receipts and actual deposits and there appears to be a pattern of decreased deposits.

Medatrix UltraScan is a POS separate from the regular accounting system. POS and the cash drawer are separate. At the beginning and end of the day $500 is left in the drawer. Daily, the office manager is to:

- pull the cash drawer, count it down, and match it to the daily POS records;
- drop the cash into a safe (accessed only by Jennifer Anderson and the store manager);
- pull all deposits, count envelopes, and make sure both totals agree;
- make sure they match computer system;
- prepare cash deposits using a deposit book, which has carbon copies;
- make deposit slips and take to bank; and,
- staple bank receipts to the carbon copy.

The office manager records the cash receipts information from the POS into the accounting system.

Teresa Padgett quarterly audits receipt data. She visits the POS activity log and looks for adjustments. After the fact, when a manager is reconciling the sales, she can use the edit run to fix errors. With the exception of the Jennifer Anderson, Teresa Padgett, and Tonya Larsen, employees do not have access to the edit function.

Anderson Internal Medicine - Cash Receipts - January 2016 to March 2016

01-09-2016 07:10:24 File: PO020711.DAT   Total: 1 Cash - Deposit   203-TONYA
    Orig. Amt: $1,897.46 New Amt: $1,747.46
01-09-2016 07:10:33 File: PO020711.DAT   Total: 3 Checks - Deposit   203-TONYA
    Orig. Amt: $0.00 New Amt: $6.00
01-11-2016 07:10:45 File: PO020711.DAT   Total: 10 Check - Deposit   203-TONYA
    Orig. Amt: $44.56 New Amt: $38.56
01-18-2016 07:13:56 File: PO022016.DAT   Total: 1 Cash - Deposit   203-TONYA
    Orig. Amt: $1,415.50 New Amt: $1,315.50
01-19-2016 07:12:36 File: PO022111.DAT   Total: 1 Cash - Deposit   203-TONYA
    Orig. Amt: $1,675.58 New Amt: $1,435.58
01-22-2016 07:13:04 File: PO022111.DAT   Total: 10 Check - Deposit   203-TONYA
    Orig. Amt: $51.00 New Amt: $44.00
01-22-2016 07:13:13 File: PO022111.DAT   Total: 3 Checks - Deposit   203-TONYA
    Orig. Amt: $0.00 New Amt: $7.00
01-23-2016 06:58:22 File: PO022211.DAT   Total: 1 Cash - Deposit   203-TONYA
    Orig. Amt: $1,387.70 New Amt: $1,262.94
01-23-2016 06:58:49 File: PO022211.DAT   Total: 3 Checks - Deposit   203-TONYA
    Orig. Amt: $117.85 New Amt: $138.85
01-25-2016 07:32:04 File: PO022411.DAT   Total: 1 Cash - Deposit   203-TONYA
    Orig. Amt: $1,396.94 New Amt: $1,276.94
01-26-2016 10:21:00 File: PO022511.DAT   Total: 1 Cash - Deposit   203-TONYA
    Orig. Amt: $2,006.13 New Amt: $1,756.13
01-29-2016 12:18:22 File: PO022611.DAT   Total: 1 Cash - Deposit   203-TONYA
    Orig. Amt: $2,487.89 New Amt: $2,187.89
02-01-2016 07:44:50 File: PO022811.DAT   Total: 1 Cash - Deposit   203-TONYA
    Orig. Amt: $1,896.94 New Amt: $1,746.94
02-01-2016 09:01:24 File: PO022811.DAT   Total: 3 Checks - Deposit   203-TONYA
    Orig. Amt: $23.71 New Amt: $91.71
02-02-2016 09:04:41 File: PO030111.DAT   Total: 1 Cash - Deposit   203-TONYA
    Orig. Amt: $2,140.09 New Amt: $1,965.09
02-02-2016 07:21:17 File: PO030211.DAT   Total: 1 Cash - Deposit   203-TONYA
    Orig. Amt: $1,541.68 New Amt: $1,366.68
02-04-2016 07:37:46 File: PO030311.DAT   Total: 1 Cash - Deposit   203-TONYA
    Orig. Amt: $1,267.76 New Amt: $1,127.76
02-05-2016 07:26:14 File: PO030411.DAT   Total: 1 Cash - Deposit   203-TONYA
    Orig. Amt: $2,589.39 New Amt: $2,289.39
02-08-2016 07:26:28 File: PO030511.DAT   Total: 1 Cash - Deposit   203-TONYA
    Orig. Amt: $1,797.36 New Amt: $1,497.36
02-08-2016 07:27:00 File: PO030611.DAT   Total: 1 Cash - Deposit   203-TONYA
    Orig. Amt: $1,481.78 New Amt: $1,181.78
02-11-2016 07:19:11 File: PO031011.DAT   Total: 1 Cash - Deposit   203-TONYA
    Orig. Amt: $1,839.18 New Amt: $1,639.18
02-12-2016 07:44:41 File: PO031111.DAT   Total: 1 Cash - Deposit   203-TONYA
    Orig. Amt: $2,196.98 New Amt: $1,796.98
02-12-2016 07:44:47 File: PO031211.DAT   Total: 1 Cash - Deposit   203-TONYA

Anderson Internal Medicine - Cash Receipts - January 2016 to March 2016

Orig. Amt:	$2,137.65	New Amt:	$1,737.65	
02-15-2016 09:03:10 File: PO031411.DAT		Total: 1 Cash - Deposit		203-TONYA
Orig. Amt:	$1,281.83	New Amt:	$1,131.83	
02-16-2016 07:15:20 File: PO031511.DAT		Total: 1 Cash - Deposit		203-TONYA
Orig. Amt:	$1,369.62	New Amt:	$1,169.62	
02-17-2016 09:29:30 File: PO031611.DAT		Total: 1 Cash - Deposit		203-TONYA
Orig. Amt:	$1,691.90	New Amt:	$1,391.90	
02-18-2016 09:09:42 File: PO031711.DAT		Total: 1 Cash - Deposit		203-TONYA
Orig. Amt:	$1,632.59	New Amt:	$1,332.59	
02-22-2016 07:56:33 File: PO031811.DAT		Total: 1 Cash - Deposit		203-TONYA
Orig. Amt:	$1,822.86	New Amt:	$1,422.86	
02-22-2016 07:56:59 File: PO031911.DAT		Total: 1 Cash - Deposit		203-TONYA
Orig. Amt:	$1,834.92	New Amt:	$1,584.92	
02-23-2016 07:46:04 File: PO032211.DAT		Total: 1 Cash - Deposit		203-TONYA
Orig. Amt:	$1,374.38	New Amt:	$1,174.38	
02-24-2016 07:59:10 File: PO032311.DAT		Total: 1 Cash - Deposit		203-TONYA
Orig. Amt:	$2,059.78	New Amt:	$1,659.78	
02-25-2016 07:59:15 File: PO032411.DAT		Total: 1 Cash - Deposit		203-TONYA
Orig. Amt:	$1,634.75	New Amt:	$1,384.75	
02-25-2016 09:11:02 File: PO032411.DAT		Total: 3 Checks - Deposit		203-TONYA
02-26-2016 07:58:49 File: PO032511.DAT		Total: 1 Cash - Deposit		203-TONYA
Orig. Amt:	$1,839.33	New Amt:	$1,439.33	
02-26-2016 07:58:59 File: PO032611.DAT		Total: 1 Cash - Deposit		203-TONYA
Orig. Amt:	$1,550.91	New Amt:	$1,150.91	
02-26-2016 07:59:26 File: PO032711.DAT		Total: 1 Cash - Deposit		203-TONYA
Orig. Amt:	$1,142.14	New Amt:	$992.14	
02-29-2016 09:00:57 File: PO032811.DAT		Total: 1 Cash - Deposit		203-TONYA
Orig. Amt:	$1,744.35	New Amt:	$1,394.35	
03-01-2016 07:52:11 File: PO033111.DAT		Total: 1 Cash - Deposit		203-TONYA
Orig. Amt:	$2,134.40	New Amt:	$1,734.40	
03-03-2016 07:47:10 File: PO030311.DAT		Total: 1 Cash - Deposit		203-TONYA
Orig. Amt:	$1,498.30	New Amt:	$1,298.30	
03-03-2016 07:47:33 File: PO030211.DAT		Total: 1 Cash - Deposit		203-TONYA
Orig. Amt:	$2,707.43	New Amt:	$2,307.43	
03-03-2016 07:47:44 File: PO030111.DAT		Total: 1 Cash - Deposit		203-TONYA
Orig. Amt:	$1,982.55	New Amt:	$1,782.55	
03-04-2016 07:56:14 File: PO030311.DAT		Total: 1 Cash - Deposit		203-TONYA
Orig. Amt:	$1,987.53	New Amt:	$1,587.53	
03-04-2016 07:54:09 File: PO030511.DAT		Total: 1 Cash - Deposit		203-TONYA
Orig. Amt:	$1,491.61	New Amt:	$1,241.61	
03-08-2016 07:06:23 File: PO030611.DAT		Total: 1 Cash - Deposit		203-TONYA
Orig. Amt:	$1,489.63	New Amt:	$1,139.63	
03-09-2016 07:27:19 File: PO030911.DAT		Total: 1 Cash - Deposit		203-TONYA
Orig. Amt:	$1,903.27	New Amt:	$1,503.27	
03-09-2016 07:27:38 File: PO030911.DAT		Total: 1 Cash - Deposit		203-TONYA

Anderson Internal Medicine - Cash Receipts - January 2016 to March 2016

```
                      Orig. Amt:      $2,013.82  New Amt:      $1,763.82
03-10-2016 07:48:19 File: PO031111.DAT  Total:  1 Cash - Deposit    203-TONYA
                      Orig. Amt:      $1,927.74  New Amt:      $1,477.74
03-10-2016 07:53:17 File: PO031211.DAT  Total:  1 Cash - Deposit    203-TONYA
                      Orig. Amt:      $1,713.93  New Amt:      $1,313.93
03-11-2016 09:03:06 File: PO031311.DAT  Total:  1 Cash - Deposit    203-TONYA
                      Orig. Amt:      $2,026.82  New Amt:      $1,551.82
03-11-2016 07:50:56 File: PO031411.DAT  Total:  1 Cash - Deposit    203-TONYA
                      Orig. Amt:      $1,873.16  New Amt:      $1,273.16
03-11-2016 07:37:00 File: PO031711.DAT  Total:  1 Cash - Deposit    203-TONYA
                      Orig. Amt:      $1,619.92  New Amt:      $1,219.92
03-11-2016 07:37:27 File: PO031511.DAT  Total:  1 Cash - Deposit    203-TONYA
                      Orig. Amt:      $1,799.92  New Amt:      $1,399.92
03-15-2016 07:37:52 File: PO031611.DAT  Total:  1 Cash - Deposit    203-TONYA
                      Orig. Amt:      $2,383.23  New Amt:      $1,783.23
03-15-2016 07:39:23 File: PO031811.DAT  Total:  1 Cash - Deposit    203-TONYA
                      Orig. Amt:      $1,448.49  New Amt:      $1,098.49
03-17-2016 07:43:17 File: PO031911.DAT  Total:  1 Cash - Deposit    203-TONYA
                      Orig. Amt:      $2,067.13  New Amt:      $1,467.13
03-17-2016 07:53:16 File: PO032016.DAT  Total:  1 Cash - Deposit    203-TONYA
                      Orig. Amt:      $1,392.96  New Amt:      $1,142.96
03-18-2016 07:57:53 File: PO032111.DAT  Total:  1 Cash - Deposit    203-TONYA
                      Orig. Amt:      $1,571.06  New Amt:      $1,121.06
03-18-2016 07:47:05 File: PO032211.DAT  Total:  1 Cash - Deposit    203-TONYA
                      Orig. Amt:      $2,487.37  New Amt:      $1,887.37
03-22-2016 07:47:32 File: PO032311.DAT  Total:  1 Cash - Deposit    203-TONYA
                      Orig. Amt:      $2,303.45  New Amt:      $1,703.45
03-24-2016 07:44:52 File: PO032511.DAT  Total:  1 Cash - Deposit    203-TONYA
                      Orig. Amt:      $1,690.92  New Amt:      $1,140.92
03-25-2016 07:57:39 File: PO032611.DAT  Total:  1 Cash - Deposit    203-TONYA
                      Orig. Amt:      $1,643.76  New Amt:      $1,068.76
03-28-2016 07:57:16 File: PO032711.DAT  Total:  1 Cash - Deposit    203-TONYA
                      Orig. Amt:      $1,676.09  New Amt:      $1,126.09
03-29-2016 09:44:28 File: PO032811.DAT  Total:  1 Cash - Deposit    203-TONYA
                      Orig. Amt:      $1,555.21  New Amt:      $1,005.21
```

DEPOSIT TICKET — 64-777/611

ANDERSON INTERNAL MEDICINE
Lawrenceville, GA
DATE 1/9/2016

CASH	CURRENCY	200.00
	COIN	
LIST CHECKS SINGLY		1,547.46
TOTAL FROM OTHER SIDE		
TOTAL		1,747.46
LESS CASH RECEIVED		
NET CASH RECEIVED		1,747.46

DEPOSITS MADE MAY NOT BE AVAILABLE FOR IMMEDIATE WITHDRAWAL.
SIGN HERE FOR CASH RECEIVED (IF REQUIRED)
BANK OF LAWRENCEVILLE
:062110777: 70018188

DEPOSIT TICKET — 64-777/611

ANDERSON INTERNAL MEDICINE
Lawrenceville, GA
DATE 1/18/2016

CASH	CURRENCY	150.00
	COIN	
LIST CHECKS SINGLY		1,765.50
TOTAL FROM OTHER SIDE		
TOTAL		1,915.50
LESS CASH RECEIVED		
NET CASH RECEIVED		1,915.50

DEPOSITS MADE MAY NOT BE AVAILABLE FOR IMMEDIATE WITHDRAWAL.
SIGN HERE FOR CASH RECEIVED (IF REQUIRED)
BANK OF LAWRENCEVILLE
:062110777: 70018188

DEPOSIT TICKET — 64-777/611

ANDERSON INTERNAL MEDICINE
Lawrenceville, GA
DATE 1/19/2016

CASH	CURRENCY	400.00
	COIN	
LIST CHECKS SINGLY		1,035.58
TOTAL FROM OTHER SIDE		
TOTAL		1,435.58
LESS CASH RECEIVED		
NET CASH RECEIVED		1,435.58

DEPOSITS MADE MAY NOT BE AVAILABLE FOR IMMEDIATE WITHDRAWAL.
SIGN HERE FOR CASH RECEIVED (IF REQUIRED)
BANK OF LAWRENCEVILLE
:062110777: 70018188

DEPOSIT TICKET — 64-777/611

ANDERSON INTERNAL MEDICINE
Lawrenceville, GA
DATE 1/23/2016

CASH	CURRENCY	300.00
	COIN	
LIST CHECKS SINGLY		976.94
TOTAL FROM OTHER SIDE		
TOTAL		1,276.94
LESS CASH RECEIVED		
NET CASH RECEIVED		1,276.94

DEPOSITS MADE MAY NOT BE AVAILABLE FOR IMMEDIATE WITHDRAWAL.
SIGN HERE FOR CASH RECEIVED (IF REQUIRED)
BANK OF LAWRENCEVILLE
:062110777: 70018188

DEPOSIT TICKET — 64-777/611

ANDERSON INTERNAL MEDICINE
Lawrenceville, GA
DATE 1/25/2016

CASH	CURRENCY	200.00
	COIN	
LIST CHECKS SINGLY		1,076.94
TOTAL FROM OTHER SIDE		
TOTAL		1,276.94
LESS CASH RECEIVED		
NET CASH RECEIVED		1,276.94

DEPOSITS MADE MAY NOT BE AVAILABLE FOR IMMEDIATE WITHDRAWAL.
SIGN HERE FOR CASH RECEIVED (IF REQUIRED)
BANK OF LAWRENCEVILLE
:062110777: 70018188

DEPOSIT TICKET — 64-777/611

ANDERSON INTERNAL MEDICINE
Lawrenceville, GA
DATE 1/26/2016

CASH	CURRENCY	400.00
	COIN	
LIST CHECKS SINGLY		1,356.13
TOTAL FROM OTHER SIDE		
TOTAL		1,756.13
LESS CASH RECEIVED		
NET CASH RECEIVED		1,756.13

DEPOSITS MADE MAY NOT BE AVAILABLE FOR IMMEDIATE WITHDRAWAL.
SIGN HERE FOR CASH RECEIVED (IF REQUIRED)
BANK OF LAWRENCEVILLE
:062110777: 70018188

184

DEPOSIT TICKET

64-777/611

ANDERSON INTERNAL MEDICINE
Lawrenceville, GA

DATE 1/29/2016

DEPOSITS MADE MAY NOT BE AVAILABLE FOR IMMEDIATE WITHDRAWAL.

CASH	CURRENCY	300.00
	COIN	
	LIST CHECKS SINGLY	1,887.89
TOTAL FROM OTHER SIDE		
	TOTAL	2,187.89
	LESS CASH RECEIVED	
	NET CASH RECEIVED	2,187.89

SIGN HERE FOR CASH RECEIVED (IF REQUIRED)

BANK OF LAWRENCEVILLE

:062110777: 70018188

DEPOSIT TICKET

64-777/611

ANDERSON INTERNAL MEDICINE
Lawrenceville, GA

DATE 2/1/2016

DEPOSITS MADE MAY NOT BE AVAILABLE FOR IMMEDIATE WITHDRAWAL.

CASH	CURRENCY	200.00
	COIN	
	LIST CHECKS SINGLY	1,546.94
TOTAL FROM OTHER SIDE		
	TOTAL	1,746.94
	LESS CASH RECEIVED	
	NET CASH RECEIVED	1,746.94

SIGN HERE FOR CASH RECEIVED (IF REQUIRED)

BANK OF LAWRENCEVILLE

:062110777: 70018188

DEPOSIT TICKET

64-777/611

ANDERSON INTERNAL MEDICINE
Lawrenceville, GA

DATE 2/2/2016

DEPOSITS MADE MAY NOT BE AVAILABLE FOR IMMEDIATE WITHDRAWAL.

CASH	CURRENCY	100.00
	COIN	
	LIST CHECKS SINGLY	1,865.09
TOTAL FROM OTHER SIDE		
	TOTAL	1,965.09
	LESS CASH RECEIVED	
	NET CASH RECEIVED	1,965.09

SIGN HERE FOR CASH RECEIVED (IF REQUIRED)

BANK OF LAWRENCEVILLE

:062110777: 70018188

DEPOSIT TICKET

64-777/611

ANDERSON INTERNAL MEDICINE
Lawrenceville, GA

DATE 2/2/2016

DEPOSITS MADE MAY NOT BE AVAILABLE FOR IMMEDIATE WITHDRAWAL.

CASH	CURRENCY	100.00
	COIN	
	LIST CHECKS SINGLY	1,266.68
TOTAL FROM OTHER SIDE		
	TOTAL	1,366.68
	LESS CASH RECEIVED	
	NET CASH RECEIVED	1,366.68

SIGN HERE FOR CASH RECEIVED (IF REQUIRED)

BANK OF LAWRENCEVILLE

:062110777: 70018188

DEPOSIT TICKET

64-777/611

ANDERSON INTERNAL MEDICINE
Lawrenceville, GA

DATE 2/4/2016

DEPOSITS MADE MAY NOT BE AVAILABLE FOR IMMEDIATE WITHDRAWAL.

CASH	CURRENCY	50.00
	COIN	
	LIST CHECKS SINGLY	1,077.76
TOTAL FROM OTHER SIDE		
	TOTAL	1,127.76
	LESS CASH RECEIVED	
	NET CASH RECEIVED	1,127.76

SIGN HERE FOR CASH RECEIVED (IF REQUIRED)

BANK OF LAWRENCEVILLE

:062110777: 70018188

DEPOSIT TICKET

64-777/611

ANDERSON INTERNAL MEDICINE
Lawrenceville, GA

DATE 2/5/2016

DEPOSITS MADE MAY NOT BE AVAILABLE FOR IMMEDIATE WITHDRAWAL.

CASH	CURRENCY	200.00
	COIN	
	LIST CHECKS SINGLY	2,089.39
TOTAL FROM OTHER SIDE		
	TOTAL	2,289.39
	LESS CASH RECEIVED	
	NET CASH RECEIVED	2,289.39

SIGN HERE FOR CASH RECEIVED (IF REQUIRED)

BANK OF LAWRENCEVILLE

:062110777: 70018188

DEPOSIT TICKET

64-777/611

ANDERSON INTERNAL MEDICINE
Lawrenceville, GA

DATE 2/8/2016

CASH	CURRENCY	500.00
	COIN	
LIST CHECKS SINGLY		997.36
TOTAL FROM OTHER SIDE		
TOTAL		1,497.36
LESS CASH RECEIVED		
NET CASH RECEIVED		1,497.36

DEPOSITS MADE MAY NOT BE AVAILABLE FOR IMMEDIATE WITHDRAWAL.
SIGN HERE FOR CASH RECEIVED (IF REQUIRED)

BANK OF LAWRENCEVILLE

:062110777: 70018188

DEPOSIT TICKET

64-777/611

ANDERSON INTERNAL MEDICINE
Lawrenceville, GA

DATE 2/8/2016

CASH	CURRENCY	200.00
	COIN	
LIST CHECKS SINGLY		987.78
TOTAL FROM OTHER SIDE		
TOTAL		1,187.78
LESS CASH RECEIVED		
NET CASH RECEIVED		1,187.78

DEPOSITS MADE MAY NOT BE AVAILABLE FOR IMMEDIATE WITHDRAWAL.
SIGN HERE FOR CASH RECEIVED (IF REQUIRED)

BANK OF LAWRENCEVILLE

:062110777: 70018188

DEPOSIT TICKET

64-777/611

ANDERSON INTERNAL MEDICINE
Lawrenceville, GA

DATE 2/11/2016

CASH	CURRENCY	500.00
	COIN	
LIST CHECKS SINGLY		1,139.18
TOTAL FROM OTHER SIDE		
TOTAL		1,639.18
LESS CASH RECEIVED		
NET CASH RECEIVED		1,639.18

DEPOSITS MADE MAY NOT BE AVAILABLE FOR IMMEDIATE WITHDRAWAL.
SIGN HERE FOR CASH RECEIVED (IF REQUIRED)

BANK OF LAWRENCEVILLE

:062110777: 70018188

DEPOSIT TICKET

64-777/611

ANDERSON INTERNAL MEDICINE
Lawrenceville, GA

DATE 2/12/2016

CASH	CURRENCY	200.00
	COIN	
LIST CHECKS SINGLY		1,596.98
TOTAL FROM OTHER SIDE		
TOTAL		1,796.98
LESS CASH RECEIVED		
NET CASH RECEIVED		1,796.98

DEPOSITS MADE MAY NOT BE AVAILABLE FOR IMMEDIATE WITHDRAWAL.
SIGN HERE FOR CASH RECEIVED (IF REQUIRED)

BANK OF LAWRENCEVILLE

:062110777: 70018188

DEPOSIT TICKET

64-777/611

ANDERSON INTERNAL MEDICINE
Lawrenceville, GA

DATE 2/12/2016

CASH	CURRENCY	200.00
	COIN	
LIST CHECKS SINGLY		1,537.65
TOTAL FROM OTHER SIDE		
TOTAL		1,737.65
LESS CASH RECEIVED		
NET CASH RECEIVED		1,737.65

DEPOSITS MADE MAY NOT BE AVAILABLE FOR IMMEDIATE WITHDRAWAL.
SIGN HERE FOR CASH RECEIVED (IF REQUIRED)

BANK OF LAWRENCEVILLE

:062110777: 70018188

DEPOSIT TICKET

64-777/611

ANDERSON INTERNAL MEDICINE
Lawrenceville, GA

DATE 2/15/2016

CASH	CURRENCY	200.00
	COIN	
LIST CHECKS SINGLY		937.83
TOTAL FROM OTHER SIDE		
TOTAL		1,137.83
LESS CASH RECEIVED		
NET CASH RECEIVED		1,137.83

DEPOSITS MADE MAY NOT BE AVAILABLE FOR IMMEDIATE WITHDRAWAL.
SIGN HERE FOR CASH RECEIVED (IF REQUIRED)

BANK OF LAWRENCEVILLE

:062110777: 70018188

DEPOSIT TICKET — 64-777/611

ANDERSON INTERNAL MEDICINE
Lawrenceville, GA
DATE 2/16/2016

CASH	CURRENCY	100.00
	COIN	
LIST CHECKS SINGLY		1,069.62
TOTAL FROM OTHER SIDE		
TOTAL		1,169.62
LESS CASH RECEIVED		
NET CASH RECEIVED		1,169.62

BANK OF LAWRENCEVILLE
:062110777: 70018188

DEPOSIT TICKET — 64-777/611

ANDERSON INTERNAL MEDICINE
Lawrenceville, GA
DATE 2/17/2016

CASH	CURRENCY	250.00
	COIN	
LIST CHECKS SINGLY		1,141.90
TOTAL FROM OTHER SIDE		
TOTAL		1,391.90
LESS CASH RECEIVED		
NET CASH RECEIVED		1,391.90

BANK OF LAWRENCEVILLE
:062110777: 70018188

DEPOSIT TICKET — 64-777/611

ANDERSON INTERNAL MEDICINE
Lawrenceville, GA
DATE 2/18/2016

CASH	CURRENCY	150.00
	COIN	
LIST CHECKS SINGLY		1,182.39
TOTAL FROM OTHER SIDE		
TOTAL		1,332.39
LESS CASH RECEIVED		
NET CASH RECEIVED		1,332.39

BANK OF LAWRENCEVILLE
:062110777: 70018188

DEPOSIT TICKET — 64-777/611

ANDERSON INTERNAL MEDICINE
Lawrenceville, GA
DATE 2/22/2016

CASH	CURRENCY	200.00
	COIN	
LIST CHECKS SINGLY		1,222.86
TOTAL FROM OTHER SIDE		
TOTAL		1,422.86
LESS CASH RECEIVED		
NET CASH RECEIVED		1,422.86

BANK OF LAWRENCEVILLE
:062110777: 70018188

DEPOSIT TICKET — 64-777/611

ANDERSON INTERNAL MEDICINE
Lawrenceville, GA
DATE 2/22/2016

CASH	CURRENCY	200.00
	COIN	
LIST CHECKS SINGLY		1,384.92
TOTAL FROM OTHER SIDE		
TOTAL		1,584.92
LESS CASH RECEIVED		
NET CASH RECEIVED		1,584.92

BANK OF LAWRENCEVILLE
:062110777: 70018188

DEPOSIT TICKET — 64-777/611

ANDERSON INTERNAL MEDICINE
Lawrenceville, GA
DATE 2/23/2016

CASH	CURRENCY	100.00
	COIN	
LIST CHECKS SINGLY		1,074.38
TOTAL FROM OTHER SIDE		
TOTAL		1,174.38
LESS CASH RECEIVED		
NET CASH RECEIVED		1,174.38

BANK OF LAWRENCEVILLE
:062110777: 70018188

DEPOSIT TICKET

ANDERSON INTERNAL MEDICINE
Lawrenceville, GA

DATE 2/24/2016

64-777/611

CASH	CURRENCY	500.00
	COIN	
LIST CHECKS SINGLY		1,159.78
TOTAL FROM OTHER SIDE		
TOTAL		1,659.78
LESS CASH RECEIVED		
NET CASH RECEIVED		1,659.78

BANK OF LAWRENCEVILLE

:062110777: 70018188

DEPOSIT TICKET

ANDERSON INTERNAL MEDICINE
Lawrenceville, GA

DATE 2/26/2016

64-777/611

CASH	CURRENCY	500.00
	COIN	
LIST CHECKS SINGLY		939.33
TOTAL FROM OTHER SIDE		
TOTAL		1,439.33
LESS CASH RECEIVED		
NET CASH RECEIVED		1,439.33

BANK OF LAWRENCEVILLE

:062110777: 70018188

DEPOSIT TICKET

ANDERSON INTERNAL MEDICINE
Lawrenceville, GA

DATE 2/26/2016

64-777/611

CASH	CURRENCY	-
	COIN	
LIST CHECKS SINGLY		992.74
TOTAL FROM OTHER SIDE		
TOTAL		992.74
LESS CASH RECEIVED		
NET CASH RECEIVED		992.74

BANK OF LAWRENCEVILLE

:062110777: 70018188

DEPOSIT TICKET

ANDERSON INTERNAL MEDICINE
Lawrenceville, GA

2/25/2016

64-777/611

CASH	CURRENCY	100.00
	COIN	
LIST CHECKS SINGLY		1,284.75
TOTAL FROM OTHER SIDE		
TOTAL		1,384.75
LESS CASH RECEIVED		
NET CASH RECEIVED		1,384.75

BANK OF LAWRENCEVILLE

:062110777: 70018188

DEPOSIT TICKET

ANDERSON INTERNAL MEDICINE
Lawrenceville, GA

DATE 2/26/2016

64-777/611

CASH	CURRENCY	200.00
	COIN	
LIST CHECKS SINGLY		950.97
TOTAL FROM OTHER SIDE		
TOTAL		1,150.97
LESS CASH RECEIVED		
NET CASH RECEIVED		1,150.97

BANK OF LAWRENCEVILLE

:062110777: 70018188

DEPOSIT TICKET

ANDERSON INTERNAL MEDICINE
Lawrenceville, GA

DATE 2/29/2016

64-777/611

CASH	CURRENCY	50.00
	COIN	
LIST CHECKS SINGLY		1,344.35
TOTAL FROM OTHER SIDE		
TOTAL		1,394.35
LESS CASH RECEIVED		
NET CASH RECEIVED		1,394.35

BANK OF LAWRENCEVILLE

:062110777: 70018188

DEPOSIT TICKET   64-777/611

ANDERSON INTERNAL MEDICINE
Lawrenceville, GA

DATE 3/1/2016

CASH	CURRENCY	500.00
	COIN	
LIST CHECKS SINGLY		1,234.40
TOTAL FROM OTHER SIDE		
TOTAL		1,734.40
LESS CASH RECEIVED		
NET CASH RECEIVED		1,734.40

DEPOSITS MADE MAY NOT BE AVAILABLE FOR IMMEDIATE WITHDRAWAL.

SIGN HERE FOR CASH RECEIVED (IF REQUIRED)

BANK OF LAWRENCEVILLE

:062110777: 70018188

DEPOSIT TICKET   64-777/611

ANDERSON INTERNAL MEDICINE
Lawrenceville, GA

DATE 3/3/2016

CASH	CURRENCY	500.00
	COIN	
LIST CHECKS SINGLY		1,807.43
TOTAL FROM OTHER SIDE		
TOTAL		2,307.43
LESS CASH RECEIVED		
NET CASH RECEIVED		2,307.43

DEPOSITS MADE MAY NOT BE AVAILABLE FOR IMMEDIATE WITHDRAWAL.

SIGN HERE FOR CASH RECEIVED (IF REQUIRED)

BANK OF LAWRENCEVILLE

:062110777: 70018188

DEPOSIT TICKET   64-777/611

ANDERSON INTERNAL MEDICINE
Lawrenceville, GA

DATE 3/4/2016

CASH	CURRENCY	500.00
	COIN	
LIST CHECKS SINGLY		1,087.53
TOTAL FROM OTHER SIDE		
TOTAL		1,587.53
LESS CASH RECEIVED		
NET CASH RECEIVED		1,587.53

DEPOSITS MADE MAY NOT BE AVAILABLE FOR IMMEDIATE WITHDRAWAL.

SIGN HERE FOR CASH RECEIVED (IF REQUIRED)

BANK OF LAWRENCEVILLE

:062110777: 70018188

DEPOSIT TICKET   64-777/611

ANDERSON INTERNAL MEDICINE
Lawrenceville, GA

DATE 3/3/2016

CASH	CURRENCY	500.00
	COIN	
LIST CHECKS SINGLY		798.30
TOTAL FROM OTHER SIDE		
TOTAL		1,298.30
LESS CASH RECEIVED		
NET CASH RECEIVED		1,298.30

DEPOSITS MADE MAY NOT BE AVAILABLE FOR IMMEDIATE WITHDRAWAL.

SIGN HERE FOR CASH RECEIVED (IF REQUIRED)

BANK OF LAWRENCEVILLE

:062110777: 70018188

DEPOSIT TICKET   64-777/611

ANDERSON INTERNAL MEDICINE
Lawrenceville, GA

DATE 3/3/2016

CASH	CURRENCY	500.00
	COIN	
LIST CHECKS SINGLY		1,282.53
TOTAL FROM OTHER SIDE		
TOTAL		1,782.53
LESS CASH RECEIVED		
NET CASH RECEIVED		1,782.53

DEPOSITS MADE MAY NOT BE AVAILABLE FOR IMMEDIATE WITHDRAWAL.

SIGN HERE FOR CASH RECEIVED (IF REQUIRED)

BANK OF LAWRENCEVILLE

:062110777: 70018188

DEPOSIT TICKET   64-777/611

ANDERSON INTERNAL MEDICINE
Lawrenceville, GA

DATE 3/4/2016

CASH	CURRENCY	500.00
	COIN	
LIST CHECKS SINGLY		741.67
TOTAL FROM OTHER SIDE		
TOTAL		1,241.67
LESS CASH RECEIVED		
NET CASH RECEIVED		1,241.67

DEPOSITS MADE MAY NOT BE AVAILABLE FOR IMMEDIATE WITHDRAWAL.

SIGN HERE FOR CASH RECEIVED (IF REQUIRED)

BANK OF LAWRENCEVILLE

:062110777: 70018188

DEPOSIT TICKET

ANDERSON INTERNAL MEDICINE
Lawrenceville, GA

DATE 3/9/2016

DEPOSITS MADE MAY NOT BE AVAILABLE FOR IMMEDIATE WITHDRAWAL.

SIGN HERE FOR CASH RECEIVED (IF REQUIRED)

BANK OF LAWRENCEVILLE

:062110777: 70018188

64-777/611

CASH	CURRENCY	500.00
	COIN	
LIST CHECKS SINGLY		1,003.27
TOTAL FROM OTHER SIDE		
TOTAL		1,503.27
LESS CASH RECEIVED		
NET CASH RECEIVED		1,503.27

DEPOSIT TICKET

ANDERSON INTERNAL MEDICINE
Lawrenceville, GA

DATE 3/10/2016

DEPOSITS MADE MAY NOT BE AVAILABLE FOR IMMEDIATE WITHDRAWAL.

SIGN HERE FOR CASH RECEIVED (IF REQUIRED)

BANK OF LAWRENCEVILLE

:062110777: 70018188

64-777/611

CASH	CURRENCY	500.00
	COIN	
LIST CHECKS SINGLY		977.74
TOTAL FROM OTHER SIDE		
TOTAL		1,477.74
LESS CASH RECEIVED		
NET CASH RECEIVED		1,477.74

DEPOSIT TICKET

ANDERSON INTERNAL MEDICINE
Lawrenceville, GA

DATE 3/11/2016

DEPOSITS MADE MAY NOT BE AVAILABLE FOR IMMEDIATE WITHDRAWAL.

SIGN HERE FOR CASH RECEIVED (IF REQUIRED)

BANK OF LAWRENCEVILLE

:062110777: 70018188

64-777/611

CASH	CURRENCY	500.00
	COIN	
LIST CHECKS SINGLY		1,057.82
TOTAL FROM OTHER SIDE		
TOTAL		1,557.82
LESS CASH RECEIVED		
NET CASH RECEIVED		1,557.82

DEPOSIT TICKET

ANDERSON INTERNAL MEDICINE
Lawrenceville, GA

DATE 3/8/2016

DEPOSITS MADE MAY NOT BE AVAILABLE FOR IMMEDIATE WITHDRAWAL.

SIGN HERE FOR CASH RECEIVED (IF REQUIRED)

BANK OF LAWRENCEVILLE

:062110777: 70018188

64-777/611

CASH	CURRENCY	500.00
	COIN	
LIST CHECKS SINGLY		639.63
TOTAL FROM OTHER SIDE		
TOTAL		1,139.63
LESS CASH RECEIVED		
NET CASH RECEIVED		1,139.63

DEPOSIT TICKET

ANDERSON INTERNAL MEDICINE
Lawrenceville, GA

DATE 3/9/2016

DEPOSITS MADE MAY NOT BE AVAILABLE FOR IMMEDIATE WITHDRAWAL.

SIGN HERE FOR CASH RECEIVED (IF REQUIRED)

BANK OF LAWRENCEVILLE

:062110777: 70018188

64-777/611

CASH	CURRENCY	500.00
	COIN	
LIST CHECKS SINGLY		1,263.82
TOTAL FROM OTHER SIDE		
TOTAL		1,763.82
LESS CASH RECEIVED		
NET CASH RECEIVED		1,763.82

DEPOSIT TICKET

ANDERSON INTERNAL MEDICINE
Lawrenceville, GA

DATE 3/10/2016

DEPOSITS MADE MAY NOT BE AVAILABLE FOR IMMEDIATE WITHDRAWAL.

SIGN HERE FOR CASH RECEIVED (IF REQUIRED)

BANK OF LAWRENCEVILLE

:062110777: 70018188

64-777/611

CASH	CURRENCY	500.00
	COIN	
LIST CHECKS SINGLY		873.93
TOTAL FROM OTHER SIDE		
TOTAL		1,373.93
LESS CASH RECEIVED		
NET CASH RECEIVED		1,373.93

DEPOSIT TICKET

ANDERSON INTERNAL MEDICINE
Lawrenceville, GA
DATE 3/11/2016

64-777/611

CASH	CURRENCY	500.00
	COIN	
LIST CHECKS SINGLY		773.16
TOTAL FROM OTHER SIDE		
TOTAL		1,273.16
LESS CASH RECEIVED		
NET CASH RECEIVED		1,273.16

DEPOSITS MADE MAY NOT BE AVAILABLE FOR IMMEDIATE WITHDRAWAL
SIGN HERE FOR CASH RECEIVED (IF REQUIRED)

BANK OF LAWRENCEVILLE

:062110777: 70018188

DEPOSIT TICKET

ANDERSON INTERNAL MEDICINE
Lawrenceville, GA
DATE 3/11/2016

64-777/611

CASH	CURRENCY	500.00
	COIN	
LIST CHECKS SINGLY		719.92
TOTAL FROM OTHER SIDE		
TOTAL		1,279.92
LESS CASH RECEIVED		
NET CASH RECEIVED		1,279.92

DEPOSITS MADE MAY NOT BE AVAILABLE FOR IMMEDIATE WITHDRAWAL
SIGN HERE FOR CASH RECEIVED (IF REQUIRED)

BANK OF LAWRENCEVILLE

:062110777: 70018188

DEPOSIT TICKET

ANDERSON INTERNAL MEDICINE
Lawrenceville, GA
DATE 3/15/2016

64-777/611

CASH	CURRENCY	500.00
	COIN	
LIST CHECKS SINGLY		899.92
TOTAL FROM OTHER SIDE		
TOTAL		1,399.92
LESS CASH RECEIVED		
NET CASH RECEIVED		1,399.92

DEPOSITS MADE MAY NOT BE AVAILABLE FOR IMMEDIATE WITHDRAWAL
SIGN HERE FOR CASH RECEIVED (IF REQUIRED)

BANK OF LAWRENCEVILLE

:062110777: 70018188

DEPOSIT TICKET

ANDERSON INTERNAL MEDICINE
Lawrenceville, GA
DATE 3/15/2016

64-777/611

CASH	CURRENCY	500.00
	COIN	
LIST CHECKS SINGLY		1,283.23
TOTAL FROM OTHER SIDE		
TOTAL		1,783.23
LESS CASH RECEIVED		
NET CASH RECEIVED		1,783.23

DEPOSITS MADE MAY NOT BE AVAILABLE FOR IMMEDIATE WITHDRAWAL
SIGN HERE FOR CASH RECEIVED (IF REQUIRED)

BANK OF LAWRENCEVILLE

:062110777: 70018188

DEPOSIT TICKET

ANDERSON INTERNAL MEDICINE
Lawrenceville, GA
DATE 3/15/2016

64-777/611

CASH	CURRENCY	500.00
	COIN	
LIST CHECKS SINGLY		598.49
TOTAL FROM OTHER SIDE		
TOTAL		1,098.49
LESS CASH RECEIVED		
NET CASH RECEIVED		1,098.49

DEPOSITS MADE MAY NOT BE AVAILABLE FOR IMMEDIATE WITHDRAWAL
SIGN HERE FOR CASH RECEIVED (IF REQUIRED)

BANK OF LAWRENCEVILLE

:062110777: 70018188

DEPOSIT TICKET

ANDERSON INTERNAL MEDICINE
Lawrenceville, GA
DATE 3/17/2016

64-777/611

CASH	CURRENCY	500.00
	COIN	
LIST CHECKS SINGLY		967.73
TOTAL FROM OTHER SIDE		
TOTAL		1,467.13
LESS CASH RECEIVED		
NET CASH RECEIVED		1,467.13

DEPOSITS MADE MAY NOT BE AVAILABLE FOR IMMEDIATE WITHDRAWAL
SIGN HERE FOR CASH RECEIVED (IF REQUIRED)

BANK OF LAWRENCEVILLE

:062110777: 70018188

DEPOSIT TICKET

64-777/611

ANDERSON INTERNAL MEDICINE
Lawrenceville, GA

DATE   3/17/2016

CASH	CURRENCY	1,142.96
	COIN	
	LIST CHECKS SINGLY	
TOTAL FROM OTHER SIDE		
TOTAL		1,142.96
LESS CASH RECEIVED		
NET CASH RECEIVED		1,142.96

DEPOSITS MADE MAY NOT BE AVAILABLE FOR IMMEDIATE WITHDRAWAL.

SIGN HERE FOR CASH RECEIVED (IF REQUIRED)

BANK OF LAWRENCEVILLE

:062110777: 70018188

DEPOSIT TICKET

64-777/611

ANDERSON INTERNAL MEDICINE
Lawrenceville, GA

3/18/2016

CASH	CURRENCY	1,127.06
	COIN	
	LIST CHECKS SINGLY	
TOTAL FROM OTHER SIDE		
TOTAL		1,127.06
LESS CASH RECEIVED		
NET CASH RECEIVED		1,127.06

DEPOSITS MADE MAY NOT BE AVAILABLE FOR IMMEDIATE WITHDRAWAL.

SIGN HERE FOR CASH RECEIVED (IF REQUIRED)

BANK OF LAWRENCEVILLE

:062110777: 70018188

DEPOSIT TICKET

64-777/611

ANDERSON INTERNAL MEDICINE
Lawrenceville, GA

DATE   3/18/2016

CASH	CURRENCY	1,887.37
	COIN	
	LIST CHECKS SINGLY	
TOTAL FROM OTHER SIDE		
TOTAL		1,887.37
LESS CASH RECEIVED		
NET CASH RECEIVED		1,887.37

DEPOSITS MADE MAY NOT BE AVAILABLE FOR IMMEDIATE WITHDRAWAL.

SIGN HERE FOR CASH RECEIVED (IF REQUIRED)

BANK OF LAWRENCEVILLE

:062110777: 70018188

DEPOSIT TICKET

64-777/611

ANDERSON INTERNAL MEDICINE
Lawrenceville, GA

DATE   3/22/2016

CASH	CURRENCY	1,703.45
	COIN	
	LIST CHECKS SINGLY	
TOTAL FROM OTHER SIDE		
TOTAL		1,703.45
LESS CASH RECEIVED		
NET CASH RECEIVED		1,703.45

DEPOSITS MADE MAY NOT BE AVAILABLE FOR IMMEDIATE WITHDRAWAL.

SIGN HERE FOR CASH RECEIVED (IF REQUIRED)

BANK OF LAWRENCEVILLE

:062110777: 70018188

DEPOSIT TICKET

64-777/611

ANDERSON INTERNAL MEDICINE
Lawrenceville, GA

DATE   3/24/2016

CASH	CURRENCY	1,740.92
	COIN	
	LIST CHECKS SINGLY	
TOTAL FROM OTHER SIDE		
TOTAL		1,740.92
LESS CASH RECEIVED		
NET CASH RECEIVED		1,740.92

DEPOSITS MADE MAY NOT BE AVAILABLE FOR IMMEDIATE WITHDRAWAL.

SIGN HERE FOR CASH RECEIVED (IF REQUIRED)

BANK OF LAWRENCEVILLE

:062110777: 70018188

DEPOSIT TICKET

64-777/611

ANDERSON INTERNAL MEDICINE
Lawrenceville, GA

DATE   3/25/2016

CASH	CURRENCY	1,068.76
	COIN	
	LIST CHECKS SINGLY	
TOTAL FROM OTHER SIDE		
TOTAL		1,068.76
LESS CASH RECEIVED		
NET CASH RECEIVED		1,068.76

DEPOSITS MADE MAY NOT BE AVAILABLE FOR IMMEDIATE WITHDRAWAL.

SIGN HERE FOR CASH RECEIVED (IF REQUIRED)

BANK OF LAWRENCEVILLE

:062110777: 70018188

DEPOSIT TICKET

64-777/611

ANDERSON INTERNAL MEDICINE

Lawrenceville, GA

DATE   3/28/2016

DEPOSITS MADE MAY NOT BE AVAILABLE FOR IMMEDIATE WITHDRAWAL

CASH	CURRENCY	1,126.09
	COIN	
LIST CHECKS SINGLY		
TOTAL FROM OTHER SIDE		
	TOTAL	1,126.09
LESS CASH RECEIVED		
	NET CASH RECEIVED	1,126.09

SIGN HERE FOR CASH RECEIVED (IF REQUIRED)

BANK OF LAWRENCEVILLE

:062110777: 70018188

DEPOSIT TICKET

64-777/611

ANDERSON INTERNAL MEDICINE

Lawrenceville, GA

DATE   3/29/2016

DEPOSITS MADE MAY NOT BE AVAILABLE FOR IMMEDIATE WITHDRAWAL

CASH	CURRENCY	1,005.27
	COIN	
LIST CHECKS SINGLY		
TOTAL FROM OTHER SIDE		
	TOTAL	1,005.27
LESS CASH RECEIVED		
	NET CASH RECEIVED	1,005.27

SIGN HERE FOR CASH RECEIVED (IF REQUIRED)

BANK OF LAWRENCEVILLE

:062110777: 70018188

193

7-4 CASE 4: USING DATA ANALYTICS: ANALYZING AND SUMMARIZING DATA WITH EXCEL PIVOT [ANDERSON INTERNAL MEDICINE (EXCEL PIVOT)]

ANDERSON BANK TRANSACTIONS (SEP OCT NOV DEC JAN FEB)
DETAILS OF TRANSACTIONS IN BANK OF LAWRENCEVILLE A/C 171499800
FROM SEPTEMBER 1, 2015 TO FEBRUARY 29, 2016
ALL TRANSACTIONS
ANDERSON INTERNAL MEDICINE
LAWRENCEVILLE, GA
CASE NUMBER: 16-023

Schedule 2

Posted Date	Check Number	Check Date	Payee of Check / Debit	Check Endorsement	Amount Check/Debit	Amount Deposit	Bank Balance	Check Category	Deposit Category
09/01/15							8,921.58	<< BEG. BALANCE	
09/01/15						1,734.40	10,655.98		Cash deposit
09/01/15	649	08/29/15	Linens to You		8,575.00		2,080.98		
09/02/15						1,241.61	3,322.59		Cash deposit
09/03/15						1,587.53	4,910.12		Cash deposit
09/03/15	650	08/31/15	Parking Co of America		53.00		4,857.12		
09/04/15	651	08/31/15	Water and Sewer Dept.		59.24		4,797.88		
09/04/15						1,139.63	5,937.51		Cash deposit
09/04/15	653	09/01/15	Georgia Professional Insurance		198.50		5,739.01		
09/04/15	654	09/01/15	Georgia Professional Insurance		207.50		5,531.51		
09/04/15	655	09/01/15	Georgia Prof Ins		248.00		5,283.51		
09/04/15	656	09/01/15	Georgia Professional Insurance		294.50		4,989.01		
09/04/15	657	09/01/15	Sensitive Waste Services		127.75		4,861.26		
09/04/15	658	09/01/15	Verizon		218.69		4,642.57		
09/04/15		09/01/15	Withdrawal		200.00		4,442.57		
09/04/15		09/01/15	Brown's Hardware		21.20		4,421.37		
09/04/15		09/01/15	UPS		89.72		4,331.65		
09/04/15		09/01/15	UPS		210.52		4,121.13		
09/05/15						1,298.30	5,419.43		Cash deposit
09/05/15	659	09/02/15	Georgia Power Company		3,234.12		2,185.31		
09/05/15	660	09/02/15	Kinko's		71.74		2,113.57		
09/05/15		09/02/15	Larry's Deli		22.72		2,090.85		
09/07/15						1,503.27	3,594.12		Cash deposit
09/07/15	661	09/04/15	Horizon Telephone Company		1,455.53		2,138.59		
09/08/15						1,763.82	3,902.41		Cash deposit
09/09/15						1,782.53	5,684.94		Cash deposit
09/10/15						2,307.43	7,992.37		Cash deposit
09/10/15	662	09/07/15	76 Church Street		29.88		7,962.49		
09/10/15	663	09/07/15	Andrew & Duvall		125.00		7,837.49		
09/10/15	664	09/07/15	Georgia Prof Ins		95.78		7,741.71		
09/10/15	665	09/07/15	Kennesaw Health Plan		195.80		7,545.91		
09/10/15	666	09/07/15	Marjorie's Cleaning Services		75.00		7,470.91		
09/10/15	667	09/07/15	Parkaire Band Boosters		75.00		7,395.91		
09/11/15						1,313.93	8,709.84		Cash deposit

DETAILS OF TRANSACTIONS IN BANK OF LAWRENCEVILLE A/C 171499800
FROM SEPTEMBER 1, 2015 TO FEBRUARY 29, 2016
ALL TRANSACTIONS
ANDERSON INTERNAL MEDICINE
LAWRENCEVILLE, GA
CASE NUMBER: 16-023

Schedule 2

Posted Date	Check Number	Check Date	Payee of Check/Debit	Check Endorsement	Amount Check/Debit	Amount Deposit	Bank Balance	Check Category	Deposit Category
09/11/15	668	09/08/15	Kinko's		77.79		8,632.05		
09/11/15	669	09/08/15	Southeast Airlines		401.94		8,230.11		
09/11/15		09/08/15	Withdrawal		700.00		7,530.11		
09/12/15						1,477.74	9,007.85		Cash deposit
09/12/15	670	09/09/15	Georgia Professional Insurance		27.98		8,979.87		
09/13/15		09/10/15	Cash		1,221.18		7,758.69		
09/13/15	670	10/13/15	Physicians Central		256.00		7,502.69		
09/14/15						1,219.92	8,722.61		Cash deposit
09/14/15	671	10/14/15	Physicians Central		768.00		7,954.61		
09/15/15						1,273.16	9,227.77		Cash deposit
09/15/15	672	09/12/15	Kennesaw HP		190.71		9,037.06		
09/15/15	673	09/12/15	Southeast Airlines		563.12		8,473.94		
09/15/15	674	09/12/15	Standard Mortgage Co.		7,050.29		1,423.65		
09/15/15	675	09/12/15	Water and Sewer Dept.		40.69		1,382.96		
09/16/15						1,399.92	2,782.88		Cash deposit
09/17/15						1,551.82	4,334.70		Cash deposit
09/17/15	676	09/14/15	Blue Jay Health		1,927.27		2,407.43		
09/17/15	677	09/14/15	North Georgia PCS		198.23		2,209.20		
09/17/15		09/14/15	Strip TZ Grille		408.00		1,801.20		
09/18/15						1,098.49	2,899.69		Cash deposit
09/18/15	678	09/15/15	Central Office Supply		48.72		2,850.97		
09/19/15						1,783.23	4,634.20		Cash deposit
09/20/15						1,142.96	5,777.16		Cash deposit
09/21/15						1,467.13	7,244.29		Cash deposit
09/22/15						1,121.06	8,365.35		Cash deposit
09/23/15						1,887.37	10,252.72		Cash deposit
09/23/15	679	09/20/15	Tonya Larsen		2,497.89		7,754.83		
09/24/15						1,703.45	9,458.28		Cash deposit
09/25/15						1,140.92	10,599.20		Cash deposit
09/26/15						1,068.76	11,667.96		Cash deposit
09/26/15	680	10/24/15	Physicians Central		256.00		11,411.96		
09/26/15	681	10/27/15	Physicians Central		768.00		10,643.96		
09/27/15		09/24/15	Food-Mart		247.63		10,396.33		
09/28/15						1,126.09	11,522.42		Cash deposit

Supporting analysis: Page 2

DETAILS OF TRANSACTIONS IN BANK OF LAWRENCEVILLE A/C 171499800
FROM SEPTEMBER 1, 2015 TO FEBRUARY 29, 2016
ALL TRANSACTIONS
ANDERSON INTERNAL MEDICINE
LAWRENCEVILLE, GA
CASE NUMBER: 16-023

Schedule 2

Posted Date	Check Number	Check Date	Payee of Check / Debit	Check Endorsement	Amount Check/Debit	Amount Deposit	Bank Balance	Check Category	Deposit Category
09/29/15						1,005.21	12,527.63		Cash deposit
09/30/15						1,005.21	13,532.84		Cash deposit
09/30/15		09/30/15	Bank Fee		21.36		13,511.48		
10/01/15						1,793.40	15,304.88		Cash deposit
10/01/15	683	09/28/15	Linens to U		8,575.00		6,729.88		
10/02/15						1,300.61	8,030.49		Cash deposit
10/02/15	684	09/29/15	Barry's Con'l Repairs		1,900.00		6,130.49		
10/03/15	685	09/30/15	Parking Co of America		53.00		6,077.49		
10/05/15						1,646.53	7,724.02		Cash deposit
10/05/15	686	10/02/15	Georgia Power Company		3,174.12		4,549.90		
10/06/15						1,198.63	5,748.53		Cash deposit
10/06/15	687	10/03/15	Kennesaw Health Plan		27.00		5,721.53		
10/07/15						1,357.30	7,078.83		Cash deposit
10/07/15	688	10/04/15	Horizon Telephone Company		1,455.53		5,623.30		
10/08/15						1,562.27	7,185.57		Cash deposit
10/09/15						1,822.82	9,008.39		Cash deposit
10/10/15						1,841.53	10,849.92		Cash deposit
10/10/15	689	10/07/15	J J Dawson	J Jason Dawson	5,800.00		5,049.92		
10/12/15						2,366.43	7,416.35		Cash deposit
10/13/15						1,372.93	8,789.28		Cash deposit
10/13/15		10/10/15	Food-Mart		349.63		8,439.65		
10/14/15						1,536.74	9,976.39		Cash deposit
10/15/15						1,278.92	11,255.31		Cash deposit
10/15/15	691	10/12/15	Standard Mortgage Co.		7,050.29		4,205.02		
10/16/15						1,332.16	5,537.18		Cash deposit
10/16/15	692	10/13/15	76 Church Street		71.99		5,465.19		
10/16/15	693	10/13/15	Kennesaw Health Plan		8.98		5,456.21		
10/16/15	694	10/13/15	Marjorie's Cleaning Services		75.00		5,381.21		
10/16/15	695	10/13/15	Marjories Cleaning Services		75.00		5,306.21		
10/16/15	696	10/13/15	Physicians Central		256.00		5,050.21		
10/16/15		10/13/15	ATM		300.00		4,750.21		
10/17/15		10/13/15	UPS		12.84		4,737.37		
10/17/15						1,458.92	6,196.29		Cash deposit
10/17/15	697	10/14/15	Always Their		150.00		6,046.29		

DETAILS OF TRANSACTIONS IN BANK OF LAWRENCEVILLE A/C 171499800
FROM SEPTEMBER 1, 2015 TO FEBRUARY 29, 2016
ALL TRANSACTIONS
ANDERSON INTERNAL MEDICINE
LAWRENCEVILLE, GA
CASE NUMBER: 16-023

Schedule 2

Posted Date	Check Number	Check Date	Payee of Check / Debit	Check Endorsement	Amount Check/Debit	Amount Deposit	Bank Balance	Check Category	Deposit Category
10/17/15	698	10/14/15	Barry's Commercial Repairs		557.00		5,489.29		
10/17/15	699	10/14/15	North Georgia PCS		198.23		5,291.06		
10/17/15	700	10/14/15	Physicians Central		768.00		4,523.06		
10/17/15	701	10/14/15	Southeast Airlines		427.70		4,095.36		
10/18/15	702	10/15/15	Agbonze Tree Service		170.00		3,925.36		
10/18/15	703	10/15/15	Always There		100.00		3,825.36		
10/18/15	704	10/15/15	Shwartz German Haus		97.91		3,727.45		
10/19/15						1,610.82	5,338.27		Cash deposit
10/20/15						1,157.49	6,495.76		Cash deposit
10/20/15	705	10/17/15	FedEx Kinko's		2.57		6,493.19		
10/20/15	706	10/17/15	Johnson Medical Coding		4.75		6,488.44		
10/21/15						1,842.23	8,330.67		Cash deposit
10/22/15						1,201.96	9,532.63		Cash deposit
10/23/15						1,526.13	11,058.76		Cash deposit
10/23/15	707	10/20/15	Always Their		125.00		10,933.76		
10/23/15	708	10/20/15	Herald, Johnson, Bates		225.99		10,707.77		
10/23/15	709	10/20/15	Organic Steam		109.67		10,598.10		
10/23/15	710	10/20/15	Sensitive Waste Services		14.71		10,583.39		
10/23/15	711	10/20/15	Sensitive Waste Services		70.92		10,512.47		
10/23/15	712	10/20/15	Tonya Larsen		2,497.89		8,014.58		
10/23/15	713	10/20/15	Verizon		218.69		7,795.89		
10/23/15	714	10/20/15	Verizon Wireless		218.69		7,577.20		
10/23/15	715	10/20/15	Verizon Wireless		218.69		7,358.51		
10/23/15	716	10/20/15	Verizon		218.69		7,139.82		
10/24/15						1,180.06	8,319.88		Cash deposit
10/24/15	717	10/21/15	Andrew & Duvall		190.00		8,129.88		
10/24/15	718	10/21/15	Georgia Professional Insurance		105.00		8,024.88		
10/24/15	719	10/21/15	KIA Finance Company		599.75		7,425.13		
10/24/15	720	10/21/15	KIA Southeast		599.75		6,825.38		
10/24/15	721	10/24/15	Browns Hardware		27.27		6,798.11		
10/25/15	721	10/22/15	Herald and Bates		209.97		6,588.14		
10/25/15	722	10/22/15	Larry's Deli		27.77		6,560.37		
10/26/15						1,946.37	8,506.74		Cash deposit
10/26/15	723	10/23/15	Always There		100.00		8,406.74		

DETAILS OF TRANSACTIONS IN BANK OF LAWRENCEVILLE A/C 171499800
FROM SEPTEMBER 1, 2015 TO FEBRUARY 29, 2016
ALL TRANSACTIONS
ANDERSON INTERNAL MEDICINE
LAWRENCEVILLE, GA
CASE NUMBER: 16-023

Schedule 2

Posted Date	Check Number	Check Date	Payee of Check / Debit	Check Endorsement	Amount Check/Debit	Amount Deposit	Bank Balance	Check Category	Deposit Category
10/27/15	724	10/24/15	Jason Dawson	J Dawson	6,700.00	1,762.45	10,169.19		Cash deposit
10/27/15	725	10/24/15	Kennesaw HP		214.00		3,469.19		
10/27/15	726	10/24/15	Kinko's		79.55		3,255.19		
10/27/15	727	10/24/15	Pest USA	Team Pent USA Co	145.00		3,175.64		
10/27/15	728	10/24/15	Physicians Central		256.00		3,030.64		
10/27/15		10/24/15	Food-Mart		256.23		2,774.64		
10/28/15						1,199.92	2,518.41		Cash deposit
10/29/15						1,127.76	3,718.33		Cash deposit
10/30/15						1,185.09	4,846.09		Cash deposit
10/30/15	729		Marjories Cleaning Services		75.00		6,031.18		
10/27/15	730		Physicians Central		768.00		5,956.18		
10/28/15	731		Herald, Johnson, Bates		201.12		5,188.18		
10/31/15	732		Johnson Medical Coding		92.05		4,987.06		
10/31/15			Bank Fee		23.58		4,895.01		
10/29/15	733		Linens to You		1,575.00		4,871.43		
11/01/15						981.60	3,296.43		Cash deposit
11/02/15	734		Barry's Commercial Repairs		922.00		4,278.03		
11/02/15	735		Schwartz German Haus		97.97		3,356.03		
11/03/15						981.60	3,258.06		Cash deposit
11/03/15	737		Johnson Coding		20.00		4,239.66		
11/03/15	738		Parking Co of America		53.00		4,219.66		
11/03/15	739		Shwartz German Haus		7.91		4,166.66		
11/03/15			Browns Hardware		95.00		4,158.75		
11/04/15						1,769.79	4,063.75		Cash deposit
11/05/15						1,277.00	5,833.54		Cash deposit
11/05/15	740		Georgia Power Company		2,998.36		7,110.54		
11/06/15						1,622.92	4,112.18		Cash deposit
11/06/15	741		Kennesaw Health Plan		19.92		5,735.18		
11/03/15	742		KIA Finance Company		599.75		5,715.18		
11/07/15						1,175.02	5,115.43		Cash deposit
11/07/15	743		Horizon Telephone Company		1,455.53		6,290.45		
11/09/15						1,333.69	4,834.92		Cash deposit
11/09/15	744		Physicians Central		256.00		6,168.61		
							5,912.61		

DETAILS OF TRANSACTIONS IN BANK OF LAWRENCEVILLE A/C 171499800
FROM SEPTEMBER 1, 2015 TO FEBRUARY 29, 2016
ALL TRANSACTIONS
ANDERSON INTERNAL MEDICINE
LAWRENCEVILLE, GA
CASE NUMBER: 16-023

Schedule 2

Posted Date	Check Number	Check Date	Payee of Check / Debit	Check Endorsement	Amount Check/Debit	Amount Deposit	Bank Balance	Check Category	Deposit Category
11/10/15						1,538.66	7,451.27		Cash deposit
11/11/15						1,799.21	9,250.48		Cash deposit
11/12/15						1,817.92	11,068.40		Cash deposit
11/13/15						2,342.82	13,411.22		Cash deposit
11/13/15		11/10/15	Food-Mart		313.33		13,097.89		
11/14/15						1,349.32	14,447.21		Cash deposit
11/14/15	745	11/11/15	76 Church Street		87.00		14,360.21		
11/14/15	746	11/11/15	Georgia Prof Ins		172.14		14,188.07		
11/14/15	747	11/11/15	Physicians Central		768.00		13,420.07		
11/15/15	748	11/12/15	Andrew and Duvall		155.00		13,265.07		
11/15/15	749	11/12/15	Std Mortgage Co.		7,050.29		6,214.78		
11/16/15						1,513.13	7,727.91		Cash deposit
11/16/15	750	11/13/15	Georgia Prof Ins		87.00		7,640.91		
11/16/15	751	11/13/15	KIA Finance Company		599.75		7,041.16		
11/17/15						1,255.31	8,296.47		Cash deposit
11/17/15	752	11/14/15	Barry's Com'l Repairs		998.00		7,298.47		
11/17/15	753	11/14/15	North Georgia PCS		198.23		7,100.24		
11/18/15						1,308.55	8,408.79		Cash deposit
11/18/15	754	11/15/15	Barry's Com'l Repairs		728.00		7,680.79		
11/19/15						1,435.31	9,116.10		Cash deposit
11/20/15						1,587.21	10,703.31		Cash deposit
11/20/15	755	11/17/15	Andrew & Duvall		200.00		10,503.31		
11/20/15	756	11/17/15	Central Office Supply		7.74		10,495.57		
11/20/15	757	11/17/15	Central Office Supply		191.95		10,303.62		
11/20/15	758	11/17/15	Johnson Medical Coding		29.99		10,273.63		
11/20/15	759	11/17/15	Kennesaw Health Plan		41.77		10,231.86		
11/20/15	760	11/17/15	Kennesaw HP		170.00		10,061.86		
11/20/15	761	11/17/15	Physicians Central		256.00		9,805.86		
11/20/15	762	11/17/15	Schwartz German Haus		70.17		9,735.69		
11/20/15	763	11/17/15	Water and Sewer		54.59		9,681.10		
11/20/15		11/17/15	Larry's Delication		29.77		9,651.33		
11/20/15		11/17/15	UPS		27.00		9,624.33		
11/21/15						1,133.88	10,758.21		Cash deposit
11/21/15	764	11/18/15	Physicians Central		768.00		9,990.21		

DETAILS OF TRANSACTIONS IN BANK OF LAWRENCEVILLE A/C 171499800
FROM SEPTEMBER 1, 2015 TO FEBRUARY 29, 2016
ALL TRANSACTIONS
ANDERSON INTERNAL MEDICINE
LAWRENCEVILLE, GA
CASE NUMBER: 16-023

Schedule 2

Posted Date	Check Number	Check Date	Payee of Check / Debit	Check Endorsement	Amount Check/Debit	Amount Deposit	Bank Balance	Check Category	Deposit Category
11/21/15	765	11/18/15	Water and Sewer Dept.		42.79		9,947.42		
11/22/15	766	11/19/15	Parkaire BB		75.00		9,872.42		
11/22/15									
11/22/15	767	11/19/15	Discount Tobacco Supply Company		900.00		8,972.42		
11/23/15						1,818.62	10,791.04		Cash deposit
11/23/15	768	11/20/15	Tonya Larsen		2,497.89		8,293.15		
11/24/15						1,178.35	9,471.50		Cash deposit
11/24/15		11/21/15	Larry's Deli		15.25		9,456.25		
11/24/15		11/21/15	Browns Hardware		405.55		9,050.70		
11/25/15						1,502.52	10,553.22		Cash deposit
11/26/15		11/23/15	Food-Mart		407.89		10,145.33		
11/27/15						1,156.45	11,301.78		Cash deposit
11/27/15	769	11/24/15	Central Office Supply		7.17		11,294.61		
11/27/15	770	11/24/15	Central Office Supply		18.77		11,275.84		
11/27/15	771	11/24/15	Central Office Sup		79.57		11,196.27		
11/27/15	772	11/24/15	Central Office Supply		99.10		11,097.17		
11/27/15	773	11/24/15	Marjories Cleaning Services		75.00		11,022.17		
11/27/15	774	11/24/15	Marjories Cleaning Services		75.00		10,947.17		
11/27/15	775	11/24/15	Water and Sewer		49.89		10,897.28		
11/27/15		11/24/15	Browns Hardware		19.77		10,877.51		
11/27/15		11/24/15	United Postal Service		23.32		10,854.19		
11/28/15						1,922.76	12,776.95		Cash deposit
11/28/15	776	11/25/15	Blue Jay Health		1,829.98		10,946.97		
11/28/15	777	11/25/15	Herald Bates		270.49		10,676.48		
11/28/15	778	11/25/15	Johnson Coding		99.49		10,576.99		
11/29/15	779	11/26/15	Always There		150.00		10,426.99		
11/29/15	780	11/26/15	Marjorie's Cleaning Services		75.00		10,351.99		
11/29/15	781	11/26/15	Marjorie's Cleaning Services		75.00		10,276.99		
11/29/15		11/26/15	UPS		25.50		10,251.49		
11/30/15						1,738.84	11,990.33		Cash deposit
11/30/15		11/31/15	Bank Fee		22.98		11,967.35		
12/01/15						1,104.15	13,071.50		Cash deposit
12/01/15	782	11/28/15	Linans to You		8,575.00		4,496.50		
12/02/15						1,161.48	5,657.98		Cash deposit

DETAILS OF TRANSACTIONS IN BANK OF LAWRENCEVILLE A/C 171499800
FROM SEPTEMBER 1, 2015 TO FEBRUARY 29, 2016
ALL TRANSACTIONS
ANDERSON INTERNAL MEDICINE
LAWRENCEVILLE, GA
CASE NUMBER: 16-023

Schedule 2

Posted Date	Check Number	Check Date	Payee of Check/Debit	Check Endorsement	Amount Check/Debit	Amount Deposit	Bank Balance	Check Category	Deposit Category
12/03/15						957.99	6,615.97		Cash deposit
12/03/15	783	11/30/15	Pkg Co of America		53.00		6,562.97		
12/03/15	784	11/30/15	Water and Sewer Dept.		43.66		6,519.31		
12/04/15						957.99	7,477.30		Cash deposit
12/04/15		12/01/15	Withdrawal		700.00		6,777.30		
12/05/15						1,746.18	8,523.48		Cash deposit
12/05/15	785	12/02/15	Georgia Power Company		3,261.45		5,262.03		
12/05/15		12/02/15	Food-Mart		388.99		4,873.04		
12/07/15						1,253.39	6,126.43		Cash deposit
12/07/15	786	12/04/15	Horizon Telephone Company		1,455.53		4,670.90		
12/08/15						1,599.31	6,270.21		Cash deposit
12/08/15	787	12/05/15	Discount Tobacco Supply Company		1,670.00		4,600.21		
12/09/15						1,151.41	5,751.62		Cash deposit
12/10/15						1,310.08	7,061.70		Cash deposit
12/11/15						1,515.05	8,576.75		Cash deposit
12/11/15	788	12/08/15	Always Their		175.00		8,401.75		
12/11/15	789	12/08/15	Central Office Sup		47.70		8,354.05		
12/11/15	790	12/08/15	Kennesaw HP		7.80		8,346.25		
12/11/15	791	12/08/15	Kinko's		47.55		8,298.70		
12/11/15	792	12/08/15	Physicians Central		256.00		8,042.70		
12/11/15		12/08/15	ATM		250.00		7,792.70		
12/11/15		12/08/15	Food-Mart		327.84		7,464.86		
12/11/15		12/08/15	Food-Mart		222.02		7,242.84		
12/12/15						1,775.60	9,018.44		Cash deposit
12/12/15	793	12/09/15	Marjorie's Cleaning Services		75.00		8,943.44		
12/12/15	794	12/09/15	Sensitive Waste Services		29.00		8,914.44		
12/14/15		12/09/15	Brown's Hardware		28.49		8,885.95		
12/14/15						1,794.31	10,680.26		Cash deposit
12/14/15	795	12/11/15	Shwartz German Haus		44.79		10,635.47		
12/14/15		12/11/15	UPS		43.63		10,591.84		
12/14/15		12/11/15	United Postal Service		22.11		10,569.73		
12/15/15						2,319.21	12,888.94		Cash deposit
12/15/15	796	12/12/15	Central Office Supply		20.52		12,868.42		
12/15/15	797	12/12/15	Standard Mortgage Co.		7,050.29		5,818.13		

Supporting analysis: Page 8

DETAILS OF TRANSACTIONS IN BANK OF LAWRENCEVILLE A/C 171499800
FROM SEPTEMBER 1, 2015 TO FEBRUARY 29, 2016
ALL TRANSACTIONS
ANDERSON INTERNAL MEDICINE
LAWRENCEVILLE, GA
CASE NUMBER: 16-023

Schedule 2

Posted Date	Check Number	Check Date	Payee of Check / Debit	Check Endorsement	Amount Check/Debit	Amount Deposit	Bank Balance	Check Category	Deposit Category
12/16/15						1,325.71	7,143.84		Cash deposit
12/17/15						1,489.52	8,633.36		Cash deposit
12/17/15	798	12/14/15	Barry's Commercial Repairs		870.00		7,763.36		
12/17/15	799	12/14/15	North Georgia PCS		198.23		7,565.13		
12/18/15						1,231.70	8,796.83		Cash deposit
12/18/15	800	12/15/15	Andrew & Duvall		175.00		8,621.83		
12/18/15	801	12/15/15	Georgia Professional Insurance		52.92		8,568.91		
12/18/15	802	12/15/15	Kennesaw Health Plan		21.99		8,546.92		
12/18/15	803	12/15/15	Kinko's		91.99		8,454.93		
12/18/15	804	12/15/15	Marjorie's Cleaning Services		75.00		8,379.93		
12/18/15		12/15/15	Food-Mart		223.56		8,156.37		
12/19/15						1,284.94	9,441.31		Cash deposit
12/19/15	805	12/16/15	Always Their		125.00		9,316.31		
12/19/15	806	12/16/15	Shwartz German Haus		25.10		9,291.21		
12/20/15	807	12/17/15	Central Office Sup		957.25		8,333.96		
12/20/15	808	12/17/15	Kinko's		472.97		7,860.99		
12/20/15		12/17/15	Food-Mart		407.44		7,453.55		
12/21/15						1,411.70	8,865.25		Cash deposit
12/21/15	809	12/18/15	Sensitive Waster Services		25.05		8,840.20		
12/21/15		12/18/15	Brown's Hardware		194.25		8,645.95		
12/22/15		12/18/15	ATM		300.00		8,345.95		
12/22/15						1,563.60	9,909.55		Cash deposit
12/22/15	810	12/19/15	Kennesaw Health Plan		98.07		9,811.48		
12/22/15	811	12/19/15	Pest USA	Team Pent USA Co	990.21		8,821.27		
12/23/15	812	12/20/15	Tonya Larsen		2,497.89		6,323.38		
12/23/15						1,110.27	7,433.65		Cash deposit
12/23/15		12/20/15	Food-Mart		247.89		7,185.76		
12/24/15						1,795.01	8,980.77		Cash deposit
12/26/15	813	12/23/15	Always There		125.00		8,855.77		
12/26/15	814	12/23/15	Blue Jaa Health		1,377.38		7,478.39		
12/26/15	815	12/23/15	Central Office Sup		219.05		7,259.34		
12/26/15	816	12/23/15	Kennesaw Health Plan		21.28		7,238.06		
12/26/15	817	12/23/15	Williams-Sonoma		149.75		7,088.31		
12/26/15		12/23/15	Brown's Hardware		45.90		7,042.41		

DETAILS OF TRANSACTIONS IN BANK OF LAWRENCEVILLE A/C 171499800
FROM SEPTEMBER 1, 2015 TO FEBRUARY 29, 2016
ALL TRANSACTIONS
ANDERSON INTERNAL MEDICINE
LAWRENCEVILLE, GA
CASE NUMBER: 16-023

Schedule 2

Posted Date	Check Number	Check Date	Payee of Check/Debit	Check Endorsement	Amount Check/Debit	Amount Deposit	Bank Balance	Check Category	Deposit Category
12/26/15		12/23/15	Toys R US		58.28		6,984.13		
12/27/15	818	12/24/15	Marjories Cleaning Services		75.00		6,909.13		
12/27/15	819	12/24/15	Water and Sewer Dept.		48.55		6,860.58		
12/28/15	820	12/25/15	Physicians Central		768.00		6,092.58		
12/28/15						1,154.74	7,247.32		Cash deposit
12/29/15	821	12/26/15	Georgia Prof Ins		14.98		7,232.34		
12/29/15	822	12/26/15	Georgia Professional Insurance		59.00		7,173.34		
12/29/15	823	12/26/15	Schwartz German Haus		9.00		7,164.34		
12/29/15						1,478.91	8,643.25		Cash deposit
12/30/15						1,132.84	9,776.09		Cash deposit
12/30/15						36,000.00	45,776.09		Check
12/31/15	828	12/31/15	Cash		3,500.00		42,276.09		
12/31/15						1,899.15	44,175.24		Cash deposit
12/31/15		12/31/15	Bank Fee		23.14		44,152.10		
01/01/16	824	12/29/15	Linens to U		8,575.00		35,577.10		
01/01/16						1,715.23	37,292.33		Cash deposit
01/02/16	832	12/30/15	Marjories Cleaning Services		75.00		37,217.33		
01/02/16	833	12/30/15	Parkaire Band Boosters		75.00		37,142.33		
01/02/16	834	12/30/15	Physicians Central		256.00		36,886.33		
01/02/16	835	12/30/15	Blue Jay Health		407.33		36,479.00		
01/02/16	836	12/30/15	Barry's Commercial Repairs		152.00		36,327.00		
01/02/16	838	12/30/15	Barry's Com'l Repairs		195.00		36,132.00		
01/02/16	839	12/30/15	Goode's Furniture		1,737.69		34,394.31		
01/02/16	845	12/30/15	Herald, Johnson, Bates		287.00		34,107.31		
01/02/16	846	12/30/15	Kennesaw HP		5.90		34,101.41		
01/02/16	847	12/30/15	Andrew and Duvall		195.00		33,906.41		
01/02/16						1,152.70	35,059.11		Cash deposit
01/03/16	831	12/31/15	Disney World		3,273.00		31,786.11		
01/03/16	840	12/31/15	Andrew and Duvall		270.00		31,516.11		
01/03/16	841	12/31/15	Southeast Airlines		375.00		31,141.11		
01/03/16	842	12/31/15	Southeast Airlines		413.53		30,727.58		
01/03/16	843	12/31/15	Southeast Airlines		397.99		30,329.59		
01/03/16	844	12/31/15	Water and Sewer Dept.		47.25		30,282.34		
01/04/16	825	12/30/15	Title Quick		10,578.67		19,703.67		

Supporting analysis Page 10

203

DETAILS OF TRANSACTIONS IN BANK OF LAWRENCEVILLE A/C 171499800
FROM SEPTEMBER 1, 2015 TO FEBRUARY 29, 2016

ALL TRANSACTIONS
ANDERSON INTERNAL MEDICINE
LAWRENCEVILLE, GA
CASE NUMBER: 16-023

Schedule 2

Posted Date	Check Number	Check Date	Payee of Check / Debit	Check Endorsement	Amount Check/Debit	Amount Deposit	Bank Balance	Check Category	Deposit Category
01/04/16	901	01/01/16	Always Their		100.00		19,603.67		
01/04/16						1,780.54	21,384.21		Cash deposit
01/05/16	826	12/30/15	Tumbler Casino		7,000.00		14,384.21		
01/05/16	827	12/30/15	Jack Gotti		7,324.23		7,059.98		
01/05/16	902	01/02/16	Georgia Power Company		2,214.15		4,845.83		
01/05/16	903	01/02/16	Kennesaw Health Plan		200.00		4,645.83		
01/05/16	904	01/02/16	Marjories Cleaning Services		75.00		4,570.83		
01/05/16	905	01/02/16	Sensitive Waste Services		7.84		4,562.99		
01/05/16						1,137.87	5,700.86		Cash deposit
01/06/16	829	12/31/15	C&S Tobacco Wholesale		3,246.00		2,454.86		
01/06/16	830	12/31/15	Nationwide Beer and Wine		1,440.00		1,014.86		
01/06/16						934.38	1,949.24		Cash deposit
01/07/16	906	01/04/16	Horizon Telephone Company		1,455.53		493.71		
01/07/16						934.38	1,428.09		Cash deposit
01/08/16	907	01/05/16	Blue J Health		901.57		526.52		
01/08/16	908	01/05/16	Parkaire BB		75.00		451.52		
01/08/16						1,722.57	2,174.09		Cash deposit
01/08/16		01/05/16	Larry's Deli		98.79		2,075.30		
01/09/16	909	01/06/16	Marjorie's Cleaning Services		75.00		2,000.30		
01/09/16						1,747.46	3,747.76		Cash deposit
01/10/16	910	01/07/16	Parkaire BB		75.00		3,672.76		
01/11/16						1,575.70	5,248.46		Cash deposit
01/12/16	911	01/09/16	Kennesaw Health Plan		19.99		5,228.47		
01/12/16						1,127.80	6,356.27		Cash deposit
01/13/16						1,286.47	7,642.74		Cash deposit
01/14/16						1,491.44	9,134.18		Cash deposit
01/15/16		01/11/16	Food-Mart		222.93		8,911.25		
01/15/16	912	01/12/16	Standard Mortgage Co.		7,050.29		1,860.96		
01/16/16						1,751.99	3,612.95		Cash deposit
01/16/16	913	01/13/16	Central Office Supply		57.94		3,555.01		
01/16/16	914	01/13/16	Kinko's		90.97		3,464.04		
01/16/16	915	01/13/16	Shwartz German Haus		79.07		3,384.97		
01/16/16	916	01/13/16	Sensitive Waste Services		15.48		3,369.49		
01/16/16	917	01/13/16	Subscription Services		9.52		3,359.97		

Supporting analysis: Page 11

DETAILS OF TRANSACTIONS IN BANK OF LAWRENCEVILLE A/C 171499800
FROM SEPTEMBER 1, 2015 TO FEBRUARY 29, 2016
ALL TRANSACTIONS
ANDERSON INTERNAL MEDICINE
LAWRENCEVILLE, GA
CASE NUMBER: 16-023

Schedule 2

Posted Date	Check Number	Check Date	Payee of Check / Debit	Check Endorsement	Amount Check/Debit	Amount Deposit	Bank Balance	Check Category	Deposit Category
01/16/16	918	01/13/16	Water and Sewer Dept.		46.32		3,313.65		
01/16/16						1,770.70	5,084.35		Cash deposit
01/17/16	837	12/30/15	Physicians Central		768.00		4,316.35		
01/17/16	920	01/14/16	North Georgia PCS		198.23		4,118.12		
01/17/16	921	01/14/16	Parkaire Band Boosters		75.00		4,043.12		
01/17/16	922	01/14/16	Parkaire Band Boosters		75.00		3,968.12		
01/18/16						1,315.50	5,283.62		Cash deposit
01/18/16	924	01/15/16	Sensitive Waste Services		22.77		5,260.85		
01/18/16	925	01/15/16	Sagget's Garage		721.63		4,539.22		
01/19/16						1,435.58	5,974.80		Cash deposit
01/19/16	926	01/16/16	Blue J Health		949.67		5,025.13		
01/20/16						1,465.91	6,491.04		Cash deposit
01/21/16						1,208.09	7,699.13		Cash deposit
01/22/16						1,261.33	8,960.46		Cash deposit
01/22/16	927	01/19/16	Blue Jay Health		870.99		8,089.47		
01/23/16						1,276.94	9,366.41		Cash deposit
01/23/16	928	01/20/16	Parking Co of America		53.00		9,313.41		
01/23/16	929	01/20/16	Parking Co of America		53.00		9,260.41		
01/23/16	930	01/20/16	Tonya Larsen		2,497.89		6,762.52		
01/23/16	931	01/20/16	Verizon		180.89		6,581.63		
01/23/16		01/20/16	United Postal Service		17.00		6,564.63		
01/25/16						1,276.94	7,841.57		Cash deposit
01/25/16	919	01/13/16	Physicians Central		256.00		7,585.57		
01/25/16	932	01/22/16	Kennesaw Health Plan		25.94		7,559.63		
01/26/16						1,756.13	9,315.76		Cash deposit
01/26/16	933	01/23/16	76 Church Street		27.01		9,288.75		
01/26/16	934	01/23/16	Cherokee Co Tax Office		910.92		8,377.83		
01/26/16	935	01/23/16	Fedex Kinko's - Alpharetta		7.09		8,370.74		
01/27/16						1,771.40	10,142.14		Cash deposit
01/28/16						1,131.13	11,273.27		Cash deposit
01/29/16						2,187.89	13,461.16		Cash deposit
01/29/16	923	01/14/16	Physicians Central		768.00		12,693.16		
01/29/16	936	01/26/16	Central Office Supply		47.49		12,645.67		
01/29/16	937	01/26/16	Johnson Coding		105.00		12,540.67		

Supporting analysis: Page 12

DETAILS OF TRANSACTIONS IN BANK OF LAWRENCEVILLE A/C 171499800
FROM SEPTEMBER 1, 2015 TO FEBRUARY 29, 2016
ALL TRANSACTIONS
ANDERSON INTERNAL MEDICINE
LAWRENCEVILLE, GA
CASE NUMBER: 16-023

Schedule 2

Posted Date	Check Number	Check Date	Payee of Check/Debit	Check Endorsement	Amount Check/Debit	Amount Deposit	Bank Balance	Check Category	Deposit Category
01/29/16	938	01/26/16	Water and Sewer		48.72		12,491.95		
01/29/16		01/26/16	Food-Mart		198.36		12,293.59		
01/30/16						1,109.23	13,402.82		Cash deposit
01/31/16	940	01/28/16	Johnson Coding		7.54		13,395.28		
01/31/16	941	01/28/16	Johnson Medical Coding		7.97		13,387.31		
01/31/16		01/31/16	Bank Fee		22.98		13,364.33		
02/01/16						1,746.94	15,111.27		Cash deposit
02/01/16	939	01/27/16	Physicians Central		256.00		14,855.27		
02/01/16	943	01/29/16	Jenson's Furniture Warehouse		595.09		14,260.18		
02/01/16	944	01/29/16	Kinko's		270.00		13,990.18		
02/01/16	945	01/29/16	Linens to You		8,575.00		5,415.18		
02/01/16	946	01/29/16	Sensitive Waste Services		29.97		5,385.21		
02/01/16	947	01/29/16	Subscription Services		7.04		5,378.17		
02/01/16	948	01/29/16	Water and Sewer		41.55		5,336.62		
02/01/16		01/29/16	Larry's Deli		90.75		5,245.87		
02/01/16		01/29/16	Food-Mart		202.19		5,043.68		
02/02/16						1,965.09	7,008.77		Cash deposit
02/02/16						1,366.68	8,375.45		Cash deposit
02/02/16	950	01/30/16	Barry's Commercial Repairs		787.00		7,588.45		
02/02/16	951	01/30/16	Village Cleaners		59.75		7,528.70		
02/03/16	953	01/31/16	Water and Sewer Dept.		47.36		7,481.34		
02/04/16						1,127.76	8,609.10		Cash deposit
02/05/16						2,289.39	10,898.49		Cash deposit
02/05/16	954	02/02/16	Always There		200.00		10,698.49		
02/05/16	955	02/02/16	Georgia Power Company		2,954.99		7,743.50		
02/05/16	956	02/02/16	Subscription Services		7.74		7,735.76		
02/06/16						910.77	8,646.53		Cash deposit
02/07/16	957	02/04/16	Cecilia Amelia Flapper	Cecilia A. Flapper	1,000.00		7,646.53		
02/07/16	958	02/04/16	Horizon Telephone Company		1,455.53		6,191.00		
02/08/16						1,497.36	7,688.36		Cash deposit
02/08/16						1,181.78	8,870.14		Cash deposit
02/08/16	959	02/05/16	Always There		125.00		8,745.14		
02/08/16	960	02/05/16	Marietta Beverage Company		1,000.00		7,745.14		
02/08/16	961	02/05/16	Firestone		792.28		6,952.86		

DETAILS OF TRANSACTIONS IN BANK OF LAWRENCEVILLE A/C 171499800
FROM SEPTEMBER 1, 2015 TO FEBRUARY 29, 2016
ALL TRANSACTIONS
ANDERSON INTERNAL MEDICINE
LAWRENCEVILLE, GA
CASE NUMBER: 16-023

Schedule 2

Posted Date	Check Number	Check Date	Payee of Check/Debit	Check Endorsement	Amount Check/Debit	Amount Deposit	Bank Balance	Check Category	Deposit Category
02/08/16	962	02/05/16	Sensitive Waster Services		27.44		6,925.42		
02/09/16	963	02/06/16	Andrew and Duvall		195.00		6,730.42		
02/09/16	964	02/06/16	Georgia Prof Ins		94.75		6,635.67		
02/09/16	965	02/06/16	Verizon		218.69		6,416.98		
02/09/16	1011	02/26/16	Shamrock Groceries		1,000.00		5,416.98		
02/10/16						1,206.17	6,623.15		Cash deposit
02/11/16						1,639.18	8,262.33		Cash deposit
02/12/16						1,796.98	10,059.31		Cash deposit
02/12/16						1,737.65	11,796.96		Cash deposit
02/12/16	966	02/09/16	Always Their		150.00		11,646.96		
02/12/16	967	02/09/16	Subscription Services		9.01		11,637.95		
02/13/16	968	02/10/16	Always There		125.00		11,512.95		
02/13/16	969	02/10/16	Always Their		100.00		11,412.95		
02/13/16	970	02/10/16	Central Office Supply		91.89		11,321.06		
02/13/16	971	02/10/16	Sensitive Waster Services		77.74		11,243.32		
02/13/16	972	02/10/16	Sensitive Waste Services		44.49		11,198.83		
02/13/16		02/10/16	UPS		15.00		11,183.83		
02/15/16						1,131.83	12,315.66		Cash deposit
02/15/16	973	02/12/16	Std Mortgage Co.		7,050.29		5,265.37		
02/15/16	974	02/12/16	Stephan T Wilson		500.00		4,765.37		
02/16/16						1,169.62	5,934.99		Cash deposit
02/16/16	975	02/13/16	Always There		125.00		5,809.99		
02/16/16	976	02/13/16	Central Office Sup		208.59		5,601.40		
02/16/16	977	02/13/16	Central Office Sup		4.54		5,596.86		
02/16/16	978	02/13/16	Georgia Professional Insurance		1,124.50		4,472.36		
02/16/16	979	02/13/16	KIA Finance Company		599.75		3,872.61		
02/16/16	980	02/13/16	Kinko's		49.02		3,823.59		
02/16/16	981	02/13/16	Water and Sewer		44.44		3,779.15		
02/16/16		02/13/16	ATM		275.00		3,504.15		
02/16/16		02/13/16	Food-Mart		459.91		3,044.24		
02/16/16		02/13/16	UPS		41.30		3,002.94		
02/16/16		02/13/16	United Postal Service		12.39		2,990.55		
02/16/16		02/13/16	UPS		17.95		2,972.60		
02/17/16						1,391.90	4,364.50		Cash deposit

Supporting analysis: Page 14

DETAILS OF TRANSACTIONS IN BANK OF LAWRENCEVILLE A/C 171499800
FROM SEPTEMBER 1, 2015 TO FEBRUARY 29, 2016
ALL TRANSACTIONS
ANDERSON INTERNAL MEDICINE
LAWRENCEVILLE, GA
CASE NUMBER: 16-023

Schedule 2

Posted Date	Check Number	Check Date	Payee of Check / Debit	Check Endorsement	Amount Check/Debit	Amount Deposit	Bank Balance	Check Category	Deposit Category
02/17/16	982	02/14/16	North Georgia PCS		198.23		4,166.27		
02/17/16		02/14/16	Strip TZ Grille		1,192.00		2,974.27		
02/18/16						1,332.59	4,306.86		Cash deposit
02/19/16						1,278.49	5,585.35		Cash deposit
02/20/16	942	01/28/16	Physicians Central		768.00		4,817.35		
02/20/16	983	02/17/16	Andrew & Duvall		449.00		4,368.35		
02/20/16	984	02/17/16	KIA Finance Company		599.75		3,768.60		
02/20/16	985	02/17/16	Schwartz German Haus		29.98		3,738.62		
02/20/16	986	02/17/16	Sensitive Waste Services		999.75		2,738.87		
02/20/16		02/17/16	Brown's Hardware		28.49		2,710.38		
02/20/16		02/17/16	Brown's Hardware		80.79		2,629.59		
02/21/16	988	02/18/16	ABC Bail Bonds LLC		2,753.00		(123.41)		
02/21/16	989	02/18/16	Parkaire Band Boosters		75.00		(198.41)		
02/21/16		02/18/16	Larry's Deli		17.21		(215.62)		
02/22/16						1,422.86	1,207.24		Cash deposit
02/22/16						1,584.92	2,792.16		Cash deposit
02/22/16	990	02/19/16	Amelia Flapper	Cecilia A Flapper	1,000.00		1,792.16		
02/23/16						1,174.38	2,966.54		Cash deposit
02/23/16	949	01/29/16	Physicians Central		256.00		2,710.54		
02/23/16	952	01/30/16	Physicians Central		256.00		2,454.54		
02/23/16	991	02/20/16	Always There		175.00		2,279.54		
02/23/16	992	02/20/16	Tonya Larsen		1,097.89		1,181.65		
02/24/16						1,659.78	2,841.43		Cash deposit
02/25/16						1,384.75	4,226.18		Cash deposit
02/26/16						1,439.33	5,665.51		Cash deposit
02/26/16						1,150.91	6,816.42		Cash deposit
02/26/16						992.14	7,808.56		Cash deposit
02/26/16	993	02/23/16	Central Office Supply		7.79		7,800.77		
02/26/16	994	02/23/16	Central Office Supply		94.01		7,706.76		
02/26/16	995	02/23/16	Central Office Supply		209.08		7,497.68		
02/26/16	996	02/23/16	Johnson Medical Coding		117.00		7,380.68		
02/26/16	997	02/23/16	Parkaire BB		75.00		7,305.68		
02/26/16	998	02/23/16	Parkaire Band Boosters		75.00		7,230.68		
02/26/16	999	02/23/16	Shwartz German Haus		9.25		7,221.43		

Supporting analysis: Page 15

DETAILS OF TRANSACTIONS IN BANK OF LAWRENCEVILLE A/C 171499800
FROM SEPTEMBER 1, 2015 TO FEBRUARY 29, 2016
ALL TRANSACTIONS
ANDERSON INTERNAL MEDICINE
LAWRENCEVILLE, GA
CASE NUMBER: 16-023

Schedule 2

Posted Date	Check Number	Check Date	Payee of Check / Debit	Check Endorsement	Amount Check/Debit	Amount Deposit	Bank Balance	Check Category	Deposit Category
02/26/16	1000	02/23/16	Schwartz German Haus		94.59		7,126.84		
02/26/16		02/23/16	Larry's Deli		4.27		7,122.57		
02/26/16		02/23/16	Strip TZ Grille		1,325.00		5,797.57		
02/27/16	1001	02/24/16	Blue Jay Health		1,977.29		3,820.28		
02/27/16	1003	02/24/16	FedEx Kinko's		9.14		3,811.14		
02/27/16	1004	02/24/16	Parkaire Band Boosters		75.00		3,736.14		
02/27/16		02/24/16	Food-Mart		209.96		3,526.18		
02/28/16	1005	02/25/16	Andrew & Duvall	Rhoda Frazier	190.00		3,336.18		
02/28/16	1007	02/25/16	Brian Frazier		670.00		2,666.18		
02/28/16	1008	02/25/16	Johnson Medical Coding		58.99		2,607.19		
02/28/16	1010	02/25/16	Kinko's		107.20		2,499.99		
02/29/16						1,394.35	3,894.34		Cash deposit
02/29/16		02/24/16	Strip TZ Grille		2,475.40		1,418.94		
02/29/16		02/26/16	Strip TZ Grille		871.08		547.86		
02/29/16		02/29/16	Bank Fee		21.65		526.21		
							526.21	<< ENDING BALANCE	
					265,513.35	257,117.98			

7-5 CASE 5: TRACING DATA ANALYTICS RED FLAGS BACK TO SOURCE DOCUMENTS USING SUBPOENAS [ANDERSON INTERNAL MEDICINE AND LARSEN CONVENIENCE (HUSBAND/WIFE LOAN FRAUD AND CONSPIRACY)]

Report of Interview

Interviewee: John Grayson, Senior Vice President, Waleska Bank
Interviewer: Raymond T. Boone, CFE
Date: May 5, 2016

John Grayson is the Senior Vice President and Branch Manager for Waleska Bank (WB) branch located on Highway 5 in Ball Ground, Georgia. Mr. Grayson said that he personally knows Greg and Tonya Larsen, both of whom have banked with WB since 2003. He sees each several times a month in the bank and at the store. In addition to having a commercial checking account, Mr. Larsen has borrowed money on and off since 2006. Mr. Larsen has had a $50,000 line of credit since 2011 that he has used on occasion to pay his vendors until he built up his receipt balance. Based on his past history, Mr. Larsen pays off the line of credit within two to four weeks.

Sometime after Christmas in late December 2015, Mr. Larsen approached him about a $50,000.00 loan to completely remodel his store. Mr. Larsen told John Grayson that he has new competition on Highway 5 from chain gas stations and needed additional funds to modernize his store and make it more appealing to customers.

Mr. Larsen provided his 2013 and 2014 IRS Schedules C and monthly Georgia Sales and Use Tax forms for the last twelve months to verify the store's gross receipts and net income. Based on the long-term relationship with Greg Larsen, WB lent him $49,000.00 so Ramey Construction could start construction in January.

When asked, John Grayson said that he was not aware when he approved the loan that Greg Larsen was having cash flow problems. Also, Mr. Grayson stated that he had not been in the store since Thanksgiving and was not aware of low inventory.

John Grayson added that WB lost no money on the loan. It filed a Financing Statement with Cherokee County to protect its interest in the inventory and leasehold improvement. Although it was a second lien, WB received full repayment of principal and interest from the insurance company.

Reset Form

Print Form

CREDIT APPLICATION

IMPORTANT APPLICANT INFORMATION: Federal law requires financial institutions to obtain sufficient information to verify your identity. You may be asked several questions and to provide one or more forms of identification to fulfill this requirement. In some instances we may use outside sources to confirm the information. The information you provide is protected by our privacy policy and federal law.

TYPE OF CREDIT REQUESTED	FOR CREDITOR USE
IMPORTANT: Check (✓) the appropriate boxes below and complete the applicable sections.	DATE _____ CLASS NO. _____
☒ SECURED ☐ INDIVIDUAL CREDIT - relying solely on my income or assets	ACCOUNT NO. _____
☐ UNSECURED ☐ INDIVIDUAL CREDIT - relying on my income or assets as well as income or assets from other sources	APPROVED ☐ BY _____
☐ JOINT CREDIT - We intend to apply for joint credit. (initials) ____	DECLINED ☐ BY _____

AMOUNT REQUESTED	FOR HOW LONG	PAYMENT DATE DESIRED	WANT TO REPAY	PROCEEDS OF LOAN TO BE USED FOR:
$ 49000	50 months	12/29/16	☒ MONTHLY ☐ 1,000	to complete remodeling of the store

SECTION A - INDIVIDUAL APPLICANT INFORMATION

NAME (Last, First, Middle)
Gregory H. Larsen

BIRTHDATE	TELEPHONE NO.	DRIVER'S LICENSE NO.	SOCIAL SECURITY NO.	NO. DEPENDENTS	AGES OF DEPENDENTS
9/27/75	770-735-9876	042771589			

ADDRESS (Street, City, State & Zip)	COUNTY		HOW LONG
213 Underwood Street, Canton, GA 30115	Cherokee	Do you ☒ own or ☐ rent?	4 1/2 yrs

PREVIOUS ADDRESS (Street, City, State & Zip) (Complete if less than 3 years at present address)	COUNTY		HOW LONG
		Did you ☐ own or ☐ rent?	

EMPLOYER (Company Name & Address)   HOW LONG
Self - Larsen Convenience Store

BUSINESS PHONE	Ext.	POSITION OR TITLE	SALARY PER MONTH	
770-735-2784		Owner	GROSS: $ 1,378,216	NET: $ 64,486

PREVIOUS EMPLOYER (Company Name & Address)   HOW LONG

NAME AND ADDRESS OF NEAREST RELATIVE NOT LIVING WITH YOU	RELATIONSHIP	TELEPHONE NO. (Include Area Code)
Jolene Larsen Cooper, 987 Gennett Drive, Jasper, GA 30143	Sister	706-253-9961

Alimony, child support, or separate maintenance income need not be revealed if you do not wish to have it considered as a basis for repaying this obligation.

Alimony, child support, separate maintenance received under: ☐ Court Order ☐ Written Agreement ☐ Oral Understanding

SOURCES OF OTHER INCOME	AMOUNT PER MONTH
	$

Is any income listed in this Section likely to be reduced before the credit request is paid off?	Have you previously received credit from us?
☒ No ☐ Yes (Explain)	☐ No ☒ Yes - When? 2011

SECTION B - JOINT APPLICANT OR OTHER PARTY INFORMATION

Complete only if: for joint credit, for individual credit relying on income or assets from other sources, or applicant is married and resides in a community property state.

NAME (Last, First, Middle)

BIRTHDATE	TELEPHONE NO.	DRIVER'S LICENSE NO.	SOCIAL SECURITY NO.	NO. DEPENDENTS	AGES OF DEPENDENTS

RELATIONSHIP TO APPLICANT (If Any)	PRESENT ADDRESS (Street, City, State & Zip)	HOW LONG

EMPLOYER (Company Name & Address)   HOW LONG

BUSINESS PHONE	Ext.	POSITION OR TITLE	SALARY PER MONTH	
			GROSS: $	NET: $

PREVIOUS EMPLOYER (Company Name & Address)   HOW LONG

Alimony, child support, or separate maintenance income need not be revealed if you do not wish to have it considered as a basis for repaying this obligation.

Alimony, child support, separate maintenance received under: ☐ Court Order ☐ Written Agreement ☐ Oral Understanding

SOURCES OF OTHER INCOME	AMOUNT PER MONTH
	$

Is any income listed in this Section likely to be reduced before the credit requested is paid off?	Has Joint Applicant or Other Party ever received credit from us?
☐ No ☐ Yes (Explain)	☐ No ☐ Yes - When?

SECTION C - MARITAL STATUS

Complete only if: for joint or secured credit, or applicant resides in a community property state or is relying on property located in such a state as a basis for repayment of the credit requested.

APPLICANT	☒ Married	☐ Separated	☐ Unmarried (including single, divorced, and widowed)
OTHER PARTY	☐ Married	☐ Separated	☐ Unmarried (including single, divorced, and widowed)

Experᴛᴀ ©1986 Bankers Systems, Inc., St. Cloud, MN Form UCA 6/30/2003   (page 1 of 2) _____ _____

SECTION D - ASSET & DEBT INFORMATION

If Section B has been completed, this Section should be completed giving information about both the Applicant and Joint Applicant or Other Person. Please mark Applicant-related information with an "A". If Section B was not completed, only give information about the Applicant in this Section.

ASSETS OWNED   (Use separate sheet if necessary.)

DESCRIPTION OF ASSETS	NAME IN WHICH THE ACCOUNT IS CARRIED	SUBJECT TO DEBT?	VALUE
CHECKING ACCOUNT NUMBER(S) (where) Harrelson Bank	Gregory H. Larsen	N/A	$ 689
SAVINGS ACCOUNT NUMBER(S) (where) Harrelson Bank	Gregory H. Larsen	N/A	53
CERTIFICATE OF DEPOSIT(S) (where)			
MARKETABLE SECURITIES (issuer, type, no. of shares)			
REAL ESTATE 213 Underwood Street, Canton, GA (location, date acquired) 7/14/2011	Greg and Tonya Larsen	Mortgage	267,800
LIFE INSURANCE (issuer, face value)			
AUTOMOBILES 2014 Ford F-150 Crew Cab (make, model, year)	Gregory H. Larsen	Auto Loan	21,777
OTHER Inventory and leasehold improvements (list)	Gregory H. Larsen	S&B Trust Co.	299,925
TOTAL ASSETS			$ 590,244

OUTSTANDING DEBTS   (Including charge accounts, installment contracts, credit cards, rent, mortgages and other obligations. Use separate sheet if necessary.)

CREDITOR	ACCOUNT NUMBER	NAME IN WHICH THE ACCOUNT IS CARRIED	ORIGINAL AMOUNT	PRESENT BALANCE	MONTHLY PAYMENTS
LANDLORD OR MORTGAGE HOLDER Appalachian Mortgage	☐ Rent Payment ☒ Mortgage	Greg and Tonya Larsen	(OMIT RENT) $ 300,000	(OMIT RENT) $ 222,500	(OMIT RENT) $ 1,393
AUTOMOBILES SE Ford Financing (describe) 2014 Ford F-150 Crew Cab	SEF 1119853769	Gregory H. Larsen	19,187	17,284	599.89
S&B Trust Company - Inventory & leasehold improvements	987-23567	Gregory H. Larsen	75,000	41,125	573.74
Georgia Dept. of Revenue - sales and use taxes		Gregory H. Larsen	7,987	7,987	Varies
A/P - regular vendors	Various	Gregory H. Larsen	N/A	95,915	95,915
TOTAL DEBTS			$	$ 384,811	$ 98,482

Complete the following information about both the Applicant and Joint Applicant or Other Person (if applicable):

Are you obligated to make Alimony, Support or Maintenance Payments? ☒ No ☐ Yes

If yes, to (Name & Address) _____ Amt. per month $ _____

Are you a co-maker, endorser, or guarantor on any loan or contract? ☒ No ☐ Yes If yes, for whom? _____ To whom? _____

Are there any unsatisfied judgments against you? ☒ No ☐ Yes If yes, to whom owed? _____ Amount $ _____

Have you been declared bankrupt in the last 10 years? ☒ No ☐ Yes If yes, where? _____ Year? _____

SECTION E - SECURED CREDIT   Complete only if credit is to be secured. Briefly describe the property to be given as security:

PROPERTY DESCRIPTION

Leasehold Improvements at Larsen Convenience Store, Hwy. 5 North, Canton, GA 30115

NAMES & ADDRESSES OF ALL CO-OWNERS OF THE PROPERTY

N/A - rented

IF THE SECURITY IS REAL ESTATE, GIVE THE FULL NAME OF YOUR SPOUSE (if any).

N/A

SIGNATURES   I certify that everything I have stated in this application and on any attachments is correct. Lender may keep this application whether or not it is approved. By signing below I authorize Lender to check my credit and employment history and to answer questions others may ask Lender about my credit record with Lender. I understand that I must update credit information at Lender's request if my financial condition changes.

Applicant's Signature	Date	Other Signature (Where Applicable)	Date

Experi™ ©1986 Bankers Systems, Inc., St. Cloud, MN Form UCA 6/30/2003

Waleska Bank
Waleska, GA 30183
www.waleskabank.com

FROM 12/1/15 TO 12/31/15
Account 7011176

Gregory Larson
213 Underwood Street
Canton, GA 30115

********************** *WALESKA BANK CHECKING - SUMMARY* ***************

Balance as of November 30, 2015		$	19,423.97
Total Deposits and Credits:	9	+	152,883.45
Total Checks and Debits:	25	-	171,389.79
Service Charges:	1	-	50.00
Interest Earned:	0	+	-
Ending Balance as of December 31, 2015		$	867.63

*** *CHECKS* ***

Date	Number	Amount	Date	Number	Amount
12/1	2843	2,876.00	12/22	2856	13,700.07
12/1	2844	13,511.59	12/22	2857	1,041.80
12/1	2845	1,028.80	12/22	2858	1,824.97
12/1	2846	1,824.60	12/22	2859	25,000.00
12/8	2847	2,878.00	12/29	2860	2,899.00
12/8	2848	13,211.21	12/29	2861	13,422.60
12/8	2849	1,031.06	12/29	2862	1,000.32
12/8	2850	1,826.60	12/29	2863	1,821.59
12/15	2851	2,870.00	12/29	2864	1,532.98
12/15	2852	13,418.60	12/30	2865	11,959.00
12/15	2853	1,026.80	12/30	2866	1,041.00
12/15	2854	1,822.20	12/30	2867	36,000.00
12/22	2855	2,821.00			

** *OTHER DEBITS* **

12/31	50.00	BUSINESS ACCOUNT SERVICE FEE

** *DEPOSITS* **

Date	Amount	Description
12/4	14,610.38	DDR REGULAR DEPOSIT
12/7	15,198.20	DDR REGULAR DEPOSIT
12/11	13,983.10	DDR REGULAR DEPOSIT
12/14	15,435.99	DDR REGULAR DEPOSIT
12/18	13,561.19	DDR REGULAR DEPOSIT
12/21	15,671.65	DDR REGULAR DEPOSIT
12/26	13,661.87	DDR REGULAR DEPOSIT
12/28	49,000.00	DDR OFFICIAL CHECK

FDIC

Waleska Bank
Waleska, GA 30183
www.waleskabank.com

Gregory Larsen
213 Underwood Street
Canton, GA 30115

| 12/29 | 14,761.07 | DDR REGULAR DEPOSIT |

** **DAILY BALANCE** ***

Date	Balance	Date	Balance	Date	Balance
12/1	182.98	12/11	25,027.79	12/23	6,171.16
12/2	182.98	12/14	40,463.78	12/24	6,171.16
12/3	182.98	12/15	21,326.18	12/26	19,833.03
12/4	14,793.36	12/16	21,326.18	12/27	68,833.03
12/7	29,991.56	12/17	21,326.18	12/28	55,833.03
12/8	11,044.69	12/18	34,887.37	12/29	49,917.61
12/9	11,044.69	12/21	50,559.00	12/30	917.61
12/10	11,044.69	12/22	6,171.16	12/31	867.61

*************************** **OVERDRAFT AND RETURN ITEM FEES** **********************************

FDIC

OFFICIAL CHECKS - ACCOUNT 7000000 - LOAN NO. 15-3989

Check 7097

OFFICIAL CHECK
WALESKA BANK, Waleska, GA

64-575/613
7097

DATE 12/28/2015

PAY TO THE
ORDER OF Gregory Larsen $49,000.00

Forty-nine thousand and 00/100 _____ Dollars

WALESKA BANK
Waleska, GA 30183

FOR Loan #16-3989

Jason K. Robards

:061110575   :007000000   :0004900000

Check 7099

OFFICIAL CHECK
WALESKA BANK, Waleska, GA

64-575/613
7099

DATE 12/28/2015

PAY TO THE
ORDER OF Waleska Bank $500.00

Five hundred and 00/100 _____ Dollars

WALESKA BANK
Waleska, GA 30183

FOR Loan #16-3989 / loan fee

Jason K. Robards

:061110575   :007000000   : 0000050000

Check 7098

OFFICIAL CHECK
WALESKA BANK, Waleska, GA

64-575/613
7098

DATE 12/28/2015

PAY TO THE
ORDER OF Southern Appalachian Insurance Company $1,045.80

One thousand forty-five and 80/100 _____ Dollars

WALESKA BANK
Waleska, GA 30183

FOR Loan #16-3989 / insurance

Jason K. Robards

:061110575   :007000000   : 0000104580

Check 8000

OFFICIAL CHECK
WALESKA BANK, Waleska, GA

64-575/613
8000

DATE 12/28/2015

PAY TO THE
ORDER OF Cherokee County Tax Commissioner $430.07

Four hundred thirty and 07/100 _____ Dollars

WALESKA BANK
Waleska, GA 30183

FOR Loan #16-3989 / ad valorem tax

Jason K. Robards

:061110575   :007000000   : 0000043007

215

For Deposit Only
Waleska Bank

Do Not Write Below This Line

Dec 1228 - 35530015

Waleska Bank

Gregory Larsen

Do Not Write Below This Line

Dec 1228 - 3227319

Waleska Bank

For Deposit Only
Cherokee County Tax
Commissioner

Do Not Write Below This Line

Bank of Cherokee
Dec 1229 - 8945631

Dec 1230- 359980

Waleska Bank

For Deposit Only
Southern Appalachian
Insurance Company

Do Not Write Below This Line

Cherokee County C.U.
Dec 1229 - 8945631

Dec 1229 - 3421819

Waleska Bank

CHECKS - ACCOUNT 701176

Gregory H. Larsen DBA Larsen
Convenience Store, Canton, GA

64-575/613

2858

PAY TO THE ORDER OF _____ Discount Tobacco Supply _____ $1,824.97

DATE 12/29/2015

One thousand eight hundred twenty-four & 97/100 _____ Dollars

WALESKA BANK
Waleska, GA 30183

FOR _____

Gregory H. Larsen

:061110575   :007011176   2858   : 0000182497

Gregory H. Larsen DBA Larsen
Convenience Store, Canton, GA

64-575/613

2859

PAY TO THE ORDER OF _____ Tumbler Casino _____ $25,000.00

DATE 12/29/2015

Twenty-five thousand & —————————no/100 _____ Dollars

WALESKA BANK
Waleska, GA 30183

FOR _____

Gregory H. Larsen

:061110575   :007011176   2859   : 0002500000

Gregory H. Larsen DBA Larsen
Convenience Store, Canton, GA

64-575/613

2860

PAY TO THE ORDER OF _____ Shamrock Grocery _____ $2,899.00

DATE 12/29/2015

Two thousand eight hundred ninety-nine & no/100 _____ Dollars

WALESKA BANK
Waleska, GA 30183

FOR payment on account

Gregory H. Larsen

:061110575   :007011176   2860   : 0000289900

Gregory H. Larsen DBA Larsen
Convenience Store, Canton, GA

64-575/613

2861

PAY TO THE ORDER OF _____ Georgia-Tennessee Fuel Partners _____ $13,422.60

DATE 12/29/2015

Thirteen thousand four hundred twenty-two & 60/100 _____ Dollars

WALESKA BANK
Waleska, GA 30183

FOR payment on account

Gregory H. Larsen

:061110575   :007011176   2861   : 0001342260

Gregory H. Larsen DBA Larsen
Convenience Store, Canton, GA

64-575/613

2862

PAY TO THE ORDER OF _____ Marietta Beverage Company _____ $1,000.32

DATE 12/29/2015

One thousand and ————32/100 _____ Dollars

WALESKA BANK
Waleska, GA 30183

FOR payment on account

Gregory H. Larsen

:061110575   :007011176   2862   : 0000100032

Gregory H. Larsen DBA Larsen
Convenience Store, Canton, GA

64-575/613

2863

PAY TO THE ORDER OF _____ Discount Tobacco Supply _____ $1,821.59

DATE 12/29/2015

One thousand eight hundred twenty-one and — 59/100 _____ Dollars

WALESKA BANK
Waleska, GA 30183

FOR payment on account

Gregory H. Larsen

:061110575   :007011176   2863   : 0000182159

For Deposit Only
Marietta Beverage Company

Do Not Write Below This Line

Dec 1229 - 37344581

Waleska Bank

For Deposit Only
Shamrock Grocery

Do Not Write Below This Line

Dec 12291 - 3670001

Waleska Bank

For Deposit Only
Discount Tobacco Company

Do Not Write Below This Line

Dec 12291 - 3670101

Waleska Bank

For Deposit Only
Discount Tobacco Company

Do Not Write Below This Line

Dec 12291 - 3770001

Waleska Bank

For Deposit Only
Georgia-Tennessee Fuel
Partners

Do Not Write Below This Line

De3 1231 - 3670001

Waleska Bank

For Deposit Only
Tumbler Casino

Do Not Write Below This Line

Dec 1229 - 3671112

Bank of Ely
Bank of Lawrenceville

Check 2864

Gregory H. Larsen DBA Larsen
Convenience Store, Canton, GA

64-575/613
2864

DATE 12/29/2015

PAY TO THE ORDER OF: Internal Revenue Service $1,532.98

One thousand five hundred thirty-two & 98/100 _____ Dollars

WALESKA BANK
Waleska, GA 30183

FOR _____

Gregory H. Larsen

:061110575   :007011176   2864   : 0000153298

Check 2865

Gregory H. Larsen DBA Larsen
Convenience Store, Canton, GA

64-575/613
2865

DATE 12/29/2015

PAY TO THE ORDER OF: Shane Wholesale Grocery $11,959.00

One hundred twenty-seven and ——————00/100 _____ Dollars

WALESKA BANK
Waleska, GA 30183

FOR payment on account

Gregory H. Larsen

:061110575   :007011176   2865   : 0001195900

Check 2866

Gregory H. Larsen DBA Larsen
Convenience Store, Canton, GA

64-575/613
2866

DATE 12/29/2015

PAY TO THE ORDER OF: Ramey Construction $1,041.00

One thousand five hundred thirty-two and – 98/100 _____ Dollars

WALESKA BANK
Waleska, GA 30183

FOR payment on account

Gregory H. Larsen

:061110575   :007011176   2866   : 0000104100

Check 2867

Gregory H. Larsen DBA Larsen
Convenience Store, Canton, GA

64-575/613
2867

DATE 12/29/2015

PAY TO THE ORDER OF: Andersen Internal Medicine $36,000.00

Thirty-six thousand and —————— no/100 _____ Dollars

WALESKA BANK
Waleska, GA 30183

FOR _____

Gregory H. Larsen

:061110575   :007011176   2867   : 0003600000

```
┌─────────────────────┐  ┌─────────────────────┐
│   For Deposit Only  │  │   For Deposit Only  │
│  Ramey Construction │  │ U. S. Department of the│
│                     │  │      Treasury       │
│                     │  │                     │
│                     │  │                     │
│ Do Not Write Below This Line │ Do Not Write Below This Line │
│                     │  │                     │
│                     │  │                     │
│                     │  │                     │
│                     │  │                     │
│ De3 12931 - 3799001 │  │ Dec 1229 - 378379051│
│                     │  │                     │
│                     │  │                     │
│    Waleska Bank     │  │    Waleska Bank     │
│                     │  │                     │
└─────────────────────┘  └─────────────────────┘

┌─────────────────────┐  ┌─────────────────────┐
│   For Deposit Only  │  │   For Deposit Only  │
│Andersen Internal Medicine│ Shane Wholesale Grocery│
│                     │  │                     │
│ Do Not Write Below This Line │ Do Not Write Below This Line │
│                     │  │                     │
│ Bankof Lawrenceville│  │                     │
│                     │  │                     │
│ Dec 1229 - 3812581  │  │ Dec 1229 - 37944581 │
│                     │  │                     │
│    Waleska Bank     │  │    Waleska Bank     │
│                     │  │                     │
└─────────────────────┘  └─────────────────────┘
```

220

AO 88B (Rev. 02/14) Subpoena to Produce Documents, Information, or Objects or to Permit Inspection of Premises in a Civil Action

UNITED STATES DISTRICT COURT
for the

_____

_____	)	
Plaintiff	)	
v.	)	Civil Action No.
	)	
_____	)	
Defendant	)	

SUBPOENA TO PRODUCE DOCUMENTS, INFORMATION, OR OBJECTS
OR TO PERMIT INSPECTION OF PREMISES IN A CIVIL ACTION

To: _____

(Name of person to whom this subpoena is directed)

❒ *Production:* **YOU ARE COMMANDED** to produce at the time, date, and place set forth below the following documents, electronically stored information, or objects, and to permit inspection, copying, testing, or sampling of the material:

Place:	Date and Time:

❒ *Inspection of Premises:* **YOU ARE COMMANDED** to permit entry onto the designated premises, land, or other property possessed or controlled by you at the time, date, and location set forth below, so that the requesting party may inspect, measure, survey, photograph, test, or sample the property or any designated object or operation on it.

Place:	Date and Time:

The following provisions of Fed. R. Civ. P. 45 are attached – Rule 45(c), relating to the place of compliance; Rule 45(d), relating to your protection as a person subject to a subpoena; and Rule 45(e) and (g), relating to your duty to respond to this subpoena and the potential consequences of not doing so.

Date: _____

CLERK OF COURT

OR

_____   _____
Signature of Clerk or Deputy Clerk   *Attorney's signature*

The name, address, e-mail address, and telephone number of the attorney representing *(name of party)* _____
_____ , who issues or requests this subpoena, are:

Notice to the person who issues or requests this subpoena
If this subpoena commands the production of documents, electronically stored information, or tangible things or the inspection of premises before trial, a notice and a copy of the subpoena must be served on each party in this case before it is served on the person to whom it is directed. Fed. R. Civ. P. 45(a)(4).

AO 88B (Rev. 02/14) Subpoena to Produce Documents, Information, or Objects or to Permit Inspection of Premises in a Civil Action (Page 2)

Civil Action No. _____

PROOF OF SERVICE
(This section should not be filed with the court unless required by Fed. R. Civ. P. 45.)

I received this subpoena for *(name of individual and title, if any)* _____

on *(date)* _____ .

    ❐ I served the subpoena by delivering a copy to the named person as follows: _____

_____ on *(date)* _____ ; or

    ❐ I returned the subpoena unexecuted because: _____

_____ .

Unless the subpoena was issued on behalf of the United States, or one of its officers or agents, I have also
tendered to the witness the fees for one day's attendance, and the mileage allowed by law, in the amount of

$ _____ .

My fees are $ _____ for travel and $ _____ for services, for a total of $ 0.00   .

I declare under penalty of perjury that this information is true.

Date: _____

_____
Server's signature

_____
Printed name and title

_____
Server's address

Additional information regarding attempted service, etc.:

[Print]   [Save As...]   [Add Attachment]   [Reset]

AO 89B (07/16) Subpoena to Produce Documents, Information, or Objects in a Criminal Case

UNITED STATES DISTRICT COURT
for the

_____

United States of America	)	
v.	)	
	)	Case No.
	)	
Defendant	)	

SUBPOENA TO PRODUCE DOCUMENTS, INFORMATION, OR OBJECTS IN A CRIMINAL CASE

To:

_____
(Name of person to whom this subpoena is directed)

YOU ARE COMMANDED to produce at the time, date, and place set forth below the following books, papers, documents, data, or other objects:

Place:	Date and Time:

Certain provisions of Fed. R. Crim. P. 17 are attached, including Rule 17(c)(2), relating to your ability to file a motion to quash or modify the subpoena; Rule 17(d) and (e), which govern service of subpoenas; and Rule 17(g), relating to your duty to respond to this subpoena and the potential consequences of not doing so.

(SEAL)

Date: _____

CLERK OF COURT

_____
Signature of Clerk or Deputy Clerk

The name, address, e-mail, and telephone number of the attorney representing *(name of party)* _____
_____ , who requests this subpoena, are:

Notice to those who use this form to request a subpoena

Before requesting and serving a subpoena pursuant to Fed. R. Crim. P. 17(c), the party seeking the subpoena is advised to consult the rules of practice of the court in which the criminal proceeding is pending to determine whether any local rules or orders establish requirements in connection with the issuance of such a subpoena. If no local rules or orders govern practice under Rule 17(c), counsel should ask the assigned judge whether the court regulates practice under Rule 17(c) to 1) require prior judicial approval for the issuance of the subpoena, either on notice or ex parte; 2) specify where the documents must be returned (e.g., to the court clerk, the chambers of the assigned judge, or counsel's office); and 3) require that counsel who receives produced documents provide them to opposing counsel absent a disclosure obligation under Fed. R. Crim. P. 16.

Please note that Rule 17(c) (attached) provides that a subpoena for the production of certain information about a victim may not be issued unless first approved by separate court order.

AO 89B (07/16) Subpoena to Produce Documents, Information, or Objects in a Criminal Case (Page 2)

Case No.

PROOF OF SERVICE

       This subpoena for *(name of individual and title, if any)* _____

was received by me on *(date)* _____ .

      ❒ I served the subpoena by delivering a copy to the named person as follows: _____

_____ on *(date)* _____ ; or

      ❒ I returned the subpoena unexecuted because: _____

_____ .

      Unless the subpoena was issued on behalf of the United States, or one of its officers or agents, I have also
tendered to the witness fees for one day's attendance, and the mileage allowed by law, in the amount of

      $ _____ .

My fees are $ _____ for travel and $ _____ for services, for a total of $ 0.00   .

      I declare under penalty of perjury that this information is true.

Date: _____

                            _____
                                     Server's signature

                            _____
                                   Printed name and title

                            _____
                                   Server's address

Additional information regarding attempted service, etc.:

| Print | Save As... | Add Attachment | | Reset |

AO 110 (Rev. 06/09) Subpoena to Testify Before a Grand Jury

UNITED STATES DISTRICT COURT
for the

___

SUBPOENA TO TESTIFY BEFORE A GRAND JURY

To:

      YOU ARE COMMANDED to appear in this United States district court at the time, date, and place shown below to testify before the court's grand jury. When you arrive, you must remain at the court until the judge or a court officer allows you to leave.

Place:	Date and Time:

      You must also bring with you the following documents, electronically stored information, or objects *(blank if not applicable)*:

Date: _____   *CLERK OF COURT*

_____
                     Signature of Clerk or Deputy Clerk

The name, address, e-mail, and telephone number of the United States attorney, or assistant United States attorney, who requests this subpoena, are:

AO 110 (Rev. 06/09) Subpoena to Testify Before Grand Jury (Page 2)

PROOF OF SERVICE

This subpoena for *(name of individual or organization)* _____

was received by me on *(date)* _____ .

❐ I served the subpoena by delivering a copy to the named person as follows: _____

_____ on *(date)* _____ ; or

❐ I returned the subpoena unexecuted because: _____

_____ .

I declare under penalty of perjury that this information is true.

Date: _____

_____
Server's signature

_____
Printed name and title

_____
Server's address

Additional information regarding attempted service, etc:

| Print | Save As... | Add Attachment | | Reset |

AO 90 (Rev. 08/09) Subpoena to Testify at a Deposition in a Criminal Case

UNITED STATES DISTRICT COURT
for the

▾|

United States of America	)	
v.	)	
	)	Case No.
	)	
Defendant	)	

SUBPOENA TO TESTIFY AT A DEPOSITION IN A CRIMINAL CASE

To:

      YOU ARE COMMANDED to appear at the time, date, and place set out below to testify at a deposition in a criminal case. If you are an organization that is _not_ a party in this case, you must designate one or more officers, directors, or managing agents, or designate other persons who consent to testify on your behalf about the following matters, or those set out in an attachment:

Place:	Date and Time:

      You must also bring with you to this deposition the following documents, electronically stored information, or objects _(blank if not applicable):_

     (SEAL)

Date: _____

                          CLERK OF COURT

                                       _____

                                         Signature of Clerk or Deputy Clerk

This subpoena has been issued on application of an attorney whose name, address, e-mail and telephone number are:

AO 90 (Rev. 08/09) Subpoena to Testify at a Deposition in a Criminal Case (Page 2)

Case No. _____

PROOF OF SERVICE

This subpoena for *(name of individual and title, if any)* _____
was received by me on *(date)* _____ .

    ❏ I served the subpoena by delivering a copy to the named person as follows: _____

_____ on *(date)* _____ ; or

    ❏ I returned the subpoena unexecuted because: _____
_____ .

Unless the subpoena was issued on behalf of the United States, or one of its officers or agents, I have also tendered to the witness fees for one day's attendance, and the mileage allowed by law, in the amount of

$ _____ .

My fees are $ _____ for travel and $ _____ for services, for a total of $ 0.00   .

I declare under penalty of perjury that this information is true.

Date: _____

_____
Server's signature

_____
Printed name and title

_____
Server's address

Additional information regarding attempted service, etc:

[Print] [Save As...] [Add Attachment] [Reset]

AO 89 (Rev. 08/09) Subpoena to Testify at a Hearing or Trial in a Criminal Case

UNITED STATES DISTRICT COURT
for the

‑|

United States of America	)	
v.	)	
	)	Case No.
_____	)	
Defendant	)	

SUBPOENA TO TESTIFY AT A HEARING OR TRIAL IN A CRIMINAL CASE

To:

YOU ARE COMMANDED to appear in the United States district court at the time, date, and place shown below to testify in this criminal case. When you arrive, you must remain at the court until the judge or a court officer allows you to leave.

Place of Appearance:	Courtroom No.:
	Date and Time:

You must also bring with you the following documents, electronically stored information, or objects *(blank if not applicable)*:

(SEAL)

Date: _____

                                   CLERK OF COURT

                                   _____
                                   Signature of Clerk or Deputy Clerk

The name, address, e-mail, and telephone number of the attorney representing *(name of party)* _____
_____ , who requests this subpoena, are:

AO 89 (Rev. 08/09) Subpoena to Testify at a Hearing or Trial in a Criminal Case (Page 2)

Case No.

PROOF OF SERVICE

This subpoena for *(name of individual and title, if any)* _____
was received by me on *(date)* _____ .

    ❑ I served the subpoena by delivering a copy to the named person as follows: _____

_____ on *(date)* _____ ; or

    ❑ I returned the subpoena unexecuted because: _____

_____ .

Unless the subpoena was issued on behalf of the United States, or one of its officers or agents, I have also
tendered to the witness fees for one day's attendance, and the mileage allowed by law, in the amount of

$ _____ .

My fees are $ _____ for travel and $ _____ for services, for a total of $ 0.00   .

I declare under penalty of perjury that this information is true.

Date: _____

                                                               _____
                                                                Server's signature

                                                                _____
                                                                Printed name and title

                                                                _____
                                                                Server's address

Additional information regarding attempted service, etc:

    [Print]   [Save As...]   [Add Attachment]   [Reset]

About the Authors

William H. Beecken teaches fraud examination courses at Brenau University, Gainesville, Georgia, and taught fraud examination at Southern Polytechnic State University (SPSU) before it merged with Kennesaw State University. The final examination at SPSU required students to write a fraud examination course, prepare trial ready schedules and audio-visuals, and then provide expert testimony before a real prosecutor and defense attorney in a court of law using the materials contained in this casebook. In addition, he mentored his SPSU students while they interned with the Cobb County District Attorney's Office, Marietta, Georgia.

Bill is a Certified Fraud Examiner (CFE) and Certified Public Accountant (CPA). He has a B.A. from Sewanee: The University of the South and M.B.A. (Accounting Concentration) from Brenau University. Bill currently serves as the Director, Fraud Services, for Assurance Forensic Accounting (where he specializes in employee dishonesty, inventory theft, fraud, and divorce cases). A retired federal employee, he previously worked as an FDIC supervisory auditor and supervisory investigator, ATF senior forensic auditor, and SEC accountant/investigator. During his 27-year federal career he trained seven times at the Federal Law Enforcement Training Center. His most notable cases were a 2,309 handgun racketeering case; 63-count arson-for-profit, check kiting, bank-mail-wire fraud case; a $1.25 million contract fraud investigation of a Big 4 CPA firm, a Ponzi scheme, and a securities-check kiting scheme. He has testified over 25 times as a witness in federal and state court on financial motive analysis; bank, bankruptcy, mail, and wire fraud; check kiting; money laundering; tax evasion; racketeering; trust fraud; divorce-related finances; employee dishonesty; and taxes.

Bill is an occasional lecturer on fraud topics. He taught *Testifying as an Expert Witness* to Georgia Tech internal auditors and a series on *Loan Fraud, Check Fraud, and Check Kiting* for the Community Bankers Association of Georgia. In addition, ACFE and the International Association of Arson Investigators have published several of his fraud articles.

Clark A. Beecken is a Certified Fraud Examiner. Clark graduated from Southern Polytechnic State University with a B.S. in Business Administration (Accounting Track). He gained fraud examination and forensic accounting experience with a federal agency, Georgia Tech Department of Internal Auditing, Special Review Unit, Legal Services Corporation, Office of Inspector General, and forensic accounting firms. Additionally, he received extensive criminal investigative training and experience while interning with the Federal Law Enforcement Training Center and the U.S. Department of State, Bureau of Diplomatic Security. Clark currently serves with a federal agency. He has twice testified in court as an expert witness in forensic accounting. In addition, Clark mentored SPSU interns with Georgia Tech and the Cobb County District Attorney's Office, Marietta, Georgia, and lectured on Digital Forensics and using IDEA Data Extraction and Analysis (Data Analytics).

About the Website

This book includes a student companion website, which can be found at www.wiley.com/go/fraudexamcases. Enter the password: beecken234. This website includes the following Excel templates and Excel document files:

203-Tonya Edits Template
Anderson Bank Transactions (Sep Oct Nov Dec Jan Feb)
Check Debit Card Larceny Case, Exercise #1 Template
Check Debit Card Larceny Case, Exercise #2 Template
Financial Statement Fraud, Exercise #1 Template
Financial Statement Fraud, Exercise #2 Template

Index

CPSIA information can be obtained
at www.ICGtesting.com
Printed in the USA
JSHW07053930123
36860JS00001B/28